Social Distinctives
OF THE
Christians
IN THE
First Century

Social Distinctives
OF THE
Christians
IN THE
First Century

PIVOTAL ESSAYS BY E. A. JUDGE

DAVID M. SCHOLER, editor

HENDRICKSON PUBLISHERS

**Social Distinctives of the Christians in the First Century:
Pivotal Essays by E. A. Judge**, edited by David M. Scholer
© 2008 by Hendrickson Publishers, Inc.
P. O. Box 3473
Peabody, Massachusetts 01961-3473

ISBN 1-978-1-56563-880-8

Printed in the United States of America

First Printing — January 2008

Cover Art: Dioscurides of Samos. Musicians. Street scene, mosaic from
Cicero's villa, 1st century C.E., from Pompeii.
Located in the Museo Archeologico Nazionale, Naples, Italy.
Photo Credit: Erich Lessing / Art Resource, N.Y. Used with Permission.

Library of Congress Cataloging-in-Publication Data

Judge, E. A.
    Social distinctives of the Christians in the first century : pivotal
essays / by E. A. Judge ; edited by David M. Scholer.
        p. cm.
    Includes bibliographical references and indexes.
    ISBN-13: 978-1-56563-880-8 (alk. paper)
    1. Christian sociology. 2. Christians—Social life and customs.
3. Church history—Primitive and early church, ca. 30–600. 4. Bible.
N.T. Epistles of Paul—Theology. I. Scholer, David M. II. Title.
    BT738.J83 2007
    270.1—dc22

                              2007022756

Table of Contents

Permissions

Chapter 1, "The Social Pattern of the Christian Groups in the First Century: Some Prolegomena to the Study of New Testament Ideas of Social Obligation" was first published as *The Social Pattern of the Christian Groups in the First Century: Some Prolegomena to the Study of New Testament Ideas of Social Obligation*. London: Tyndale, 1960. Used with permission.

Chapter 2, "Paul's Boasting in Relation to Contemporary Professional Practice," was first published as "Paul's Boasting in Relation to Contemporary Professional Practice, *Australian Biblical Review* 16 (1968): 37–50. Used with permission.

Chapter 3, "St Paul and Classical Society," was first published as "St Paul and Classical Society," *Jahrbuch für Antike und Christentum* 15 (1972): 19–36. Used with permission.

Chapter 4, "St Paul as a Radical Critic of Society," was first published as "St Paul as a Radical Critic of Society," *Interchange* 16 (1974): 191–203. Used with permission.

Chapter 5, "The Social Identity of the First Christians: A Question of Method in Religious History," was first published as "The Social Identity of the First Christians: A Question of Method in Religious History," *Journal of Religious History* 11:2 (1980): 201–17. Used with permission.

Chapter 6, "Rank and Status in the World of the Caesars and St Paul" was first published as *Rank and Status in the World of the Caesars and St Paul*. University of Canterbury Publications 29. Christchurch: University of Canterbury, 1982. Used with permission.

Chapter 7, "Cultural Conformity and Innovation in Paul: Some Clues from Contemporary Documents," was first published as "Cultural Conformity and Innovation in Paul: Some Clues from Contemporary Documents," *Tyndale Bulletin* 35 (1984): 3–24. Used with permission.

Chapter 8, "The Teacher as Moral Exemplar in Paul and in the Inscriptions of Ephesus," was first published as Chapter 12 in *In the Fullness of Time: Biblical Studies in Honour of Archbishop Donald Robinson.* Edited by D. Peterson and J. Pryor. Homebush West, NSW: Lancer/ Anzea, 1992: 185–201. Used with permission.

A few typographical adjustments have been made (notably to standardize the biblical references), and a very few orthographic errors corrected, but otherwise the content of the original publications has not been updated, correlated, or modified at all.

Abbreviations

GENERAL

A.D.	anno Domini
ad loc.	*ad locum,* at the place discussed
Append.	Appendix
art.	article
Aufl.	Auflage (Edition)
B.C.	before Christ
Bd.	Band (Volume)
bis	twice
cf.	*confer,* compare
col.	column
Diss.	dissertation
ed(s).	editor(s), edition(s)
e.g.	*exempli gratia,* for example
ep.	*epistula*
esp.	especially
E.t./ET/E.T.	English translation
et al.	*et alii,* and others
etc.	*et cetera,* and the rest
f(f).	and the following one(s)
F.t.	French translation
Gk.	Greek, referring to lexical forms, not translation
G.t.	German translation
hrsg.	herausgeben (edited)
ib./ibid./id.	*ibidem,* in the same place
i.e.	*id est,* that is
intro.	introduction
inv. nr.	inventory number
Lat.	Latin

MS(S)	manuscript(s)
n(n).	note(s)
no(s).	number(s)
op. cit.	*opere citato,* in the work cited
p(p).	page(s)
passim	here and there
pt.	part
repr.	reprinted
RSV	Revised Standard Version
s.v.	*sub verbo,* under the word
trans.	translator, translated by
u.	und (and)
usw.	und so weiter (and so on)
v(v).	verse(s)
vol(s).	volume(s)

BOOKS OF THE BIBLE

Matt	Matthew
Rom	Romans
1–2 Cor	1–2 Corinthians
Gal	Galatians
Eph	Ephesians
Phil	Philippians
Col	Colossians
1–2 Thess	1–2 Thessalonians
1–2 Tim	1–2 Timothy
Tit	Titus
Phlm	Philemon
Heb	Hebrews
Jas	James
1–2 Pet	1–2 Peter
Rev	Revelation

OTHER PRIMARY SOURCES

1 Clem	1 Clement
Ann.	Tacitus, *Annales*
Ant.	Josephus, *Jewish Antiquities*

ap. Dig.	*Apud Digest*
Att.	Cicero, *Epistulae ad Atticum*
Cic. *Orator*	Cicero, *De oratore*
comm. Ephes.	*Commentariorum in Epistulam ad Ephesios*
comm. in ep. ad Gal.	*Commentariorum in Epistulam ad Galatas*
CPR	*Corpus Papyrorum Raineri*
Doctr. chr.	Augustine, *de Doctrina Christiana*
Ep.	Pliny the Younger, *Epistulae*
Hist.	*Historia*
OGIS	*Orientis Graecae Inscriptiones Selectae*
Orat.	Cicero, *De oratore*
Paed.	Clement of Alexandria, *Paedagogus*
Plut. *Cic.*	Plutarch, *Cicero*
Plut. *Ti. Gracchus*	Plutarch, *Tiberius et Caius Gracchus*

SECONDARY SOURCES

AGJU	Arbeiten zur Geschichte des antiken Judentums und des Urchristentums
ANRW Principat	*Aufstieg und Niedergang der römischen Welt: Geschichte und Kultur Roms im Spiegel der neueren Forschung.* Edited by H. Temporini and W. Haase. Berlin, 1972–
AustBiblRev	*Australian Biblical Review*
CompStSocHist	*Comparative Studies in Society and History*
EntrFondHardt	*Entretiens Fondation Hardt*
HdbAlt-Wiss	Handbuch der Altertumswissenschaft
J. Chr. Ed.	*Journal of Christian Education*
J. Rel. Hist.	*Journal of Religious History*
JbAC	*Jahrbuch für Antike und Christentum*
JournBiblLit	*Journal of Biblical Literature*
JournChristEd	*Journal of Christian Education*
JournTheolStud	*Journal of Theological Studies*
JRS	*Journal of Roman Studies*
JSNTSup	Journal for the Study of the New Testament: Supplement Series
Lex. d. Alten Welt	*Lexikon der Alten Welt*
MusHelv	*Museum Helveticum*
NABPR	National Association of Baptist Professors of Religion

NewTestStud	*New Testament Studies*
NovTest	*Novum Testamentum*
NovTSup	Novum Testamentum Supplements
PG	Patrologia graeca [= Patrologiae cursus completus: Series graeca]. Edited by J.-P. Migne. 162 vols. Paris, 1857–1886
Proc. Israel Acad. Sci. Hum.	Proceedings of the Israel Academy of Sciences and Humanities
ProcCambPhilolSoc	*Proceedings of the Cambridge Philological Society*
RAC	*Reallexikon für Antike und Christentum.* Edited by T. Kluser et al. Stuttgart, 1950–
RechScRel	*Recherches de Science Religieuse*
RefTheolRev	*Reformed Theological Review*
RivStorIt	*Rivista storica italiana*
StudClasPhil	*Studies in Classical Philology*
StudEv	*Studia Evangelica*
StudItFilClass	*Studi italiani di filologia classica*
SymbOsl	*Symbolae Osloenses*
TU	Texte und Untersuchungen
TynBull	*Tyndale Bulletin*
WdF	Wege der Forschung
ZNW	*Zeitschrift für die neutestamentliche Wissenschaft und die Kunde der älteren Kirche*
ZPE	*Zeitschrift für Papyrologie und Epigraphik*
ZsPapEpigr	*Zeitschrift für Papyrologie und Epigraphik*

Introduction

IT WAS SOMETIME in 1960–1961 during my first year in graduate studies in New Testament (Wheaton College Graduate School) that the small booklet (77 pages) by E. A. Judge, *The Social Pattern of the Christian Groups in the First Century: Some Prolegomena to the Study of New Testament Ideas of Social Obligation* (London: Tyndale Press, 1960) came into my hands. I read the book with considerable interest, but I surely did not at that time appreciate the significance of this small study either for its own merits or its place in the history of New Testament scholarship.

By the time I began my teaching career as a New Testament professor in 1969 (at Gordon-Conwell Theological Seminary) I was beginning to understand the importance of the work of Professor E. A. Judge and used it in my teaching. Judge was a pioneer in emphasizing the social levels with the church and the implications of that for the structures and activities of the church. I was struck at that point in time, when there was so much emphasis in the United States on the presumption that the early church was comprised (only) of poor, socially disenfranchised people, with Judge's emphasis on the social levels within the church.

In March 1985 I had the wonderful opportunity to visit the Sydney, Australia area for almost two weeks to give various lectures in support of women in ministry. Professor Judge very kindly invited me to give a major lecture for a conference on ancient history being held at Macquarie University at the time I was there (I lectured on 1 Timothy 2:9–15). This was my first meeting with Judge, who was so gracious to me in every way. Frankly, I was in awe of him, his work and that of the Ancient History Documentary Research Centre, which was producing the new series *New Documents Illustrating Early Christianity* (the first volume had appeared in 1981). I again visited Judge in Sydney in 1989 and subsequently had several visits with him at various conferences in both Canada and the United States.

What is it that made the work of Judge in 1960 and in subsequent years so important? Judge was the first in scholarship after the mid-twentieth century to clarify early Christian ideals about society by defining what the social institutions of the broader cultural context were and how they influenced the social institutions of the early Christian communities. Judge points out that earlier scholars had entered into this field of inquiry, but that, in general, they failed due to the lack of careful definitions of the [Greco-Roman] social institutions at the time based on a thorough use of the primary sources.

Thus, Judge was the "new founder" (a turning point in scholarship) of what came to be called social-scientific criticism of the New Testament. Social-scientific criticism is the term in scholarship that refers to the use of social realities (e.g., institutions, class, factors of community organization) in the critical study of the literary sources available (this as an advance over "merely" literary and traditional historical questions). Of course, there were earlier movements that anticipated these approaches. One of the most important of these is what is called the "Chicago School," a group of faculty at the University of Chicago who, especially in the 1920s and 1930s, devoted themselves to sociohistorical study of the New Testament. Ernest DeWitt Burton was the founder, Shailer Mathews and Shirley Jackson Case were the main representatives, and Edgar Johnson Goodspeed was a colleague.[1]

As the field of social-scientific criticism developed, it became more complex. John H. Elliott, in his excellent book on these matters, defined five categories of such social-historical studies: 1) investigations of social *realia*; 2) integrating social, economic and political data to construct a social history; 3) an attempt to describe the social organization of early Christians; 4) the study of social and especially cultural factors which influence and constrain social interaction; and 5) the use of the theory and models of the social sciences (outside of biblical studies) to analyze biblical texts.[2] J. H. Elliott points out that these five approaches are not necessarily mutually exclusive.

The work of Judge, particularly as a pioneer, is focused on the first two categories described above, with some attention to the third (and

---

[1] An excellent summary of the Chicago School is found in William Baird, *History of New Testament Research; Volume Two: From Jonathan Edwards to Rudolf Bultmann* (Minneapolis: Fortress, 2003), 305–30 (Baird lists in his notes other studies of the Chicago School).

[2] John H. Elliott, *What Is Social-Scientific Criticism?* (Guides to Biblical Scholarship, New Testament Series; Minneapolis: Fortress, 1993). See here especially his Chapter Three: "The Recent Emergence of Social-Scientific Criticism" (pages 17–35).

virtually no engagement with the last two categories).[3] Judge's work on the social *realia* of the Roman Empire dealt with issues such as demographics, social classes, the structure of social institutions, and cultural conventions related to social class (e.g., the uses of rhetoric). Applying this data to various issues in New Testament interpretation provided new understandings of the character of the early church as a social institution within and reflecting its culture. This groundbreaking work helped scholarly study move beyond a more traditional focus limited to literary and historical questions. Judge brings to this task his extensive knowledge of the Greek and Latin languages and of Roman history, along with his study of the New Testament and the history of the early church, especially as recorded in various formal and informal papyrus documents. Virtually all of Judge's work was on Paul; his work contributed significantly to understanding Paul, his rhetoric, his relationship with his churches, and his understandings of church structure, social organization, and conflicts (e.g., the parties and tensions within Corinth as seen in 1 Corinthians; cf. Theissen) in a better and deeper way. At the most basic level, Judge's work helped scholars to understand the early church as a social institution and as a social movement, concerned with its identity in its world. Later developments in the method often focused on Jesus, which accounts, in some ways, for many of the different directions the movement took from the earlier work of Judge. In these studies, the Jesus movement was understood as a social movement with its own cultural/political agendas. As all of this developed, various scholars began to use sociological theories (drawn from other contexts, often contemporary) to attempt understanding the nature of the social realities and developments within the early church (e.g., the works of Malina, Pilch, and others; Gager; Stark).

Professor Judge is an outstanding scholar. Born on January 27, 1928, in Christchurch, New Zealand, his early education took place in New Zealand. He studied at King's College, Cambridge, England. Later he wrote the essay which became his seminal book of 1960. After holding various university posts in New Zealand, England, and Australia between 1950 and 1968, in 1969 he became Professor of History at Macquarie University in Sydney, which post he held until his retirement in 1993. During these years he held many other posts and received various honors. He became the Director of the Ancient History Documentary Research Centre at Macquarie University (1981–1996), the center of

---

[3] Chapter 5 in this book reprints Judge's essay of reflection on the methodological issues twenty years after the publication of his seminal book; see also the next note for Judge's reflections yet another ten years later.

significant work on the social history of early Christianity. At Macquarie University he also served as Pro-Vice-Chancellor 1990–1991) and as Deputy Vice-Chancellor (1992–1994). He was an Alexander von Humbolt Fellow at Cologne (1962) and at Bonn (1972; 1977). He was a visiting fellow at Yale Divinity School (1980) and Visiting Professor of Classics and History at the University of California, Berkeley (1984). He was a founding co-editor of *Antichthon*, an Australian journal devoted to classical studies. He was elected to membership in the Studiorum Novi Testamenti Societas, in recognition of his many contributions to New Testament studies. This litany of achievements does not, of course, include all that could be said about Judge, but it is enough to show his lifelong devotion to the sociological study of early Christianity that has characterized so much of his work.[4]

Although Judge's influence and publications are significant, it is unfortunately the case that his work is too little known and read today by New Testament students (both professors and students). His work had a significant impact on a limited group of scholars who sought access to his work. Judge also frequently attended scholarly conferences in the United States and Europe, which spread his influence in limited, but important, circles. As time went by, Judge was eclipsed in some ways by later developments in social-scientific study (see the paragraph above giving Elliott's analysis of the discipline). It is the purpose of this project to bring together a few of Judge's most important publications in a relatively small and accessible volume in order to enable this generation of New Testament students and professors to learn from his work. Many of the publications of Judge are not readily accessible to a North American (or even British) audience, because the Australian journals and books in which they have been published do not have wide circulation beyond Australia or New Zealand. Four of the articles in this collection fall into this category (Chapters 2 ["Paul's Boasting in Relation to Contemporary Professional Practice"], 4 ["St Paul as a Radical Critic of Society"], 5 ["The Social Identity of the First Christians"], and 8 ["The Teacher as Moral Exemplar in Paul and in the Inscriptions of Ephesus"]). Two other pieces in this collection, both small booklets, are out-of-print and difficult to acquire: *The Social Pattern of the Christian Groups in the First Century* (Chapter 1) and *Rank and Status in the World of the Caesars and St Paul* (Chapter 6). Only two essays here (Chapters 3 ["St Paul and

---

[4] There is a very useful and delightful published interview with Judge, conducted on September 12, 1990; it appears in the journal of the Australian Evangelical History Association: Mark Huchinson, "Professing History II: An Interview with Professor Edwin Judge," *Lucas* 11 (April 1991), 28–40.

Classical Society"] and 7 ["Cultural Conformity and Innovation in Paul"]) appear in sources that are found in most North American theological libraries, but even then are not often easily consulted by New Testament students.

These eight studies gathered here are perhaps the most important works of Judge in his tradition of the social study of early Christianity, selected first by me and later approved by Judge for inclusion. Later in this book I have provided a virtually complete bibliography of the works of Judge for those who want to do further study of his work. Those interested in access to all of Judge's work should look for two forthcoming volumes: *The First Christians in the Roman World: Augustan and New Testament Studies*, edited by James R. Harrison (a former student of Judge), to be published by Mohr Siebeck; and *What Jerusalem Had to Do with Athens: Cultural Transformation in Late Antiquity*, by Alanna M. Nobbs.

Most readers of this book will want to engage in further studies of the social-scientific criticism of the New Testament. In addition to the works of Judge (given later), a short bibliography for further study seems appropriate here.

There are two important books to consult for a beginning study. First is David M. May, *Social-Scientific Criticism of the New Testament: A Bibliography* (NABPR Bibliographic Series 4 [Series Editor, David M. Scholer]; Macon, Ga.: Mercer University Press, 1991). After a brief introduction to the discipline (11 pages), the book provides a topically classified bibliography of 972 entries. Second is the superb study of John H. Elliott, *What Is Social-Scientific Criticism?* (Guides to Biblical Scholarship, New Testament Series; Minneapolis: Fortress, 1993). Elliott provides a comprehensive, critical analysis of the discipline, accompanied by helpful appendices, especially the one entitled "Data Inventory for Synchronic Social Analysis of Early Christian Groups" (pages 110–21). He also provides an excellent, substantial, classified bibliography (pages 138–74). These volumes bring one to a point now about fourteen years ago.

It seems appropriate to list here a few of the classic and more recent works in the field of the social-scientific criticism of the New Testament mostly published after the bibliographies of May and Elliott (this method is now also applied to the Old Testament, but no attempt is made here to provide bibliography in that area).

Some of these works fall very closely to the interests and concerns of Judge; others are developments and approaches somewhat distant from the immediate concerns of Judge. Yet, this very selective sample will serve the reader who wishes to follow the various lines of the discipline of social-scientific criticism of the New Testament.

Barton, S. C. "Historical Criticism and Social-Scientific Perspectives in New Testament Study," in *Hearing the New Testament: Strategies for Interpretation* (ed. Joel B. Green; Grand Rapids: Eerdmans/Carlisle: Paternoster, 1995), 61–89.

Berding, Kenneth. "The Hermeneutical Framework of Social-Scientific Criticism: How Much Can Evangelicals Get Involved?" *Evangelical Quarterly* 75 (2003), 3–22.

Blasi, A. J., P. Turcotte, and J. Duhaime, *Handbook of Early Christianity: Social Science Approaches.* Walnut Creek, Calif.: AltaMira, 2002.

Bossman, David M. "International Conference on the Social Sciences and Second Testament Interpretation," *Biblical Theology Bulletin* 23 (1993), 4–39.

Clarke, Andrew D. *Secular and Christian Leadership in Corinth: A Socio-Historical and Exegetical Study of 1 Corinthians 1–6.* (AGJU 18.) Leiden/New York: Brill, 1993.

Dutch, Robert S. *The Educated Elite in 1 Corinthians: Education and Community Conflict in Graeco-Roman Context.* (JSNTSup 271.) London/New York: T&T Clark, 2005.

Esler, P. F. *The First Christians in Their Social Worlds: Social-Scientific Approaches to New Testament Interpretation.* London/New York: Routledge, 1994.

―――. *Modelling Early Christianity: Social-Scientific Studies of the New Testament in Its Context.* London/New York: Routledge, 1995.

Gager, J. C. *Kingdom and Community: The Social World of Early Christianity.* Englewood Cliffs, N.J.: Prentice-Hall, 1975.

Halligan, J. M. " 'Where Angels Fear to Tread': An Account of the Development of the Social-Scientific Approach to the Study of the Ancient World," in *"Imagining" Biblical Worlds: Studies in Spatial, Social and Historical Constructs in Honor of James W. Flanagan* (ed. David M. Gunn and Paula M. McNutt; London: Sheffield Academic Press, 2003), 202–18.

Horrell, D. "Models and Methods in Social-Scientific Interpretation: A Response to Philip Esler," *Journal for the Study of the New Testament* 78 (2000), 83–105.

―――. *Social Scientific Approaches to New Testament Interpretation.* Edinburgh: T&T Clark, 1999.

Kloppenborg, John S., and Stephen G. Wilson. *Voluntary Associations in the Graeco-Roman World.* London and New York: Routledge, 1996.

Malina, Bruce J. *The New Testament World: Insights from Cultural Anthropology.* 3d ed. Louisville: Westminster John Knox, 2001.

Malina, Bruce J., and John J. Pilch. *Social-Science Commentary on the Book of Revelation.* Minneapolis: Fortress, 2000.[5]

———. *Social-Science Commentary on the Letters of Paul.* Minneapolis: Fortress, 2006.

Malina, Bruce J., and Richard L. Rohrbaugh. *Social-Science Commentary on the Synoptic Gospels.* 2d ed. Minneapolis: Fortress, 2003.

Mott, S. C. "The Power of Giving and Receiving: Reciprocity in Hellenistic Benevolence," in *Current Issues in Biblical and Patristic Interpretation: Studies in Honor of Merrill C. Tenney* (ed. G. F. Hawthorne; Grand Rapids: Eerdmans, 1975), 60–72.

Neyrey, Jerome H. *The Social World of Luke-Acts: Models for Interpretation.* Peabody, Mass.: Hendrickson, 1991.[6]

Pilch, John J. *Social Scientific Models for Interpreting the Bible: Essays by the Context Group in Honor of Bruce J. Malina.* (Biblical Interpretation Series 53.) Leiden/Boston: Brill, 2001.[7]

Pilch, John J., and Bruce J. Malina. *Biblical Social Values and Their Meaning: A Handbook.* 2d ed. Peabody, Mass.: Hendrickson, 1998.

Rohrbaugh, R. L. *The Social Sciences and New Testament Interpretation.* Peabody, Mass.: Hendrickson, 1996.

Stark, Rodney. *The Rise of Christianity: A Sociologist Reconsiders History.* Princeton: Princeton University Press, 1996.

Stegemann, Wolfgang et al. *The Social Setting of Jesus and the Gospels.* Minneapolis: Fortress, 2002.

Theissen, Gerd. *The Social Setting of Pauline Christianity: Essays on Corinth.* Edinburgh: T&T Clark/Philadelphia: Fortress, 1982.

White, L. Michael, and O. Larry Yarbrough. *The Social World of the First Christians: Essays in Honor of Wayne A. Meeks.* Minneapolis: Fortress, 1995.

Winter, Bruce W. *After Paul Left Corinth: The Influence of Secular Ethics and Social Change.* (First-Century Christians in the Graeco-Roman World.) Grand Rapids: Eerdmans, 2001.

———. *Roman Wives, Roman Widows: The Appearance of New Women and the Pauline Communities.* Grand Rapids: Eerdmans, 2003.

---

[5] Bruce J. Malina, often with John J. Pilch (or some other scholar), has written a whole series of books such as this one, covering most of the documents in the New Testament. Malina and Pilch generally combine classic social-scientific criticism with insights from cultural anthropology.

[6] This is a volume of collected essays. J. H. Neyrey has also authored other books in the area of social-scientific criticism of the New Testament.

[7] John J. Pilch has also authored other books in the area of social-scientific criticism of the New Testament.

————. *Seek the Welfare of the City: Christians as Benefactors and Citizens.* (First-Century Christians in the Graeco-Roman World.) Grand Rapids: Eerdmans/Carlisle: Paternoster, 1994.

It is my hope that this volume will honor Professor Judge and his important work and will introduce a whole new audience to his work, as well as assist those who have known his work by providing them with a convenient text. It has been a joy to work on this project; I thank especially Shirley Decker-Lucke of Hendrickson Publishers for her patience, encouragement, and friendship. I also received significant help from Susan Carlson Wood of Fuller Seminary's Faculty Publication Services; she has been a faithful worker with me on many projects. I also received some help from my Research Assistants at Fuller Seminary, especially Jennifer Garcia Bashaw and Steven Brian Pounds. I received a diagnosis of cancer in February 2002, just as we were ready to move ahead on this project. Over the last five years, I have had difficulty in finding the time and energy to bring this project to completion, but rejoice now to see the day.

David M. Scholer
Fuller Theological Seminary
Pasadena, California
July 24, 2007

1

The Social Pattern of the Christian Groups in the First Century

PREFACE

THIS ESSAY OFFERS a new approach to a familiar topic. It is an attempt to clarify certain early Christian ideas about society by defining the particular social institutions that are presupposed, and showing how the behaviour of the Christians was related to them. At first it was thought that an analysis of the social stratification of the Christian groups would suffice, but on investigation the conception of society as a series of strata seemed increasingly anachronistic. Instead it became apparent that the contemporary writers were thinking in terms of a series of overlapping but not systematically related circles. The description of these circles occupies the main body of the essay.

For a topic of this kind the primary material is mostly well known, and the interpretation of many of the points is under constant discussion. The present study however is not pieced together from modern works. Many of these are referred to where they are relevant, for comparison or elaboration, so that the footnotes constitute a partial bibliography of recent work on some aspects of the subject. Inevitably in a field where so much is common ground, ideas that are in fact adopted tend to be thought one's own. It would be hard to trace the debt, and in the present case the means are not to hand. But it must be emphasized that whether or not any details here presented as new have been anticipated elsewhere, the study may claim a substantial originality in the design and formulation of the whole. The pattern emerged from an examination of the primary sources which began, as stated above, along somewhat different lines; it must be judged therefore on its correspondence with the documents, and to this end full internal references have been provided.

In origin this is a by-product of studies undertaken through the generosity of the Trustees of the late Sir James Knott at King's College, Newcastle upon Tyne, in the University of Durham. It is indebted generally to teachers in New Zealand and at Cambridge, and in its present form to discussions with the many enthusiastic students of ancient history in the University of Sydney.

The essay is based on the 1957 Tyndale New Testament Lecture, and was awarded the 1958 Hulsean Prize by the University of Cambridge. In the original publication it was subtitled, "Some Prolegomena to the Study of New Testament Ideas of Social Obligation." It appeared in German translation (with a new introduction) as *Christliche Gruppen in nichtchristlicher Gesellschaft: Die Sozialstruktur christlicher Gruppen im ersten Jahrhundert* (Wuppertal, 1964). The first section, "Interpreting New Testament Ideas," was reproduced in B. S. Rosner, ed., *Understanding Paul's Ethics: Twentieth-Century Approaches* (Grand Rapids: Eerdmans, 1995), 75–84.

I. INTERPRETING NEW TESTAMENT IDEAS

A generation ago the attempt to discover the principles of social obligation held by the early Christians was still common. Since then interest has largely petered out. This need not necessarily mean that there were no such principles to be found; it may simply have been that the enquiry itself was misdirected. It is the object of this study to support a revival of the issue by opening up some new lines of interpretation.

Earlier writers, failing to define adequately the social institutions assumed in the New Testament, often formulated the problems in anachronistic terms. Indeed one is still confronted with discussions of 'Church' and 'State' in the New Testament,[1] or with tirades against slavery and the enormities of Imperial Rome.[2] We are still the victims of Tacitean cynicism, it seems. But the New Testament writers would have found much of this puzzling. They were not thinking in such terms. Modern students have thus created for themselves the problems of New Testament acquiescence and inconsistency, through neglecting to identify the situation to which the New Testament writings were actually addressed. This lack will perhaps justify an ancient historian's trespassing on New Testament ground. For while the religious background to the New Testament has been thoroughly searched, the political and social

---

[1] E.g. T. M. Parker, *Christianity and the State in the Light of History,* 1955; and O. Cullmann, *Der Staat im Neuen Testament,* 1956 (English version, 1957).

[2] E.g. E. F. Scott, *Man and Society in the New Testament,* 1947.

material summed up here does not seem to be familiar enough to students of theology.[3] Ancient historians, too, it is hoped, will not find the reassessment useless.

Although interest in the social ideas of the New Testament writers has waned, the new appreciation of their eschatological views will inevitably reopen the question. We already have new treatments of their idea of history,[4] but more needs to be done in applying the recovered eschatology to government and society.[5] Obviously if the New Testament groups saw themselves standing at the climax of the ages, and anticipated an imminent end, this must have profoundly affected their view of their obligation to society. The old search has thus been unexpectedly provided with a new and revolutionary starting-point. There still remains however the lack of definition that partly stultified earlier efforts.

It may be asserted that ideas are never satisfactorily explained merely by discovering their philosophical connections. They must be pinned down in relation to the particular circumstances in which they were expressed. The meaning is fixed at this point, and cannot be certainly ascertained until it is identified. This view has presumably been axiomatic in earlier New Testament criticism, but it seems to be implicitly called in question by certain modern methods of interpretation. Demythologizing may result in looking for the meaning not primarily in terms of the situation in which the ideas were originally expressed, but in the existential realization of the truth concerned.[6] The eliciting of patterns of symbolism may also lead to a neglect of the historical situation.[7] However illuminating these approaches may seem to be, they are misleading if they attract attention away from the original situation. At the very least this ought to be properly explored before it is abandoned in favour of other modes of interpreting the meaning.

---

[3] Two newly translated collections should help to fill the gap: E. Barker, *From Alexander to Constantine: Passages Illustrating the History of Social and Political Ideas*, 1956; C. K. Barrett, *The New Testament Background: Selected Documents*, 1956.

[4] E.g. C. H. Dodd, *History and the Gospel*, 1938; O. Cullmann, *Christus und die Zeit*, 2 Aufl. 1948 (English version, 1951); E. Dinkler, *The Idea of History in the Ancient Near East*, ed. R. C. Dentan, 1955; R. Bultmann, *History and Eschatology*, 1957.

[5] Cf. A. N. Wilder, "Kerygma, Eschatology and Social Ethics," in *The Background of the New Testament and Its Eschatology: Studies in Honour of C. H. Dodd* (ed. W. D. Davies and D. Daube, 1956), 509–36.

[6] Cf. R. P. C. Hanson, 'History and Revelation', *Theology*, 1957.

[7] Cf. H. Gardner, *The Limits of Literary Criticism: Reflections on the Interpretation of Poetry and Scripture*, 1956.

In accepting this as its method, however, New Testament criticism encounters a notorious difficulty. While Christianity originated in Galilee, it flourished in the great cosmopolitan cities of the eastern Mediterranean. The New Testament is itself the product of this shift. Its writers are mainly Jews of Palestinian associations; their readers the Greek-speaking members of Hellenistic communities. It interprets the religious significance of certain events in Judaea to a public unfamiliar with that situation. It applies ideas derived from it to their own situation.

This tension between Hebraic origins and Hellenic application can be resolved in strikingly different ways. The tendency in recent years has been to stress the Hebraic as primary, and to regard the Hellenic as incidental.[8] But the material is also being reassembled for a detailed review of the Hellenic affinities of early Christianity.[9] The greatest progress towards a balanced appraisal of this duality has been in lexicography.[10] Here the most painstaking classification of word usage in the New Testament and related literatures has demonstrated what ought in any case to be obvious, that the meaning of a word is not ultimately determined by antecedent, parallel, or derived instances, but by its situation in its own context. A word means whatever its writer meant it to mean.

In the interpretation of the ideas the same standard should be applied. They must not be treated simply as stages in a system of thought. The New Testament is not an orderly statement of dogma, but a heterogeneous collection of writings addressed to various occasions. While the affiliation of the ideas will generally govern their content, there will normally be a particular construction to be placed on them in relation to the particular situation. Neglect of this may result in imprecision or even error.

Thus the present study concentrates not on the writers, but on the readers. We must know who they were and what they thought if we are

---

[8] E.g. the works of A. Schlatter, inadequately appreciated.

[9] E.g. C. Schneider, *Geistesgeschichte des antiken Christentums*, 1954; T. Klauser, hrsg., *Reallexikon für Antike u. Christentum usw.*, 1950 (in progress). [Ed.: T. Klauser, et al., *Reallexikon für Antike und Christentum* (Stuttgart: A. Hiersmann, 1950–).]

[10] E.g. G. Kittel, *Theologisches Wörterbuch zum Neuen Testament*, 1933 (in progress) [Ed.: This was completed in 1960. The English translation is G. Kittel and G. Friedrich, eds., *Theological Dictionary of the New Testament* (trans. G. W. Bromiley; Grand Rapids, Mich.: Eerdmans, 1985).]; W. Bauer, *Griechisch-Deutsches Wörterbuch zu den Schriften des N. Testaments usw.*, 4 Aufl. 1952 (English adaptation, W. F. Arndt and F. W. Gingrich, 1957). [Ed.: This is now available as Danker, F. W., W. Bauer, W. F. Arndt, and F. W. Gingrich, *A Greek-English Lexicon of the New Testament and Other Early Christian Literature* (3d ed., Chicago: University of Chicago Press, 2000).]

to understand completely what was being said to them. The teaching of Jesus is therefore not the starting-point. We do not possess the teaching of Jesus, *tout court*. We possess the teaching of Jesus, an itinerant Aramaic preacher, as collated and formulated in Greek for the information of religious societies in Hellenistic cities. If it is to be understood properly, it must be understood from their point of view. The only meaning that can be certainly recovered from the Gospels in their present form is the meaning they were intended to convey to their original readers. We must therefore begin with the readers, and explain their social situation as it is shown in the Acts and Epistles. It was very different from that of Jesus, which may now be summed up in order to clear the ground for this central enquiry.

The region to which Jesus belonged was notoriously backward by the standards of contemporary civilization. Its population was economically rural, and resident in villages or small towns. Jesus himself thought in terms of this circumscribed manner of life—witness the parables. His followers, if not he himself, were thoroughly out of sympathy with the sophisticated classes of the cities. Financial, legal, and religious professionals (the publicans, scribes, and Pharisees) were mistrusted by them, and retorted with open contempt. It was the same with intellectuals (the Sadducees) and the administration (the rulers and chief priests).

The form of government the disciples most readily understood was monarchy. The sayings of Jesus make this plain. The social distinctions involved are accepted. 'Behold, they which are gorgeously apparelled, and live delicately, are in kings' courts' (Luke 7:25). International affairs can still be talked of in terms of rival kingdoms. 'What king, going to make war against another king, sitteth not down first, and consulteth whether he be able with ten thousand to meet him that cometh against him with twenty thousand? Or else, while the other is yet a great way off, he sendeth an ambassage, and desireth conditions of peace' (Luke 14:31, 32). Royal methods of internal administration are sufficiently familiar to be used in depicting the character of the kingdom of God. A nobleman 'went into a far country to receive for himself a kingdom, and to return' (cf. the dependence of the Herods on Roman approval for legitimacy). He was hated by his subjects, and took reprisals on them for their insubordination, selecting governors of tested loyalty for the administration of groups of cities (Luke 19:11–27).

Now the evangelist himself shows by his careful dating (Luke 3:1) that the old royal government of Judaea was in commission at the beginning of the ministry of Jesus, though the Galilaean tetrarch still lived in sufficient state to impress the popular mind and keep tongues wagging (Mark 6:21–28). The disciples of course belonged to this principality, but their political interests ran beyond it. Their thinking was still dominated by the idea of a national monarchy established in Judaea proper, which had now been administered for a generation by the priestly authorities under Roman supervision. One of the things that appealed to them most about Jesus was that he promised the inauguration of a new kingdom which looked like fulfilling their wildest dreams. 'I appoint unto you a kingdom, as my Father hath appointed unto me; that ye may eat and drink at my table in my kingdom, and sit on thrones judging the twelve tribes of Israel' (Luke 22:29, 30). They clung persistently to their ambition. 'Lord, wilt thou at this time restore again the kingdom to Israel?' (Acts 1:6). They thought of themselves then in nationalistic terms, and the rest of the world was similarly lumped together as 'the nations'.

The eschatological fervour that motivated the disciples was of course not unparalleled among the non-Hellenized Palestinians of the day, as the discovery of the Qumran community has emphasized.[11] A similar mood of expectation governed most of the early Christian groups. But while the fundamental conviction that the end is being realized is common to all three cases, its expression took remarkably different forms. The covenanters of Qumran, withdrawn and fastidious, must have abhorred the vulgarity and opportunism of the disciples. But a narrow provincial outlook distinguishes both of them from the first Christian societies. The peculiar orientation of Palestinian political thought ('councils', 'synagogues', 'rulers', 'kings', 'nations', Mark 13:9, 10) was thoroughly alien to the Hellenized peoples of the rest of the eastern Mediterranean.

Even the original Christian group at Jerusalem, though certainly not typical of early Christianity, is to be sharply marked off from other Palestinian religious movements. As will be shown later (section V), it was drawn from a population with broad international links, imposing social conditions on it that were very different from those governing either the Galilaean peasantry or the secluded community in the Dead Sea hills. Qumran is only a few miles away from Jerusalem as the crow flies, but from a social point of view its inhabitants lived in another world. Much the same could be said of Galilee.

Nevertheless Jerusalem must also be distinguished from the Hellenistic cities abroad. Sophisticated and cosmopolitan though its population was, it remained Jewish in faith and was administered under peculiar local arrangements.[12] Apart from the Jerusalem group, how-

---

[11] Cf. J. M. Allegro, *The Dead Sea Scrolls*, 1956; F. F. Bruce, *Second Thoughts on the Dead Sea Scrolls*, 1956; M. Burrows, *The Dead Sea Scrolls*, 1956; T. Gaster, trans., *The Scriptures of the Dead Sea Sect*, 1957.

[12] Cf. A. H. M. Jones, *The Herods of Judaea*, 1938.

ever, the Christians known from the New Testament were practically all drawn from communities living under civil institutions of the republican kind. The thirty or more places from Caesarea to Rome for which such groups are specifically attested are all republican. Moreover since they are widely distributed across areas where this was regarded as the normal constitution of society, such other groups as are implied for these parts by a number of general references in the Acts and Epistles may safely be placed in the same category. Other forms of public organization were only retained in backward areas where penetration by Christianity is likely for that very reason to have been delayed.

The only clear exceptions to this occur in certain parts of Palestine itself where, as in Jerusalem, republican institutions had not yet been introduced. For Judaea proper neither the topographical references nor the evidences for Christianity are very explicit. The early apostolic activities attracted 'a multitude out of the cities round about unto Jerusalem' (Acts 5:16), and refugees were later 'scattered abroad throughout the regions of Judaea and Samaria' (Acts 8:1). It is not at all certain what places are meant,[13] and in the first instance it cannot be asserted that they became Christians, nor in the second that they remained in these parts. General references, such as that to Judaea in Acts 9:31, need imply no more than Jerusalem itself. We do know however that the coastal towns were visited by Christian preachers (e.g. Acts 8:40), and there were certainly Christians at Lydda and Joppa (Acts 9:32, 36), which did not enjoy republican constitutions at this period.[14] The Christians in Galilee and Samaria (Acts 9:31) could have been members of the republics of Tiberias and Sebaste respectively, but in so far as they were the former adherents of Jesus this is unlikely. Although he frequented the region around the sea of Tiberias, it is not recorded that he visited the city itself. Its peculiarly heterogeneous population (Josephus, *Ant.* 18.2.3) was perhaps uncongenial. Sebaste may have been the place where Philip preached (Acts 8:5), but the text is uncertain,[15] and the rest of the terminology (Acts 8:9, 25) does not support the idea. Both cities in any case controlled only small territories.[16] The Galilaean and Samaritan Christians may therefore safely be left in the non-republican category.

But the situation that was to become characteristic is already found in the case of Caesarea, which appears in the Acts as the most important

---

[13] Cf. F. F. Bruce, *The Acts of the Apostles*, 1951, *ad loc.*
[14] Cf. A. H. M. Jones, *Cities of the Eastern Roman Provinces*, 1937.
[15] Cf. F. F. Bruce, *The Acts of the Apostles*, 1951, *ad loc.*
[16] Cf. A. H. M. Jones, 'The Urbanisation of Palestine', *Journal of Roman Studies*, 1938.

Palestinian centre of Christianity after Jerusalem. It is not surprising that the first conversion of a non-Jew, an event to which the writer pays great attention, should take place here. Caesarea was a republic, and the seat of the Roman administration. Cornelius himself was an officer of the occupation forces (Acts 10:1). Even earlier than this (Acts 11:19) the new cult had spread northwards up the Phoenician coast, and a series of seaport republics each had its group of Christians, Ptolemais (Acts 21:7), Tyre (Acts 21:3, 4), and Sidon (Acts 27:3). They were drawn however from the Jewish population (Acts 11:19); it was not till the Syrian metropolis of Antioch was reached that there was a mass conversion of non-Jews sufficient to excite the alarm of the original group in Jerusalem (Acts 11:20–22), and the curiosity of the local public (Acts 11:26). Success in Antioch established Christianity socially on a new footing. From here the lines of communication run westwards to the other great cities of the Mediterranean. 'Syrus in Tiberim defluxit Orontes' (Juvenal, *Sat.* 3.62). What is heard today on the Orontes, is repeated tomorrow on the Tiber.

Thus once the sect is established beyond the homeland of its parent religion, at least within the Roman area, which is as far as our records go, it belongs inevitably, as a social phenomenon, to the Hellenistic republics. Its thinking and behaviour naturally reflect the social institutions of these states. In political terminology it is not now so much a matter of rulers, kings, and nations, as of republics, assemblies, and magistrates.

The word *polis* is of course regularly used in the New Testament as a general term for a town or city. That this is sometimes inconsistent with its republican connotation reflects the fact that parts of the New Testament, as already pointed out, deal with an area that was peculiar, in that its population was not yet incorporated on a republican basis. It only emphasizes the extent to which republican government was taken for granted in the Hellenistic area, that when writing in Greek the standard terms should have been applied indiscriminately. Where the Hellenistic cities proper are referred to, the technical sense is naturally apparent in constitutional connections (e.g. Acts 13:50; 16:12, 20; 19:35; 21:39; 26:11; Rom 16:23; Tit 1:5). It will be noticed that the one blanket term covers Roman colonies, too; the distinction did not affect their basically republican character. Contrary to what has usually been thought, the word *demos* is not used except in its technical sense of the assembly of a citizen body (cf. Acts 12:22 [at Caesarea, as is stated in Josephus 19.8.2], 17:5; 19:30, 33). The various magistrates referred to[17] need not be enumerated here; the terminology reflects the variety of local traditions; but

---

[17] Cf. H. J. Cadbury, *The Book of Acts in History*, 1955.

it ought not to obscure the fact that the communities concerned had long been assimilated to a broadly uniform pattern of society.

How narrow a backwater, on the other hand, Galilee and the other unincorporated regions were may be seen from the fact that even the itinerary of Jesus frequently took him into the territories of neighbouring republican centres. But it is obviously in the Aramaic-speaking rural communities dependent on them, and not in the Hellenized urban centres themselves, that his interests lie. He passes through 'the coasts (namely, territory) of Tyre and Sidon', and 'the midst of the coasts of Decapolis' (Mark 7:31). He visits 'the towns (namely, villages) of Caesarea Philippi' (Mark 8:27). To these villagers republicanism was presumably as foreign as it was to Jesus himself. They were after all the subjects of the republic, not its citizens.

This distinction is also implied in the Gospels. Jesus performed a sensational exorcism across the sea of Tiberias, in 'the country (namely, the region of administration) of the Gadarenes' (Mark 5:1). The variant reading 'Gerasenes' is geographically improbable, but does not affect the present point in any case: both communities were constituted as republics, and grouped together with a number of others as the Decapolis (Mark 5:20). The exorcist was not welcomed for his feat. 'The whole city came out to meet Jesus: and when they saw him, they besought him that he would depart out of their coasts' (Matt 8:34). The reaction was mutual. To the plea of a woman who was 'a Greek, a Syrophenician by nation' (namely, a member of the Hellenized citizen class of one of the Phoenician republics, Tyre or Sidon), the retort was 'it is not meet to take the children's bread, and to cast it unto the dogs' (Mark 7:27).

Thus though the non-republican area was geographically very limited, emotionally the gulf between it and the civilized world was profound. The real division was of course cultural. When a community was incorporated its population was usually augmented from abroad to stimulate its Hellenization, and distinguish it from the peasantry newly subjected to it. Cultural gap and political boundaries were kept artificially in alignment. Thus while within the republican area the innumerable boundaries were culturally meaningless, the borders of the Jewish territories symbolized their alienation. When Jesus cryptically threatened to put himself beyond the reach of the authorities, his opponents replied in scorn, 'Whither will he go, that we shall not find him? Will he go unto the dispersed among the Gentiles (lit. Greeks), and teach the Gentiles?' (John 7:35). The original Jerusalem Christians, though assiduously propagating their faith in the other coastal towns, automatically avoided the neighbouring republic of Caesarea, and were scandalized at the idea of admitting even a very respectable and pro-Jewish resident of it to their circle (Acts 10–11). Even Paul, himself dually qualified as a member of the Hellenistic citizen class, conforms to the isolationist terminology when addressing a Jewish ruler. His 'strange (namely, foreign) cities' (Acts 26:11) need refer only to Damascus, but as a republic Damascus belongs irrevocably to the undifferentiated heathendom beyond the shrinking frontiers of the chosen land.

It was nevertheless among communities living in this alien world that the New Testament writings circulated. That many of the readers practised the Jewish religion does not make their situation irrelevant to their thinking. They still lived under the Hellenistic social institutions and largely shared in the common tradition of civilization. It is the pattern of society in the Hellenistic republics that must be determined if New Testament social precepts are to be understood.

If there is a risk of distortion in approaching the subject from the Palestinian end, there is at least an equal danger in working from the non-biblical literary material. Practically all that survives was produced in circles patronized by the Roman administration or by the members of that government itself. It consequently has a pronounced Roman slant. The concentration on the affairs of the Roman capital leads to the facile view that the Mediterranean was run by a centralized, totalitarian administration for the benefit of a vicious imperial house. Many popular accounts of the situation of the New Testament Christians are falsified by this assumption. Many problems of New Testament interpretation are created by it. But the New Testament itself shows it up as absurd. These writings, limited though they are, offer one of the few accounts we have of the general life of the eastern Mediterranean that does not reflect the Roman outlook.

What follows, then, is an attempt to illustrate the basic social institutions of Hellenistic communities from the New Testament documents. The classes from which the Christians were drawn will be discussed, followed by an examination of their relations with public authorities. Finally a quick survey of New Testament ideas will be offered, showing to what extent they represent a reaction to the situation as defined.

II. Republican Institutions: Politeia

The question of the obligation of the individual to society had frequently been debated among the Greeks.[18] Was society not the product

---

[18] Cf. for the progress of the argument, T. A. Sinclair, *A History of Greek Political Thought,* 1951; for its bearing on Christianity, R. Bultmann, *Das Urchristentum im Rahmen der Antiken Religionen,* 1949 (English version, 1956).

of convention? If so, was it not better to revert to the natural conditions of man, and to be guided by natural laws? The classical resolution of this dilemma had been to insist that the opposition was after all unreal. Man is naturally a political animal. Far from convention being alien to man, it is precisely from his membership in an ordered community that his humanity springs. To live in other states might be more or less than human; but one cannot be said to be truly man unless one belongs to a commonwealth. That is man's natural condition.

Hence the fascination of Greek political theorists with providing to the fullest possible degree for the integration of the individual into society. Plato's *Republic* is the classical expression of this. Even though his particular method of implementing the ideal was obviously unrealistic, becoming a byword for utopianism (e.g. Cicero, *Att.* 2.1.8), its critics, together with the general run of their contemporaries, worked equally from the assumption that humanity was only given its proper expression through the association of individuals in a republican community.

On a practical level this displayed itself in the extraordinary spontaneity of Greek democracy. The maximum and equal participation of all members of the republic in its administration was ensured by a variety of means. Sortition was preferred to election in order to cut out the effects of family connection, wealth, and even ability, on the filling of public offices, such qualifications being undemocratic. The delegation of power was reduced well below what a modern democracy would regard as the minimum for efficiency. Even day-to-day decisions were retained in the hands of the popular assembly. Small payments were made to prevent people being distracted by work from such duties as voting in the assemblies, sitting on a jury, or attending public festivals. The taxation of citizens was considered an unfitting expedient, except in emergencies. Essential public works were therefore undertaken at the personal charges of the wealthy, the competition in honour being relied upon to keep the system working.

The Athenian democracy of the fourth century before the Christian era is admittedly the only well-documented instance of this. It was probably abnormal in its own day, at any rate in its physical proportions. Moreover it was to a greater or less extent disapproved of by most Athenian intellectuals,[19] partly, no doubt, as a result of their own political predilections, but certainly also because it did not conform to the rules of the ideal society as defined by purists. Nevertheless the success of the

---

[19] Cf. A. H. M. Jones, 'The Athenian Democracy and Its Critics', *Cambridge Historical Journal*, 1953.

Athenian system could not be denied. Its peculiar practical advantages ensured it many imitators, and the unprecedented blossoming of the arts and letters associated with it, reactionary though many of the individuals concerned were, enshrined it in tradition as classical. For a thousand years educated men persisted in thinking of the republic as the standard form of political organization. In meaning the term inevitably adapted itself to the changing ideas of new generations, and even new peoples, such as the Romans; but the classical notion was sufficiently tenacious for the process of definition to lag far behind the changing methods of government itself.[20] It still remained the necessary formula when the preambles to Justinian's legal collections were drafted, though by then even the theory of government had been altered practically out of all recognition.

But already in the centuries immediately following Alexander its democratic character and the sovereignty of the individual republican state were being noticeably compromised.[21] Needless to say this was generally against the overt intentions of those who held the real political power from time to time. The Hellenistic monarchs frequently insisted on the autonomy of the republics they physically dominated.[22] Admittedly autonomy needed protection, and protection meant subordination, but as long as there was competition among protectors, everyone could claim to be a liberator. Expediency dictated this policy, no doubt, but at least it shows that the ideal persisted.[23] It was still believed that the local republic was the only kind of civilized community. Many of the monarchs demonstrated their sensitivity to this belief, and thus the realism of their politics, by multiplying their number.

Nevertheless the protecting hand induced a slow paralysis, particularly once the Romans began to gain a monopoly in protection. With the growth of that nation, most of the kingdoms were superseded, being retained only in particularly difficult areas where the people were unfit for political responsibility, or even recalcitrant towards the republican idea, as in Judaea. Apart from their obvious interest in decentralizing political power, and thrusting responsibility onto local shoulders, it seemed natu-

---

[20] Cf. M. Hammond, *City-State and World State in Greek and Roman Political Theory until Augustus*, 1951.

[21] Cf. A. H. M. Jones, *The Greek City from Alexander to Justinian*, 1940.

[22] Cf. the documents collected in C. B. Welles, *Royal Correspondence in the Hellenistic Period*, 1934.

[23] Cf. M. Pohlenz, *Griechische Freiheit. Werden und Wesen eines Lebensideals*, 1955; C. Wirszubski, *Libertas as a Political Ideal*, 1950 (later Roman parallel).

ral for the Romans to encourage further development, being themselves a republic. At first, under the stress of wars both foreign and civil, there were high-handed acts, but with the consolidation of the Mediterranean under the Roman imperial system, a more scrupulous regard for local rights was maintained.

Under Augustus there were in Asia Minor, for example, nearly a hundred states issuing their own currency, which was the coveted symbol of autonomy. By the end of the broad century with which the New Testament is concerned this number had been raised beyond 300.[24] There is a wealth of diplomatic material illustrating relations between these republics and the Romans. Josephus, for instance, has preserved a collection of documents (*Ant.* 14) by which various Roman officials required the consent of associated governments to privileges for Jewish minorities. Most of them belong to the civil war period, and the element of constraint is apparent. The punctilious constitutionalism of easier times, a century and a half later, is revealed by the tenth book of Pliny's *Letters.* It is the dossier containing a provincial supervisor's reports to his senior in the capital, and the official replies. The formal status of the local governments varied, but each is dealt with strictly within the terms of its agreement with the Romans, even though this meant the frustration of imperial policy on a particular point (cf. *Ep.* 47, 48, 92, 93, etc.). Nevertheless there was no doubt as to who sponsored the agreements to begin with.

The Greeks themselves devoted a good deal of thought to the reconciliation of their autonomy with Roman supervision. The generation of Dio Chrysostom and Plutarch, smarting under the recent affronts of the Flavians, cultivated an independent air.[25] Co-operation with the Romans was obviously prudent, but they did not essentially qualify the others' autonomy. They merely guaranteed it. The next generation, in so far as it is represented by the unctuous orations of Aelius Aristides, seems to have mellowed under the benevolent internationalism of the Antonines. Local loyalty is played down in anticipation of the common universal citizenship that was steadily being realized. The ideal kingship represented by the Roman rulers is invoked to justify universal subordination.[26]

---

[24] Cf. D. Magie, *Roman Rule in Asia Minor,* 1950.

[25] Cf. H. Bengtson, *Griechische Geschichte,* 1950; T. Renoirte, *Les Conseils Politiques de Plutarque,* 1951.

[26] Cf. for a study of the adjustments involved, C. G. Starr, *Civilisation and the Caesars: The Intellectual Revolution in the Roman Empire,* 1954; C. N. Cochrane, *Christianity and Classical Culture: A Study in Thought and Action from Augustus to Augustine,* 1944.

The New Testament comes from the transitional period when local nationalisms were still vigorous, and international bonds not yet fully developed. The brief account of the conflict between the republics of Tyre and Sidon on the one hand and Herod Agrippa I, King of Judaea, then enjoying a short-lived restoration, shows how independent the lesser governments could be (Acts 12:20). The situation on this occasion had degenerated at least into a cold war, and Herod was applying economic sanctions, the republics being dependent on his territories for essential foodstuffs. The affair was settled through regular diplomatic channels, including apparently graft in high places, without being submitted to the Romans at all.

The conjunction of authorities in a particular territory was sometimes complex. The republic of Damascus granted powers of extradition of criminals to the Jewish government in Jerusalem (Acts 9:2), and also allowed certain rights to a local governor appointed by their eastern neighbour, Aretas, King of the Nabataean Arabs (2 Cor 11:32). Both of these concessions were presumably made with the approval of the Romans, and were perhaps designed to protect the interests of resident minorities drawn from the two peoples concerned.

The delicacy of the legal complications arising from the decentralization of power is well illustrated by the proceedings at Caesarea over Paul of Tarsus (Acts 25:23–27). The Roman official appointed for the supervision of the various authorities in the area found himself obliged to clarify the charges brought by the government of the Jewish ethnic community against one of their nationals, who was unfortunately also entitled to Roman jurisdiction as a citizen of that republic. The accused had declined to have the case heard in the presence of the Jewish court in Jerusalem, and was not even content to accept the jurisdiction of the Roman deputy at Caesarea. Trading on the fact that this official was not finally responsible, but held his powers merely by delegation from the titular governor in the capital itself,[27] he had insisted that the case be transferred to the fully competent authority ('I stand at Caesar's judgment seat, where I ought to be judged'). Faced with this embarrassing demand, the deputy, to help draft his report, constituted a commission of enquiry that included the officers of his own Roman forces, the principal citizens of the republic in which he was stationed, and the rulers of a neighbouring kingdom who were paying a complimentary visit, and

---

[27] This explanation avoids the need to interpret the much canvassed appeal to Caesar as evidence for his appellate jurisdiction, which would be unparalleled at this period, cf. A. H. M. Jones, in *Historia*, 1955.

being themselves Jews might be expected to help unravel the involved legal position.

The idea of numerous lesser governments working in association with the Romans was plainly not simply a hypocritical fiction. On the other hand it must not be explained entirely in terms of sentimental republicanism. The Romans worked pragmatically, and were well aware of the limits to their own power. It is a mark of their political maturity that they had learned to govern not by destroying the individuality or self-esteem of their subjects, but by accommodating it, and exploiting it as a prop to their own administration. Their reward was normally the enthusiastic co-operation of the dependants. A feeling of futility began to get the upper hand, however, after New Testament times, when it slowly became more difficult to prevail upon the associated peoples to exercise their rights.

But the New Testament documents make it plain that at this period the ideal of autonomy was still sufficiently familiar for the tension between it and the growing awareness of the realities of the situation to be acutely felt. In the back of every political leader's mind was the realization that the power he enjoyed was ultimately by permission only, on condition of good behaviour. Inefficiency could lead to suspension of privileges.

It was this fear that compelled the Jerusalem authorities to work for the suppression of Jesus. There was a long history of popular unrest, and if public order was disturbed again, the Romans might feel obliged to make further experiments in the government of Judaea. 'The Romans shall come and take away both our place and nation' (John 11:48). As it turned out, the local authorities must have congratulated themselves on a completely successful operation. The official Roman view is laconically expressed by the later historian, Tacitus (*Hist.* 5.9), in his review of the troubles in Judaea. '*Sub Tiberio quies.*' 'Under Tiberius nothing happened.'

The same anxiety was expressed by the officials of the Ephesian republic in insisting that an irregular assembly be broken up. Regular meetings were provided for, but this one could be misconstrued as a revolution, and lead to embarrassing enquiries. 'We are in danger to be called in question for this day's uproar, there being no cause whereby we may give an account of this concourse (namely, assembly)' (Acts 19:40). It was not simply the riotousness, but the danger of being called in question for irregularity that was alarming. The Ephesians enjoyed privileges which might easily be jeopardized, and were no doubt particularly touchy. Nervousness of this kind need not have been as marked in the reaction of other peoples to the Romans, particularly beyond the centres where the governors were most frequently seen. The experiences of Paul in some places suggest no great degree of control (e.g. Acts 14:5, 19). Much more prominent than mistrust, in any case, was the feeling of appreciation for the benefits gained through the Roman association. The calculated rhetoric of the professional pleader, Tertullus, may be specious, but at least expresses the conventional hopes placed in a governor. 'Seeing that by thee we enjoy great quietness, and that very worthy deeds are done unto this nation by thy providence, we accept it always, and in all places, most noble Felix, with all thankfulness' (Acts 24:2, 3). Except for doctrinaire nationalists, a realistic approval of the contribution the Romans made seems normally to have outweighed any feelings of humiliation at being subjected to them.

The Hellenistic republics had traditionally mitigated their dependent status by honouring their royal patrons as benefactors. 'The kings of the Gentiles exercise lordship over them; and they that exercise authority upon them are called benefactors' (Luke 22:25). By allotting heroic status to royal benefactors, they could be accommodated within a republican community among its protecting deities without encroaching on its constitutional liberties in any formal way. Thus the republic of Caesarea acclaimed Herod in the accepted manner: 'the people gave a shout, saying, It is the voice of a god, and not of a man' (Acts 12:22).

To Hebrew minds apotheosis was anathema. Herod was eaten of worms, and gave up the ghost. But Hellenistic opinion was by no means reluctant to detect in a great man the genius of divinity. The well-being of any community was wrapped up with the favour of its gods, and the superstitious welcomed visitations. Paul twice disillusioned hopes of this kind placed in himself. After his healing a paralytic at Lystra, the rumour went round, 'The gods are come down to us in the likeness of men' (Acts 14:11), and again at Malta, on his surviving the snake-bite, it was decided that he was not after all a criminal as the portent had at first suggested. 'They changed their minds, and said that he was a god' (Acts 28:6).

This propensity for deification also proved an embarrassment to Christians in a more sophisticated form. Prominent leaders of the Roman republic were given formal honours in a similar way, a custom that was becoming popular during the New Testament period. The Roman government judiciously encouraged this so-called imperial cult. It was a useful demonstration of international solidarity.[28] But its use-

---

[28] Cf. the data assembled in L. R. Taylor, *The Divinity of the Roman Emperor*, 1931.

fulness depended very largely on its being spontaneous. Its development was more likely to be hurried on by local governments anxious to express their loyalty, than by the Romans. Compulsion would have destroyed its quality. Apart from certain megalomaniacs, the Caesars even indulged in mild deprecation of its extravagances. It is significant that though Pliny reported that he had included an offering to the imperial bust among the tests for establishing the identity of Christians, Trajan in his reply (Pliny, *Ep.* 10.97) omitted to specify this, requiring simply that the offering be made to the national gods.

The cult of the ruler, then, had never been felt to be an imposition on republicanism. It was an accepted method of recognizing the individual benefactor. The Romans now tactfully developed this into a cult of their own leadership in a universal and permanent form, thus creating a loyalty that certainly transcended that to the local republic. Its religious character was fundamental to its success.

Common religious observances had always been an essential expression of a community's social cohesion. With the increasing inadequacy of the political machinery as a unifying factor, religion may well have bulked even larger in people's minds as a demonstration of their nationality. When Paul and Barnabas were recognized as gods, there was an official ceremony of the republic planned, and the direction of the national priesthood (Acts 14:13), that of Zeus Propolis, was naturally invited. The Roman citizens of the colony of Philippi objected to Jewish proselytizing as a threat to their national identity (Acts 16:21). The court of the Areopagus, the guardian of the Athenian public religion, felt it incumbent upon them to conduct an enquiry into the ideas of the same preacher (Acts 17:19). The fanatical anti-Jewish demonstration at Ephesus took the form of a two hours' ovation to the national goddess, and was eventually pacified by a speech that appealed openly to religious exclusiveness (Acts 19:34–37). 'Ye men of Ephesus, what man is there that knoweth not how that the city of the Ephesians is a worshipper (namely, privileged guardian) of the great goddess Diana, and of the image which fell down from Jupiter? Seeing then that these things cannot be spoken against, ye ought to be quiet, and to do nothing rashly. For ye have brought hither these men, which are neither robbers of churches, nor yet blasphemers of your goddess.'

Religious nationalism of this kind however was no adequate compensation for the growing constitutional deficiencies of republicanism. Although democratic forms were necessarily retained for ideological reasons, the loss of real sovereignty in favour of external powers, and the fact that the Romans bolstered the position of the aristocratic minorities, induced an inertia which led eventually to their fossilization.

Not that they were yet totally defunct. A prosecution before the public assembly was mooted at Thessalonica. 'The Jews . . . sought to bring them out to the people' (Acts 17:5). But as the point at issue was resolved by direct magisterial action, it did not go ahead, and it is not clear what the proceedings would have been. At Ephesus the assembly still functioned regularly, but lacked criminal jurisdiction (Acts 19:38, 39).

Another outlet through which the citizen body could make its opinions plain was in the unofficial but organized demonstrations that are a feature of Hellenistic city life.[29] If not constitutionally valid, they often gained their point in a rough and ready way. The mass chanting of a crowd was difficult to resist. 'The voice of a god, and not of a man' (Acts 12:22), and 'Great is Diana of the Ephesians' (Acts 19:34), both show plainly the emotional potency of such acclamations. In the heavenly city the seer envisaged 'ten thousand times ten thousand, and thousands of thousands; saying with a loud voice, Worthy is the Lamb that was slain to receive power, and riches, and wisdom, and strength, and honour, and glory, and blessing' (Rev 5:11, 12). Even absolutism justified itself with demonstrations of universal consent.

But though the popular will might still apply itself effectively on ceremonial occasions or in times of crisis, the fact remained that the regular government was increasingly concentrated in the hands of the well-to-do. When even they showed a growing reluctance to accept duties that lacked the compensations of real power, compulsion had to be resorted to by the Romans to keep the local administrative machinery going, leading eventually to a municipal system without apology. By this time, well after our period, the many local citizen bodies had been absorbed into a common Roman citizenship, and the Roman republic itself, faced with the demand for continuity and decisiveness in action created by its own growth, had allowed an overriding combination of powers to be vested permanently in a single official, the Caesar.

Quite apart from this slowly failing effectiveness of republicanism, it had never represented a fully egalitarian sentiment within the societies concerned. On the contrary, the very cohesion of the republican body, which was the test of its quality, was partly achieved by the exclusion of large sections of the population from its privileges. Citizenship conferred financial (cf. Matt 17:25) and legal immunities (Acts 16:37). It was carefully advertised as a mark of social distinction. Witness the self-conscious discrimination of the citizens of Philippi and of their magis-

---

[29] Cf. T. Klauser, in *Reallexikon für Antike und Christentum, usw.*, 1950, s.v. Akklamation.

trates (Acts 16:21, 38); the indignant retort of Paul of Tarsus to the suggestion that he was a non-Hellenized Egyptian ('a citizen of no mean city', Acts 21:39); and the rival pretensions of Claudius Lysias and Paul over their acquisition of Roman citizenship (Acts 22:28).

Lack of citizenship was a humiliating barrier to social acceptance in many cases. The New Testament writers frequently reflect the feelings of the disqualified in their metaphors for the idea of moral alienation from the world. The familiar group of terms: 'strangers', 'foreigners', 'aliens', 'pilgrims', 'sojourners' (e.g. Eph 2:19; Heb 11:13; 1 Pet 1:1, 17; 2:11), are all drawn from the technical vocabulary of republican exclusiveness. Addressed to persons who were undoubtedly often under civil disabilities in their own communities, they must have added peculiar point to the demand for moral detachment.

Foreigners were not the only inferior persons in a republic. They at least formed a recognized bloc, which might enjoy its own corporate organization, as with the Jewish minorities (e.g. Acts 18:15), or if they had talents to offer might be treated as honoured guests, as were the international colony at Athens (Acts 17:21). On the other hand, freedmen, though sometimes in citizenship, might suffer irksome legal restrictions, and still carried the stigma of their origins (Acts 22:28). But it is of course slavery that is the most fundamental instance of discrimination, and the most difficult to assess.[30] Though intimately involved in the day-to-day affairs of the community, classical theory had defined persons held in slavery as chattels. Lacking citizenship, they lacked the essential qualification of humanity. Stoic thought, and Christian, queried the validity of the distinction, but convenience dictated its retention even where the undermining of its theoretical basis was admitted. Widespread humanitarianism did not alter the fact of legal degradation. Paul's letter to Philemon shows that it could by no means be assumed that a Christian owner would not exact his legal due. On the contrary, his right is studiously defended.

This inadequacy of republican society both in its external sovereignty and its internal arrangements led to a disillusionment which showed itself in the deflection of loyalty to other institutions. Thinking men contemplated the idea of a universal republic, the commonwealth of all mankind, the City of God. This was a commonplace of many philosophical schools. Philo, the Alexandrian Jew; Epictetus, brought up in slavery; the Stoic ruler, Marcus Aurelius; all appeal to this overriding

---

[30] Cf. a recent review of the whole subject, W. L. Westermann, *The Slave Systems of Greek and Roman Antiquity*, 1955.

obligation. Christianity offered similar consolations: 'our conversation (namely, commonwealth) is in heaven' (Phil 3:20).

But the social needs of the masses were hardly to be satisfied with philosophy. Many found a compensation for public disabilities in the mutual society and help of the household.

III. THE HOUSEHOLD COMMUNITY: OIKONOMIA

The idea of the household as a unit of society, which might be compared with republic or kingdom, was familiar. 'Every kingdom divided against itself is brought to desolation; and every city or house divided against itself shall not stand' (Matt 12:25). Economics, or the principles of household management, was studied among the Greeks from the point of view of moral philosophy. The relation between household and republic was a matter of controversy. The republican idea had risen in a patriarchal society, and in conflict with its traditions. Thus although Greek political theorists recognized that the household was fundamental, its interests tended to be subordinated to those of the republic, in some cases even to the extent of controlling marriage in the public interest. For a picture of the household community of the Greeks in its untrammelled autonomy, one has to go back to the Homeric poems.[31]

But in an area where republican institutions had never been established, the autonomy of the household under its despotic head was still taken for granted in New Testament times. Lords and masters, servants and stewards; they are familiar figures in the parables of Jesus. Within the household the subject members might rise to positions of power and wealth, controlling the activities of the other servants (Matt 24:45), or the owner's financial affairs (Matt 25:15). But all remained equally exposed to the arbitrary decisions of the master; Jesus frequently dwelt on the catastrophic reversals that might occur; maladministration (Matt 24:49), or even being loyal but unenterprising (Matt 25:25), earned merciless penalties. A trusted servant might be allowed to run up enormous debts on the household account, but if magnanimity turned to vindictiveness he was subject to distraint upon property and person without discrimination, wife and children being disposed of into the bargain (Matt 18:23–34). The dependants of the household included not only the owner's servants, but labourers hired on a daily basis (Matt 20:1), and tenants installed on the property under the super-

---

[31] Cf. M. I. Finley, *The World of Odysseus,* 1956.

vision of the central household to which the products of their labour
went (Matt 21:33–41).

It was this kind of economy that the republican institutions were
designed to prevent, or at least to break up sufficiently for each citizen to
be his own master. But throughout the history of the republic the household in its broader sense remained a rival body. Wealthy proprietors
commanded the support of their economic dependants, such as the labourers who worked on their land or in their businesses, even though
not held in slavery. Provided one had the means to gratify the needs of
one's dependants there were practically no limits to household groupings of this sort. Family connections could be exploited for the pooling
of resources, with the result that even in a democracy political affairs
were frequently dominated by aristocratic coalitions whose real power
was derived from their social following.

In the Roman republic particularly this was a regular phenomenon,
the Romans not having suffered the inroads of the democratic ideology
to the same extent as the Greeks. The republic recognized not only the
sweeping powers the Roman *pater familias* enjoyed over his personal
family, bond and free alike, but also the rights and duties imposed by the
relationship of *clientela*. Freedmen, who had formerly been members of
a household through slavery, retained their link with it, and in some respects their obligation, as its clients. Others also freely associated themselves with it for their mutual benefit. But clientship once accepted was
binding. Loyalty to the household interest was expected, though the authority of the patron was grounded in his trustworthiness, which guaranteed that the material and social needs of the client's family were met.

The intimacy of this grouping offered the kind of security that an
over-extended republic was no longer felt to afford. Its solidarity in turn
could therefore be turned to their own account by politically-minded patrons, with the result that political competition in the Roman republic
consisted of alignment and realignment within the aristocracy, success
going to the combination which commanded the greatest voting strength
through its *clientela*. Many of the paradoxes which Roman politics present
to political theory may be explained in terms of these institutions.[32]

The New Testament comes from a period when this monopoly of
political power through the control of social groupings had recently
been carried to novel proportions. The success of Caesarism is perhaps
basically a social phenomenon. Augustus states in his political testament

---

[32] Cf. H. H. Scullard, *Roman Politics*, 1951; L. R. Taylor, *Party Politics in the
Age of Caesar*, 1949; R. Syme, *The Roman Revolution*, 1939.

that what was undoubtedly at the critical moment a usurpation of political power was in fact carried out on the basis of an oath of personal loyalty applied to the whole population. It would be hard to say that this was explained at the time as a universal *clientela*, but the fact that it was not imposed upon the clients of his principal opponent suggests that the validity of that relationship may have been peculiarly vital to Octavian's own position. This anomalous situation was shortly afterwards rectified, but the implication was plain. He had asserted the priority of the personal obligation over public duty. The institutions of the republic had been converted to the aggrandizement of the household community.

This is the key to the success of the imperial system. Technically the Caesars were republican officials, but filling out and substantiating their agglomeration of legal powers was the undefined but supremely influential authority derived from the patronal link with the other members of the republic.[33] The feeling of personal indebtedness to the Caesar was sedulously cultivated. The *Res Gestae* of Augustus is a manifesto addressed to the public, putting on permanent record the long list of benefits they had received, and the honours they had returned him, and culminating in the act that expressed the essential character of their relation to him, the formal and universal acknowledgment of him as *Pater Patriae*. This paternalism reveals the emotional basis upon which the power of the Caesars rested. It was neither novel in kind, nor alarming. Being always a familiar factor in Roman society, its new universal application was welcomed. The opposition to Augustus centred in the other leading houses, who resented their dispossession. Republican politics had traditionally consisted of open competition among them; the new monopoly of the government by one of their number marked the end of the republic as they conceived of it. But to the great bulk of the population the republic meant constitutional government, public order, legality. This they saw restored and confirmed.[34] There was no inconsistency in the fact that it was permanently sponsored by one leader. Authoritarian leadership was understood and accepted. Augustus neither concealed his domination, nor was it misinterpreted by his contemporaries. In Roman politics credit always accrued to success; a reputation conferred authority; everything was to be gained by judicious advertisement. Moreover an established position conferred on one's heirs the right, and indeed the duty, of succeeding to it. The perpetuation of the Caesarian system was not the result of a sinister dynasticism: it was

---

[33] Cf. H. Mattingly, *The Emperor and His Clients*, 1948.
[34] Cf. R. Syme, *A Roman Post-mortem: An Inquest on the Fall of the Roman Republic*, 1950.

the product of the characteristic Roman sentiments of the family's obligation to its own tradition, and the loyalty of dependants to the patronal household.

The ramifications of this establishment imposed duties on persons at all levels of society. The family proper must maintain high standards of ability and responsibility in its own members. Its continuity must be ensured by strategic marriages, and by adoption if the regular succession failed. Augustus himself was plagued with difficulties of this kind. A hierarchy of carefully selected friends must be established. Friendship was not simply a spontaneous relationship of mutual affection. It was a status of intimacy conferred on trusted companions, such as the associates of one's youth (cf. 'Manaen, which had been brought up with Herod the tetrarch', Acts 13:1), or else on persons whose help was essential. Friendship conferred authority and prestige, the greater because undefined; it was from among his friends that the Caesar drew his principal advisers.[35] But its indefiniteness was also its weakness. What had been granted to an inferior might as arbitrarily be renounced, with disastrous consequences. In a position of such delicacy, blackmail could be applied with paralysing effect. 'If thou let this man go, thou art not Caesar's friend' (John 19:12).

More securely placed, because standing in a recognized legal relationship, though one of inferiority, were dependants held in slavery. Upon them fell much of the day-to-day administration of such public affairs as were entrusted to the Caesar; they constituted a kind of imperial bureaucracy. Their occupation conferred social distinction upon them; among their legal equals they were regarded as a special class. The letter to the Philippians carried greetings from the Christians in the capital, 'chiefly they that are of Caesar's household' (Phil 4:22). Their services in the administration frequently earned them emancipation, leading in turn to rapid promotion and high honours that scandalized the traditional aristocracy. Felix, the procurator of Judaea who investigated the charges against Paul, was a freedman of the imperial household. His brother Pallas was the financial expert in the government of Claudius.

Beyond these privileged circles of clients, dependants, and friends, lay the masses of the population pledged to support the Caesarian cause. The oath sworn by the Paphlagonians and the Roman businessmen resident in that area[36] calls to witness Zeus, Earth, Sun, all the gods and

---

[35] Cf. J. Crook, *Consilium Principis*, 1955.
[36] V. Ehrenberg and A. H. M. Jones, *Documents Illustrating the Reigns of Augustus and Tiberius*, 1949, no. 315.

goddesses, and Augustus himself, and invokes utter destruction of body and soul, children, kindred, and descendants, in the event of any act contrary to or inconsistent with its terms. It pledges loyalty of word, deed, and thought to Augustus, his children, and his descendants; full identification with them in their personal friendships and enmities, to the extent of sacrificing life and children in their support; and the duty of reporting any word, plan, or act that was discovered to be against their interests. 'They drew Jason and certain brethren unto the rulers of the city, crying, These that have turned the world upside down are come hither also; whom Jason hath received: and these all do contrary to the decrees of Caesar, saying that there is another king, one Jesus. And they troubled the people and the rulers of the city, when they heard these things' (Acts 17:6–8). The oath may not have been taken seriously by individuals, but it was public knowledge that everyone was committed to it, and the accusation of disloyalty could be damaging. Whatever one's personal feelings, public displays of conformity were expedient. 'We have no king but Caesar' (John 19:15).

The Caesarian system is easily the best documented case of the bearing of personal loyalties on the functioning of republican institutions, and it is of course abnormal in the degree of its success. But it does illustrate plainly how fundamental the household community was in ancient society.[37] There were many such lesser groupings, and large sections of society clearly found compensation for the disabilities imposed by the limits on citizenship and the failure of democracy in the benevolence and community feeling enjoyed within the circle of wealthy patrons.

The household, like the republic, expressed its solidarity in a common religion.[38] The new paternal government appealed to both sentiments in an imperial cult (cf. above, pp. 16–17) that was at the same time public and personal in the objects of its devotion: *Roma et Augustus*. This religious character of the household community, added to its fundamental position in society, explains much of the behaviour of the New Testament groups. Where the head of a house was converted, its religious unity was preserved. The members were apparently baptized as a group.

Cornelius was a fairly low ranking Roman army officer. Yet his household has all the usual ramifications, and all deliberately involved in its religious interests ('a devout man, and one that feared God with all

---

[37] Cf. for a Marxist treatment of the topic, N. A. Maschkin, *Prinzipat Augusta*, 1949 (German version, 1954).

[38] Cf. G. Bardy, *La Conversion au Christianisme durant les premiers siècles*, 1949.

his house', Acts 10:2). Servants and batmen are at his disposal for his own religious ends ('he called two of his household servants, and a devout soldier of them that waited on him continually', Acts 10:7). Contemplating an important innovation, he made certain that his own family and circle of personal associates were included (he 'had called together his kinsmen and near friends', Acts 10:24). The company that was finally baptized into the new faith was a large one (Acts 10:27, 48).

Detailed information is not available in other cases, but the fact that the first converts in certain places were wealthy or prominent persons who were baptized together with their households is significant for the way the movement spread. At Philippi it began with a pro-Jewish woman who was the business agent for the luxury textile industry based in Thyatira in Asia Minor (Acts 16:15). The baptism of her household was followed by that of the city's jailor (Acts 16:33). The first baptism at Corinth was of the household of one Stephanas, who earned a reputation as a benefactor of the Christians (1 Cor 1:16; 16:15), but the accession that attracted most attention at the time was that of the household of the chief ruler of the synagogue (Acts 18:8).

Not only was the conversion of a household the natural or even the necessary way of establishing the new cult in unfamiliar surroundings, but the household remained the soundest basis for the meetings of Christians. In several of the cases above the preachers were entertained and begged to carry on their activities from that platform. The Christians in a particular city are thought of not as an undifferentiated unit; individual household groups are commonly singled out. Among the persons to whom greetings are sent in one letter, for instance, there are three sets representing full households (Rom 16:5, 14, 15), and two others apparently drawn from the inferior members of households whose heads are by implication not Christians (Rom 16:10, 11). This latter phenomenon suggests some kind of looseness in the groups concerned, though it is still significant that even when detached from their group for religious reasons they remain a coherent body.

It is not clear whether the common New Testament phrase 'the church (namely, meeting) in one's house' denotes the meeting of a larger body of Christians through the hospitality of a particular household, or the members of the Christian meeting as separately constituted who happen to belong to the household concerned. The latter sense would certainly apply where the early habits of the Jerusalem group were followed, 'breaking bread from house to house (namely, in their own houses)' (Acts 2:46). These household celebrations were in addition to the general meetings (Acts 2:44), but in Corinth both ceremonial and communal meals apparently took place at a joint gathering (1 Cor 11:22). This was presumably held in the premises of 'Gaius mine host, and of the whole church' (Rom 16:23), a person whose distinction earned him his baptism at the hands of Paul (1 Cor 1:14) along with Crispus, the chief ruler of the synagogue, and Stephanas (cf. above, p. 25). The groups referred to at Colossae (Phlm 2), Laodicea (Col 4:15), and Ephesus (1 Cor 16:19) seem to be distinguished from the main body of Christians in those places, though more likely as households which corporately belonged to the general meeting than as meetings in their own right on a household basis.

As with the republican institutions, the terminology of the household community was regularly used by the New Testament writers to express their theological ideas. In one passage the two sets of terms are strikingly run together. The non-Jewish believers have been relieved of their former civil disabilities, admitted to a joint citizenship in the republic of Israel, and accepted as members of God's household (Eph 2:19). Although the problem under discussion is that of reconciling the position of Greek converts with the peculiar religious privileges of Israel, and the terminology may have been familiar to Hellenized Jews when thinking of their national tradition, there can be little doubt that addressed to Greeks as in fact it is, its forcefulness depends on their familiarity with the words as applied in their own political and social situation.

The gradations within 'the household of faith' (Gal 6:10) are as various as in any other. Jesus had spoken of himself both as Son (Matt 11:27) and as Servant (Matt 12:18). He pictured the disciples as his own servants (Matt 10:25). At one point his words clearly reveal the peculiar combination of intimacy and subordination that was characteristic of the institutionalized friendship conferred by the great patrons on trusted clients. 'Ye are my friends, if ye do whatsoever I command you. Henceforth I call you not servants; for the servant knoweth not what his lord doeth: but I have called you friends; for all things that I have heard of my Father I have made known unto you. Ye have not chosen me, but I have chosen you' (John 15:14–16). Paul carried the idea of emancipation one step further with his metaphors from the institution of adoptive sonship, which, properly attested, was not only legally but morally liberating, since it guaranteed rights of succession and afforded an unchallengeable security. 'For ye have not received the spirit of bondage again to fear; but ye have received the Spirit of adoption, whereby we cry, Abba, Father. The Spirit itself beareth witness with our spirit, that we are the children of God: and if children, then heirs; heirs of God, and joint-heirs with Christ' (Rom 8:15–17; cf. Gal 4:5–7).

But the most illuminating adaptation of household terms to theological ideas is the constant assertion that Christians are the servants of God. Their leaders are his stewards (1 Cor 4:1; Tit 1:7; 1 Pet 4:10), and the duty with which they are entrusted is the administration of his goods for the benefit of his household (1 Cor 9:17; Eph 3:2; Col 1:25). More commonly still, they are simply his servants, stressing the subjection rather than the trust. These metaphors from slavery suggest how far the institution was appreciated as a means of support for the otherwise unrepresented and helpless. The bond frequently excited feelings not of resentment, but of personal devotion and loyalty towards the master. Moreover, as with the centurion whose servant 'was dear unto him' (Luke 7:2), the bond could be the basis of mutual affection.

Nevertheless there were many who found their needs unsatisfied either in the republican or the household community. Though both of these could give expression to high ideals of humanity, they both fortified a paternalistic order. The democratic ideology had certainly once worked against this, but the great patrons, by exploiting their personal followings for political ends, had converted the very democratic institutions into an outlet for their own paternalism. But the democratic instinct persisted among sections of society that lacked access to any official means of expression.

IV. Unofficial Associations: Koinonia

One of the critical steps towards breaking the original family domination of Greek society had been the defining of rights of spontaneous association. Combinations of individuals might be formed on their own terms, providing no public law was infringed. In its ideal form, the republic had been designed to satisfy fully the needs of its members in communal activity, but with its increasing inadequacy unofficial societies of all kinds multiplied.

As with the republic and the household, they were always religious societies to the extent that they gave formal expression to their unity in the worship of a god. The members frequently belonged to a common profession or industry, of which the god was patron. The silversmiths at Ephesus were obviously devotees of their national goddess, Diana, the popularity of whose cult was not unrelated to their own livelihood (Acts 19:24, 27). But the direct economic interest in the cult must have been unusual. It was otherwise important principally as an occasion for convivial gatherings; it was under the aegis of the deity that they celebrated the dinners which were their characteristic activity. For this reason Christians found their membership in such societies an embarrassment; 'for if any man see thee which hast knowledge sit at meat in the idol's temple, shall not the conscience of him which is weak be emboldened to eat those things which are offered to idols' (1 Cor 8:10). They also acted as friendly societies, holding common funds for charity, and in particular offering security of burial. They normally constituted themselves along republican lines ('proprium est ad exemplum rei publicae habere res communes', Gaius, *ap. Dig.* 3.4.1), electing officials and holding formal business meetings. Not much information can be gathered about unofficial associations from the literary remains of classical antiquity, as these emanate principally from the aristocratic circles which were preoccupied with public activities. A great number of their own epigraphic records survives, but is concerned mainly with constitutional or ceremonial details. The literary references and legal texts in turn deal almost exclusively with the attempts of the public authorities to keep them under some sort of control. But there is a serious lack of information about their membership and activities in themselves.

The result of this disproportion in the primary material is that modern students are obliged to follow the official preoccupation with their effects on public order. The government had no wish to limit their innocent activities, but was nevertheless worried by the fact that they were not subject to regular supervision, and could therefore become centres of agitation.[39] How justified such fears were may be judged from the alarming results of the grievances of the Ephesian silversmiths. Their economic difficulties led them to stage a demonstration which took on a nationalistic character. Another association, that of the Jews, though not themselves the cause of the original complaints, attempted to get a hearing, probably with a view to dissociating themselves from the charges. This however resulted in an outburst of mass hysteria which the local government feared might lead to enquiries by the Roman authorities (Acts 19:24–41).

The case of the Jewish associations shows that the unrest centering on such bodies need not be caused by agitation on their own part. The exclusiveness of a group, particularly when devoted to a foreign religion, might attract public antipathy through little fault of its own. The leader of the Jewish association at Corinth ('Sosthenes, the chief ruler of the synagogue', Acts 18:17), on his society's suit being disallowed in the pub-

---

[39] Cf. B. Reicke, *Diakonie, Festfreude und Zelos in Verbindung mit der altchristlichen Agapenfeier*, 1951; C. G. Starr, *Civilization and the Caesars*, 1954.

lic court, was physically assaulted by a non-Jewish crowd. On the other hand the Jews frequently acted as a pressure group in politics to compel public action against a heretical sect that threatened their own solidarity. This might be achieved either by using influence with the authorities themselves ('the Jews stirred up the devout and honourable women, and the chief men of the city', Acts 13:50), or by using mob action to force the authorities' hands ('the Jews which believed not, moved with envy, took unto them certain lewd fellows of the baser sort, and gathered a company, and set all the city on an uproar, and assaulted the house of Jason, and sought to bring them out to the people', Acts 17:5).

It was because of this kind of behaviour that the Roman government clamped down on certain kinds of association from time to time. The Jews themselves sometimes found their privileges suspended ('Claudius had commanded all Jews to depart from Rome', Acts 18:2). At Philippi they may even have been prevented from forming an association, or at any rate sufficiently discouraged from settlement for it not to be possible under the terms of their own law. The sabbath was observed by a small group of women, though not in the normal manner, and the only one of their number who is named was not herself a Jewess (Acts 16:13, 14). The complaint made to the authorities and the official penalty imposed show that there was a ban on proselytization that was sufficiently strictly enforced to make conditions particularly awkward for a proper Jewish settlement ('These men, being Jews, do exceedingly trouble our city, and teach customs, which are not lawful for us to receive, neither to observe, being Romans. . . . And the magistrates rent off their clothes, and commanded to beat them', Acts 16:20–22).

Restrictions of this kind on Jewish associations were not at all normal however; on the contrary the Romans went out of their way to protect their autonomy. This privileged position might even be an embarrassment, as at Corinth where the proconsul refused public arbitration on an internal matter ('if it be a question of words and names, and of your law, look ye to it; for I will be no judge of such matters', Acts 18:15). The official disinterest in the religion of its subjects was characteristic of the Roman government. When restrictions had to be imposed on the freedom of the unofficial associations, their specifically religious functions, including charities and the necessary meetings, were safeguarded.

The eventual solution to the problems of the disorder and divisiveness of the associations was typical of Roman pragmatism. They were accommodated within the public framework of society and thus rendered innocuous. This began with the legal incorporation of those which applied for and secured official approval,[40] a process which was going on in New Testament times, and reached its end two centuries later when their membership was made hereditary and binding in an attempt to fix the pattern of society.

But within this general trend there was a good deal of variation of official policy. The legal material on the control of associations comes mostly from the latter part of the process and thus creates the risk of anachronism if applied to New Testament times. It is also practically entirely Roman which means that its validity in other territories depended on specific arrangements being made with their governments. Another important qualification is that the enforcement of the laws must have depended greatly on the sense of urgency that a particular administrator felt in the matter. Trajan's administrator in Bithynia, for example, treated even that ruler's clear-cut policy of suppression as sufficiently elastic to admit of exceptions, and though this particular request was refused, Trajan himself insisted that the policy did not bind the autonomous republics (Pliny, *Ep.* 10.34, 93). Moreover the policy was designed in any case for the needs of the moment in Bithynia, and ought not to be assumed to have been a permanent or universal ruling. The fluctuations of official policy suggest that the societies were both multifarious and popular. The question of public recognition mainly affects their capacity as incorporated bodies. Lack of recognition need not mean that they ceased to exist as groups, but simply that they had no rights at law. They were unincorporated rather than illegal. Bodies of this kind may have been numerous at all times. They only attracted the attention of the authorities in the event of malpractices or disorder, when the members would be dealt with as individuals.

Unfortunately we lack detailed information on the internal affairs and attitudes of the associations from an unofficial point of view, with the exception of the Jews and the Christians. The New Testament writings are therefore an invaluable supplement to the legal material. A serious difficulty is that both of these kinds of association are in some ways untypical. Not of course in their having interest in the cult itself as the principal common factor rather than occupation, for there were many unofficial religious movements whose appeal was similar.[41]

The Jews were unusual in their feeling that they were a distinct nationality. This was sustained even though many of them were fully accepted and qualified in the communities where they lived, and their

---

[40] Cf. P. W. Duff, *Personality in Roman Private Law*, 1938.
[41] Cf. K. Prümm, *Religionsgeschichtliches Handbuch für den Raum der Altchristlichen Umwelt*, 1954.

religion attracted widespread interest among the other inhabitants.[42] It
was apparently positively fashionable in many of the cities Paul visited
for the 'honourable women which were Greeks' to bestow their attentions on the Jewish cult (cf. Acts 13:50; 16:14; 17:12). The legal status of
Jewish associations is disputed[43] but plainly there was at least a body
that was fully incorporated and a form of meeting that was unofficial
(cf. above, pp. 28–29). But whatever the local arrangements, Judaism
was a phenomenon that was perfectly well understood by the authorities
and public alike.

The groups of Christians shared with the Jews the peculiarity of
maintaining international links, but lacking a recognized national seat
for their cult, this habit can hardly have seemed so justifiable to the authorities as in the case of the Jews. Compared with other associations,
they were probably also abnormal in the broad constituency from which
their members were drawn. This might also be deemed undesirable.
There are great difficulties in determining their legal status,[44] but there
need be no doubt that whatever it was they were not distinguished in the
public's mind from the general run of unofficial associations. Like many
others they could be labelled conveniently from the god whose patronage they claimed. 'Christ-ites' is certainly not the sort of name they
would have chosen for themselves; but they seem to have had no agreed
terminology, and most of the phrases they used, such as 'the sanctified'
and 'the brothers', were hardly likely to pass over into general usage
when they merely denoted in a vague way the kind of satisfaction offered
by many other parallel societies. The Jews are the last persons who
would have coined such a word as 'Christian', which to them would have
conceded the very point about the Messiahship of Jesus that they denounced as heretical; the followers of Jesus were simply 'the sect of
the Nazarenes' (Acts 24:5). The word concerned (i.e. 'Christian') is
a latinized form, invented at Antioch (Acts 11:26) when an accession
of non-Jews to the movement first made its separate identity from the
Jewish associations apparent. A generation later it was still used contemptuously, knowing that it would hurt (Acts 26:28), and was achiev-
ing popularity as an expression of the odium excited by Christians
('quos per flagitia inuisos uulgus Christianos appellabat', Tacitus, *Ann.*
15.44). Its admission in the courts at this time as incriminating proof of

[42] Cf. S. W. Baron, *A Social and Religious History of the Jews*, 1952.
[43] Cf. S. L. Guterman, *Religious Toleration and Persecution in Ancient Rome*, 1951.
[44] Cf. J.-P. Waltzing, art. 'Collegia', in *Dictionnaire d'Archéologie Chré-tienne*, etc.

membership led to its reluctant acceptance by Christians themselves (1 Pet 4:16).

This distaste of the Christians for the name that was gratuitously bestowed upon them, however, certainly does not mean that they were unwilling to be thought of as forming an association of the usual kind. On the contrary it would hardly have occurred to them to raise the question in the first place. It was taken for granted. Whatever the original Jerusalem group may have thought about the character of their society and its government, and whatever affinities it may have had with contemporary Palestinian religious movements, the person who wrote up its affairs a generation later for the information of a Hellenistic public presented it in terms that could not fail to identify it as a religious association of the kind familiar to them. The term *ecclesia* (namely, meeting) itself, and the names for the various officials may have developed special connotations within the Christian community, but to non-Christians, and to Christians themselves in the early stages, they need have suggested nothing out of the ordinary.

The first vacancy in the board of special commissioners who administered the community was filled by the recognized republican method of sortition from a preselected field (Acts 1:23, 26). When an additional board was needed to deal with financial affairs, it was elected by the membership summoned in an assembly by the original board, who then asserted their own right of appointment by confirming the election (Acts 6:2–6). This relationship between board of management and assembly of members was developed into a regular system of government, with the addition of an advisory council of senior members. This latter body was bracketed with the board of management who consulted it. Business was submitted to the two jointly, but reports were first made to the assembly. When a proposition was made from the floor of this meeting, the board and council withdrew for a full discussion, during which controversial views were aired and a decision reached. They then returned to the assembly, the originators of the business presented a formal report on the situation that had provoked it, and a spokesman for the board (not the person who had resolved the conflict in council) introduced a formal motion, inviting the assembly to act. The decision was expressed as taken in concert by board and council, together with the assembly. The document conveying it was drafted in the name of board and council (acting as executors), referring to the joint enactment (Acts 15:2, 4, 6, 12, 19, 22, 23, 25). It cannot be shown that other Christian groups were constituted in this form; indeed the association to which the communication in question is addressed, that at Antioch, seems to be constituted simply as an assembly, under charismatic leadership (Acts

13:1–3; 15:23, 30, 32–35). But if the group in non-republican Jerusalem governed itself in a manner so thoroughly in harmony with the customs of Hellenistic corporations, both republics and lesser bodies alike, it would be most surprising if the Christian associations in the Hellenistic cities themselves presented any constitutional novelty to their contemporaries. The international direction, as seen applied in the case cited above, and in the activities of the principal travelling member of the board of management (e.g. 'For this cause left I thee in Crete, that thou shouldest set in order the things that are wanting, and ordain elders in every city, as I had appointed thee', Tit 1:5), may be unusual, but does not seriously qualify the similarity at the local level.

But even if the constitutional and legal situation of the Christian associations could be shown to be distinctive, they would still have to be classified under this heading on the grounds of their objects and activities. The summary description of the behaviour of the first group at Jerusalem, would, with a few technical terms changed to suit, do very nicely as an idealized version of the activities of many other Hellenistic religious associations. All the elements are familiar: initiation, the mysteries, equal partnership, ceremonial meal, the cult, wonder-working, mutual benefits ('Then they that gladly received his word were baptised . . . , and they continued steadfastly in the apostles' doctrine and fellowship, and in breaking of bread, and in prayers. And fear came upon every soul: and many wonders and signs were done by the apostles. And all that believed were together, and had all things common; and sold their possessions and goods, and parted them to all men, as every man had need', Acts 2:41–45).

The first bliss did not last however. The impassioned expositions of the ideal which make up the bulk of the Epistles attest the degree of its frustration. Factions supported rival leaders (1 Cor 1:12); members sued each other in the public courts (1 Cor 6:7); the common meal was poisoned by selfishness (1 Cor 11:21); social discrimination split up the group (1 Cor 12:23); they were reluctant to support each other financially (1 Cor 16:1).

Nevertheless the ideal persisted: 'We being many are . . . one body' (1 Cor 10:17). Eighty years after the beginning, at the end of the New Testament period, an official investigator discovered the same essential practices going on (Pliny, *Ep.* 10.96). Lapsed members who were interrogated would only admit to the fact that there had been regular meetings of the community (held before dawn, which was hardly the time for scandalous behaviour); that this was for cult purposes (an antiphonal hymn to Christ as in honour of a god was the detail that impressed Pliny); that their ceremonies involved pledges against moral delinquency (a good point for the governor); and that there had been a second gathering for a communal meal (but no indulgence or indecencies).

This however had been abandoned on the announcement of Trajan's edict banning fraternities, an important point which shows that the Christians were distinguished from the other unofficial associations neither by the authorities nor by themselves, and also that the ban was not intended to apply to the strictly religious gatherings of any association, but merely to its social occasions. That these depositions were substantially true in spite of their suspect origin, Pliny himself established by a third-degree examination of two girls who were attendants at the Christian meetings. He had been alarmed by the calculated reference of his previous informants to the precaution the Christians had taken against infringing the law on associations. But the only extra points he could unearth were a mass of perverted and unbalanced beliefs. Apparently his subjects had insisted on giving him lessons in 'the apostles' doctrine' to correct the previous information.

But though the Christians shared so many of the characteristics of the other associations, including the problems of administration their disorders posed the government, they also threatened to become a disintegrating factor in a strained social order in a way that was peculiar to themselves, through the odium they generated.[45] Their novel theological ideas, that is partly their monotheism, though this was not unparalleled, but more particularly their eschatology, which was disconcertingly final, led them into serious breaches of social convention. The resultant alienation generated fantastic charges, but also the secretiveness that made the unravelling of them impossible. Popular alarmism dragged halting public authorities into a series of haphazard actions against Christians. Mutual hostility ended in repression and insubordination, until a solution was eventually contrived along familiar lines. The Christian associations were themselves incorporated, and recognized as part of the normal social order, in the hope that their energies might be converted to its preservation.

One of the features that had made the movement so disconcerting was the unusual social character of its membership. This must therefore be clarified, and the early conflicts with the authorities studied, if its social precepts and practices are to be understood.

V. THE SOCIAL CONSTITUENCY OF CHRISTIAN GROUPS

Any demographic study of New Testament times that aims at detailed accuracy is doomed to failure from the start by the inadequacy of

---

[45] Cf. E. M. Blaiklock, *The Christian in Pagan Society,* 1951.

the statistical material.[46] A few statistics may even be worse than none, since they may have been recorded simply because they were not typical, and therefore of particular interest at the time. There is plenty of general information that can be brought to bear, but the interpretation of it is still controversial. Prosopography, for example, provides innumerable details of prominent persons, but prominence is by definition useless for determining the norm. The normal is never interesting, except to statisticians. Vaguer, and therefore safer, are the general implications of the organization of Christian groups, their social and charitable activities, their educational standard as seen in the surviving writings, their relations with the general public and the government, and so on. Insufficiency of material is of course the historian's livelihood, but when other than historical interests can become involved in his reconstruction, as on this topic, it is also a test of his integrity. Not that there is ultimately any such thing as a disinterested statement about the past. The mere fact of selection guarantees the relativity of historical judgments. A neutral statement, listing all the data, or a random selection of them, would be incoherent, and therefore defeat its own end, which is to interpret the past to the present. But the canon of selection must always be identified if the interpretation is not to acquire a specious air of objectivity. The idea of the oecumenicity of the Christian faith nicely illustrates the bearing of dogma on the description of events.

The Christian preachers worked from the assumption that they had a universal obligation. 'Go ye into all the world, and preach the gospel to every creature' (Mark 16:15). With the limitations of their information and their unlimited enthusiasm, they readily anticipated the fulfilling of this duty. It was not only a duty, however, but an article of faith. 'This gospel of the kingdom shall be preached in all the world for a witness unto all nations; and then shall the end come' (Matt 24:14). It was the express precondition of the expected end. The more imminent they conceived the end to be, then, the more freely they talked in terms of a universal preaching. It could be spoken of as already achieved (Col 1:23). Not only was this outlook involved in the formulation of the faith (cf. 1 Tim 3:16), but it developed a usefulness on other grounds. It was a good point to stress in the face of suspicion or contempt, for the encouragement of the faithful (e.g. 1 Thess 1:8; Rom 1:8), or for the confusion of their enemies. The literary form of the book of Acts suggests an apologetic intention along these lines. It begins by showing that the Pentecostal gift

---

[46]Cf. F. G. Maier, 'Römische Bevölkerungsgeschichte und Inschriftenstatistik', in *Historia*, 1954.

was designed to carry the testimony 'unto the uttermost part of the earth' (Acts 1:8). The realization of this is at once foreshadowed when on the first day the preachers address themselves to a crowd representing 'every nation under heaven' (Acts 2:5). When the preaching is carried beyond Jerusalem, three conversions are singled out for detailed treatment, those of an Ethiopian statesman, a Jewish religious leader, and a Roman army officer. There are other obvious reasons for the interest in these persons, but they could also be intended to symbolize the reaching of the goal (Acts 8–10). The book then traces the progress from Jerusalem to Rome, the centre of the civilized world, where Paul is dramatically left 'preaching the kingdom of God . . . , with all confidence, no man forbidding him' (Acts 28:31). Suppression later converted this optimism into a defiant apocalyptic which envisaged in heaven the success that was denied on earth, 'a great multitude, which no man could number, of all nations, and kindreds, and people, and tongues' (Rev 7:9).

Subsequent to New Testament times the extent of the movement became a matter of embittered contention between its protagonists and their critics. But all this must be evaluated as debating-material, not as direct historical data. Where so much is said in hatred, fear, or anger, the conclusions based upon it must be very tentative, taking as an overriding consideration the fact that no-one can have had any certain means of ascertaining the situation beyond his immediate experience. The prophetic assurance of the first Christians was exploited by a later romanticism as the basis for the idea that certain prominent centres of Christianity went back to the founding generation. Another extraneous factor appeared with the dissensions among Christians themselves, when the claim to catholicity proved a useful stick to beat ecclesiastical opponents with.

The geographical expansion of the Christian movement in its early years is no longer a matter of strong feeling in any of these ways. Its main outlines are agreed upon.[47] But the question of its penetration within the framework of society can still be the subject of tendentious treatment. Modern Christians, uneasy about the respectability of a faith that is supposed to have revolutionary implications, like to cultivate the idea that it first flourished among the depressed sections of society. Others again have an ideological interest in identifying its impetus as that of social discontent.[48] Given a belief in the class struggle, it is easy to take a group of Galilean peasants, add the community of goods, Paul 'working

---

[47] Cf. K. S. Latourette, *A History of the Expansion of Christianity*, 1953.
[48] Cf. J. Morris, 'Early Christian Orthodoxy', in *Past and Present*, 1953.

with his hands', and the 'not many wise . . . , not many mighty, not many noble' at Corinth, and thus discover a movement of protest among the working classes; or alternatively an internal proletariat breaking down the old civilization in favour of the emergent new one, given that one has been initiated into the rhythms of civilizations. But unfortunately the social stratification of the Christian groups has never been properly investigated, and is perhaps beyond recovery. Quite apart from the difficulties of the Christian sources, the patterns of contemporary society in general need further clarification if the Christians are to be fitted into them. What follows here is merely an attempt to show that from a different selection of data, or even the same data differently evaluated, a picture can be obtained very different from that caricatured above.

If the common assertion that the Christian groups were constituted from the lower orders of society is meant to imply that they did not draw upon the upper orders of the Roman ranking system, the observation is correct, and pointless. In the eastern Mediterranean it was self-evident that members of the Roman aristocracy would not belong to a local cult association. Their social needs were very amply gratified by the exclusiveness of the circles to which they were admitted. The concentration of literary talent within these circles has won them a familiarity out of all proportion to their numbers (cf. above, p. 10), which amounted to an infinitesimally small fraction of the total population.

The only Roman aristocrats likely to be found in the east were the provincial governors themselves and a few members of their staffs; distinguished local politicians who had been elevated for their services in order that outstanding talent for leadership should have a vested interest in the Roman loyalty;[49] and millionaires on business from the capital, together with the local magnates who attracted official attention by public benefactions. It might occasionally happen that Christians met such persons, but plainly not on their own ground. It was as Jews that the contact was made. An interest in Judaism was not at all uncommon among the Roman aristocracy, and within the leisured classes generally, particularly the women (cf. above, p. 31), whose idleness called for a decent attention to religion. Judaism was presumably felt to offer the respectability of antiquity and a certain austerity of manners which appealed to the Roman mentality. The cultivation of Jewish manners by members of the nobility was a useful pretext for political purges.

The proconsul of Cyprus, Sergius Paulus, who summoned Barnabas and Saul ('who also is called Paul', being allotted his Roman name

---

[49] Cf. W. M. Ramsay, *The Social Basis of Roman Power in Asia Minor*, 1941.

for the occasion) to explain their ideas, and 'believed, being astonished at the doctrine of the Lord', did so because he was already undergoing indoctrination from a Jewish 'prophet' who challenged the Christian teaching (Acts 13:6–12). Other encounters with Roman governors which are recorded all took place in connection with legal proceedings initiated by Jews (cf. *infra*, section VI). Among the local authorities it is difficult to say which are likely to have ranked high in Roman eyes, but the friendship of Paul with 'certain of the chief of Asia' (namely, Asiarchs)[50] is probably the nearest thing to an association between Christianity and the local Romanized aristocracy in our texts. The gentleman depicted entering a meeting in state (Jas 2:2) is clearly of Roman equestrian status, as the gold ring must imply. It need not mean that he belonged to the metropolitan aristocracy, however, and even if he did, he might still be a *parvenu* among them, as the equestrian insignia could be awarded to freedmen to distract attention from their origins[51] (cf. above, p. 23). But it is much more likely that the writer is thinking in terms of the big businessmen of the eastern cities who were certainly familiar to his readers, if not included among them (Jas 4:13). Such persons were not concerned with political careers in the capital; the equestrian insignia were useful to them simply as a mark of their being millionaires. It is most unlikely that James is thinking of a canvassing visit by a local politician, as has been suggested.[52] The much neglected view that James is a Palestinian writing not to Christians as such, but as he says himself to Israel in general, not thinking of 'the faith of our Lord Jesus Christ (namely, Messiah)' (Jas 2:1) as anything but the proper end of Israel's religion,[53] has received unexpected support from the Dead Sea scrolls.[54] If it is correct, it hardly helps to support the idea that Hellenistic politics were in the writer's mind. The passage in question is merely a schematized contrast between the recognized types of luxury and pauperism. Far from suggesting that visits from such men could be expected, it appeals rhetorically to improbable extremes in order to make the point as bluntly as possible. This method is characteristic of the writer. But in any case, granted

---

50 Cf. D. Magie, *Roman Rule in Asia Minor,* 1950; H. J. Cadbury, *The Book of Acts in History,* 1955; J. A. O. Larsen, *Representative Government in Greek and Roman History,* 1955.

51 Cf. A. M. Duff, *Freedmen in the Early Roman Empire,* 1928.

52 By B. Reicke, *Diakonie, Festfreude und Zelos in Verbindung mit der altchristlichen Agapenfeier,* 1951.

53 A. Schlatter, *Jakobusbrief;* cf. *Church in the New Testament Period,* 1955.

54 Cf. T. Gaster, trans., *The Scriptures of the Dead Sea Sect,* 1957.

that the letter is addressed to an undifferentiated Jewry, the equestrian gentleman tells us nothing of relations between Christians and the Roman upper orders, since the 'assembly' (Gk. *synagoge*) he was visiting was a Jewish one.

But the question which needs clearing up is largely untouched by the discovery that Christians rarely met members of the Roman aristocracy; very few people did. What we want to discover are the affiliations of Christians within their own communities. There is nothing in the New Testament to suggest that at this level the groups concerned represented any sectional interest at all. On the contrary their membership seems to have been drawn from a surprising variety of stations. This can be well illustrated even at points that have been taken as supporting the idea of a movement of the depressed classes.

The initial group at Jerusalem centred on the following of Jesus still resident in that city. If they were all Galilaeans, as their spokesmen certainly were (Acts 2:7), and the tradition assumed (Acts 1:11), they had nevertheless successfully established themselves on new ground. It may be that they enjoyed the support of some of the wealthy and influential persons who had entertained Jesus ('Joanna the wife of Chuza Herod's steward, and Susanna, and many others, which ministered unto him of their substance', Luke 8:3). Despite the antipathy between Galilaeans and the professional classes of the city (cf. above, p. 5), Jesus won the secret approval of persons in high places ('among the chief rulers also many believed on him; but because of the Pharisees they did not confess him', John 12:42), at least two of whom remained loyal to his memory (John 19:38, 39; cf. John 3:1; Mark 15:43; Matt 27:57). The Jerusalem group was later openly joined by both priests (Acts 6:7) and Pharisees (Acts 15:5), but this was probably provoked by much more momentous changes that were already taking place.

Whatever secret sympathy there was for the Galilaean group at the start they remained publicly branded as 'unlearned and ignorant men' (Acts 4:13). But the startling expansion of the movement drew precisely on the cosmopolitan crowds who looked down on such villagers (Acts 2:7). The long list of nationalities mentioned (Acts 2:9–11) is meant to show that they represented Jewish communities from all over the civilized world. The list may be due to the writer's universalizing interest (cf. above, pp. 35–36), but it is not for that reason improbable. There were sufficiently large numbers of Jews from abroad in Jerusalem for study, as tourists, on business, or living there in retirement, and they were sufficiently conscious of the background that distinguished them from Palestinian Jewry for there to be at least one, and possibly several, synagogues catering for them (Acts 6:9). There was also a settlement of

Roman citizens, who retained their identity as a body. The phrase 'strangers of Rome' is found in epigraphic parallels as a technical term of constitutional affairs for the Roman citizens resident in a particular place and acting corporately in concert with the local public bodies. In this instance the phrase 'Jews and proselytes' makes the point that the Romans concerned were of course attending a Jewish festival in their religious capacity as members of Israel. But socially they remained distinguished as 'Greeks' (John 12:20), and were treated as a different class by the local population (Acts 2:14). Quite apart from the political and cultural distinction they enjoyed, there was a significant economic gap that marked them off.

That the foreign community in an international resort should be persons of means would be reasonably assumed without specific confirmation. But in this case the evidence is unequivocal. It was explicitly their contribution to the funds raised by the Christians that ensured the solvency of the new community (Acts 4:34–37). With this must be contrasted the notorious impoverishment of the Jerusalem group after they had left (Acts 11:29, 30). The Hellenistic members nevertheless agreed under persuasion, though some did it willingly, to keep up their fraternal support by remitting money from the groups now formed in their own homelands, which mostly had good financial resources to be tapped (e.g. 1 Cor 16:1–3; 2 Cor 8:1–4; 9:1–5).

In the early stages, when they had been personally well represented at Jerusalem, grievances had developed precisely over this financial disproportion, as a result of which they had successfully demanded that the business affairs of the community be entrusted to a new board. This body directly represented them, being composed entirely of Hellenists, including one who was not even a Jew by birth (Acts 6:1–5).

The new leadership later involved itself in a violent theological conflict within the foreign community at Jerusalem, of which they were part, resulting in legal action being taken against this section of the Christians (Acts 6:9; 8:1). The Judaean members were not implicated, but the many foreign converts had to be hurriedly evacuated, which had the unexpected result of bringing many new groups into being abroad. Philip, for example, first visited Samaria, and then the coastal towns (Acts 8:5, 40), before settling finally in the republic of Caesarea (Acts 21:8). This was not the only occasion on which Caesarea provided security against the Jewish authorities. During a period when controls were imposed on the Judaean Christians as well, one of their leaders took refuge there (Acts 12:19). Apparently there was no extradition arrangement as there was with Damascus (cf. above, p. 14). But the repatriation of the Hellenists had its main effects along the routes leading to the big centres of population to the northwest. The cities of Phoenicia and Cyprus, and above all Antioch, saw the establishment of Christian groups (cf. above, p. 8).

The only member of the Hellenist section who had certainly stayed in Jerusalem was Barnabas (Acts 9:27), who was now commissioned to look into the disconcerting developments at Antioch. He was himself a Cypriot, and a notable benefactor of the Christians at Jerusalem (Acts 4:36, 37), thus giving him an affinity with either section of the movement. He associated with himself in his responsibility at Antioch the prominent Jewish leader, Saul of Tarsus, whom he had himself earlier introduced to the Jerusalem group (Acts 9:27), and the two of them very successfully launched the new non-Jewish Christianity on its course (Acts 11:22–26). Thus far they were catching up with events, but they subsequently took matters into their own hands, by undertaking a calculated programme of extension, independently of Jerusalem, and leading in the end to conflict with them (Acts 15:2). Apart from Barnabas and Saul, the Antioch leaders responsible for this action included two who used Latin names, one being a Jew, but the other not necessarily, and a personal friend of Herod the Tetrarch. No others are named (Acts 13:1).

It was out of the action of these persons that the organized expansion of Christianity proceeded, and particularly its vigorous propagation among non-Jews. Their success called for a restatement and development of a Palestinian Messianic faith for the population of the Hellenistic cities. They thus created the New Testament. Christianity in its canonical form, then, is not so much the work of Galilaeans, as of a very cultivated section of international Jewry; they were at any rate its principal sponsors. This can be confirmed by a good deal of other information offered in the texts. It is obvious in the many cases where the new groups enjoyed the hospitality of wealthy and respectable patrons (cf. above, p. 25). It also accounts for the constant travelling that was maintained. Entertainment could be asked for as a matter of course (Phlm 22). Not only were individuals provided for, but regular delegations could be handled. Paul's party on the final journey from the Aegean to Jerusalem consisted of nine persons at least (Acts 20:4), who were all accommodated for generous periods at the main points on the way (Acts 21:4, 8, 10, 16).

The most detailed illustration of all this is of course the career of Paul. He was himself one of the distinguished circle of foreign Jews in Jerusalem among whom the clash over Stephen's teaching occurred; if one may judge from the fact that the synagogue concerned is said to have included the Cilicians, he was probably personally involved in the controversy. Certainly it was he who was appointed by the authorities to see to the execution of the resultant court judgment against the Hellenistic section of the Christians, a mark of the high esteem in which his abilities were held (Acts 8:3; 9:1, 2). Although of non-Palestinian origin, his credentials in Judaism were beyond question. His ancestry was impeccable (Rom 11:1), and he had deliberately been sent from his homeland to Jerusalem to ensure a classical training in the Jewish faith (Acts 22:3). This reversion produced the not unprecedented ostentatious archaism (Gal 1:14), and resulted in his joining the rigorist sect of the Pharisees (Acts 26:5).

On the other hand, he was in full standing in the republican society of his homeland (Acts 21:39), belonging to the privileged group of Hellenistic families which had also been accorded Roman citizenship in return for services rendered (Acts 22:28) (cf. above, p. 37). He thus possessed an unusually well balanced set of social qualifications, a combination shared with only a very small minority of persons in the eastern Mediterranean. This fact he demonstrated when it suited him by moving freely in the best circles in that society. Among his connections were, at Athens, a member of the Areopagus, the upper house of the government (Acts 17:34); at Corinth, prominent religious (Acts 18:8) and civil (Rom 16:23) leaders; at Ephesus, members of the titled aristocracy (Acts 19:31) (cf. above, p. 38). When in custody at Malta, he was entertained by 'the chief man of the island', though this may simply have been an act of charity on his part (Acts 28:7).

This social distinction explains his constant sensitivity to the humiliations he suffered from time to time. 'We are made as the filth of the world, and are the off-scouring of all things unto this day' (1 Cor 4:13) is certainly not the complaint of a person to whom social affronts were normal. On the contrary, they are felt as indignities he ought not to have been subjected to. Under the same heading come his occasional periods of manual labour. It was part of his Jewish traditionalism to have practised a manual skill, but it was only exercised in order to establish a point of honour, as his advertisement of it admits. Normally he expected to be supported at the charges of the groups who enjoyed his religious leadership (1 Cor 9:4; 2 Cor 11:8; 12:13; Acts 20:33–35).

Paul's touchiness was exposed principally in connection with the Corinthian group, who forced him into an embarrassing position by their own airs. He was hurt by their criticism of him (1 Cor 4:4; 9:3), and because of the tension felt it politic to keep away (2 Cor 1:23). He replied instead with a very self-conscious outburst in a letter, heavily ironical in its contrast between their behaviour and his, which left him feeling extremely awkward. 'I am become a fool in glorying; ye have compelled me: for I ought to have been commended of you: for in nothing am I behind the very chiefest apostles, though I be nothing' (2 Cor 12:11). The difficulty was that his leadership had been challenged, resulting in factions developing under the names of his supposed rivals (1 Cor 1:12). The Corinthian social pretensions are not surprising. They were riddled with snobbery and divisions (cf. above, p. 33): 'debates, envyings, wraths, strifes, backbitings, whisperings, swellings, tumults' (2 Cor 12:20). But this was natural in a group that had enjoyed the attentions not only of the mercurial Paul, but also of the impressive Alexandrian theologian, Apollos (Acts 18:24–28), and others, and was entertained by a number of generous patrons (Rom 16:1, 2, 23; and also cf. above, pp. 25, 37–38). Far from suggesting anything else, the overworked exclamation 'not many wise . . . , not many mighty, not many noble, are called' (1 Cor 1:26) plainly admits this situation. Taking the words at their face value, they merely imply that the group did not contain many intellectuals, politicians, or persons of gentle birth. But this would suggest that the group did at least draw upon this minority to some extent. However, it is hardly intended as a factual statement. Properly evaluated as a piece of impassioned rhetoric, it leaves no doubt that in their own opinion, and presumably also in that of their contemporaries, they were anything but a collection of unintelligent nonentities. Paul in fact states this later. 'Now ye are full, now ye are rich, ye have reigned as kings without us. . . . We are fools . . . , but ye are wise . . . ; we are weak, but ye are strong; ye are honourable, but we are despised' (1 Cor 4:8, 10). His aim is to disabuse them of such ideas, and to clear his gospel of any suggestion of depending on human qualifications for success. The stress on his own humiliation is meant to drive the point home by contrast with their behaviour.

Far from being a socially depressed group, then, if the Corinthians are at all typical, the Christians were dominated by a socially pretentious section of the population of the big cities. Beyond that they seem to have drawn on a broad constituency, probably representing the household dependants of the leading members (cf. above, pp. 24–25). The interests brought together in this way probably marked the Christians off from the other unofficial associations, which were generally socially and economically as homogeneous as possible. Certainly the phenomenon led to constant differences among the Christians themselves, and helps to explain the persistent stress on not using membership in an association of equals to justify breaking down the conventional hierarchy of the household (e.g. 1 Cor 7:20–24). The interest of the owner and patron class is obvious in this. It was they who sponsored Christianity to their dependants.

But the dependent members of city households were by no means the most debased section of society. If lacking freedom, they still enjoyed security, and a moderate prosperity. The peasantry and persons in slavery on the land were the most underprivileged classes. Christianity left them largely untouched. There seems to have been a certain following in the country parts where Jesus had preached (cf. above, p. 7). James refers to the peasantry in his denunciations of the well-to-do landowners. 'Behold, the hire of the labourers who have reaped down your fields, which is of you kept back by fraud, crieth: and the cries of them which have reaped are entered into the ears of the Lord of sabaoth' (Jas 5:4). But it is not at all certain that his letter is addressed to such persons, who would not have understood Greek, and in any case the assumption that his readers were Christians, except incidentally, is ill-founded (cf. above, p. 38). Except for Palestinians, then, there is nothing to suggest that Christianity penetrated beyond the civilized Greek-speaking classes. When Hellenistic Christians met such persons, they treated them with the same superciliousness they had originally bestowed on the Galilaean preachers (Acts 2:7). Barnabas and Paul found the Lycaonian-speaking crowd at Lystra incomprehensible and alarming (Acts 14:11–19). Paul resented being mistaken for an illiterate agitator, not because of the criminal imputation, but because of the cultural slight (Acts 21:37–39). When the ship's company were rescued from disaster at Malta, the writer notes with an air of relief that underlines the conventional assumption of superiority, 'the barbarous people showed us no little kindness' (Acts 28:2). Sixty years later Pliny accepted the fact that Christians represented a broad cross-section of society, from Roman citizens downwards, but reserved his surprise, apart from their numbers, in which he is an alarmist, for the ominous fact that the new religion was infecting not merely the cities, but the countryside. Until then however we may safely regard Christianity as a socially well backed movement of the great Hellenistic cities.

VI. Legal Proceedings Involving Christians

The character of the judicial hearings in which Christians were involved from time to time must also be taken into account if their ideas of social obligation are not to be misunderstood. The trial of Jesus himself is by no means irrelevant to this topic, partly because it was actuated by considerations that always applied in the minds of the governments associated with the Romans, and partly because his followers must have looked upon it as the prototype of their own difficulties. Identification with Christ in his suffering was a favourite theme of Christian mysticism (cf. Gal 2:20; 6:14; 2 Tim 2:12). The sensitivity of John's Gospel to the political motivation of the crucifixion suggests that this work may well have been produced in a situation where the affinities were becoming painfully apparent.

The execution of Jesus was decided upon by the Jewish authorities after an anxious consideration of the political risk involved in doing nothing (cf. above, p. 15). From the start there had been a revolutionary tendency in the movement. 'They would come and take him by force, to make him a king' (John 6:15). Whatever Jesus might say most of his followers inevitably thought of Messiah in terms of a military leader who would 'restore again the kingdom to Israel' (Acts 1:6). At least one of the twelve was known as a member of the terrorist underground, 'Simon called Zelotes' (namely, the partisan) (Luke 6:15), and another probably was: it has been suggested that Iscariot (Luke 6:16) is an Aramaic form of *sicarius* (namely, the assassin) (Acts 21:38); 'Sons of thunder' (Mark 3:17) does not suggest a particularly pacific disposition. It was not unknown for them to carry arms, nor to use them (John 18:10).[55]

The Jerusalem government was perfectly familiar with revolutionary movements of this kind. Apart from the followers of Jesus, at least four others crop up in the New Testament (Mark 15:7; Acts 5:36, 37; 21:38). There was no doubt about their responsibility in the matter. If they failed to check the movement, the Romans would be compelled to act. It would be a national disaster. 'It is expedient for us that one man should die for the people, and that the whole nation perish not' (John 11:47–50). An order was put out for his arrest (John 11:57), but if badly handled it could lead to the very outbreak it was supposed to prevent (Matt 21:5). An attempt to trap him in a political indiscretion and thus secure Roman action against him failed (Luke 20:20). He was eventually arrested out of the public eye, with Roman authorization, and through the good offices of one of his own supporters who was probably disillusioned, ironically enough, precisely by the fact that he had renounced direct action (John 18:3).

The controversy over the procedure involved in the trial of Jesus cannot be reviewed here. What follows is an attempt to show how the several accounts may be reconciled. That the execution was Roman and

---

[55] Cf. O. Cullmann, *Der Staat im Neuen Testament*, 1956; E. Stauffer, 'Geschichte Jesu', in *Historia Mundi*, vol. 4, 1956.

not Jewish in method need not mean that the Jewish council had not passed a formal judgment. They naturally preferred that the Romans incur the expected public odium, and insisted on crucifixion by the governor instead of stoning. Nevertheless they needed a watertight religious conviction (Luke 22:66–71), perhaps to pacify public opinion which would be less enthusiastic about a person properly convicted of blasphemy, but certainly in order to be able to offer the governor a firm ground for action if the real accusations failed to carry conviction. They preferred him to act on his own responsibility, and anxiously impressed upon him the treasonable interpretation that could be placed upon his (namely, Jesus') activities (Luke 23:2, 5). The decision on such a matter was entirely in his hands, and he rejected their accusations, as had been feared (Luke 23:14). The emergency arrangement was now brought into play; the religious conviction was cited, and its execution requested (John 19:7). It only remained to stampede the governor into doing the job himself and all would still be well. To this end popular agitation was organized (Mark 15:11), which took Pilate by surprise. The revulsion of opinion was probably of much the same character as Judas' change of heart. Jesus was not looking at all like a determined national leader at the critical moment, while on the other hand the opportunity had suddenly been presented to them of regaining a well tried revolutionary whom the Romans were holding. The demonstrators therefore insisted that the prerogative of mercy that was available for one prisoner be exercised in favour of Barabbas. There was no point in further opposition. After all Jesus was legitimately condemned, as the Jewish authorities had ensured. The governor therefore felt justified in ratifying their decision, while humouring the basic accusation by undertaking the execution himself. He washed his hands as a demonstration of the fact that the judgment was not his. He was merely the agent.

The satisfaction of the Jewish council at thus eliminating the risk of another insurrection was shattered when the movement reappeared at Pentecost, making the claim that was politically electrifying, and which they believed they had squashed by branding it as blasphemy, that Jesus was Messiah (Acts 2:36). The statement that he had been raised from the dead was an added provocation to a certain section, and is recorded as the point that first attracted official attention. It was apparently this that was cited as the grounds for the arrest of Peter and John (Acts 4:2). But the hearing itself was certainly not concerned with theological questions. The council was only interested in confirming their suspicions of the political character of the movement. They secured a formal admission of the identity between it and the one recently suppressed ('they took knowledge of them, that they had been with Jesus', Acts 4:13), but having no valid legal basis for proceeding against it, were reduced simply to binding them over to refrain from carrying it on ('not to speak at all nor teach in the name of Jesus', Acts 4:18). They carefully noted the danger of its getting a hold on the people, but the current flush of enthusiasm made caution essential (Acts 4:16, 17).

The movement however continued unchecked, and the renewed activity of the men who had been placed under a bond presented to the council clear-cut grounds for action against them. In addition to their contempt of court, they were also attacked for calling in question the judicial decision against Jesus ('ye . . . intend to bring this man's blood upon us', Acts 5:28). That the council was only concerned to do the best in the interest of political stability is plain. A capital penalty was proposed, but after a consideration of two earlier revolutionary movements that had petered out after alarming beginnings, the policy of restraint was adhered to. The accused were convicted, and after corporal punishment, dismissed on the same conditions as before (Acts 5:33–40).

The retort of the Christians to these judgments was openly defiant, they claiming that they had a higher obligation (Acts 4:23–30; 5:29, 42). It is noteworthy that at the very outset there appeared that mutual incomprehension of public authorities and Christian groups that bedevilled their later relations. The authorities objected to the groups because of the political or criminal charges inextricably associated with them. The Christians defied the objection, on the grounds that it amounted to an attack on their faith itself. The only possibility of solution lay in establishing a clear distinction between the faith and its alleged criminal aspects. During the New Testament period the point was not uncommonly tested in the courts, but even where favourable verdicts were obtained, the risk of the magistrates giving up in despair in the face of persistent accusations was always real. The law must ultimately move with public opinion.

The execution of Stephen for blasphemy, precipitate though it was, must have rested upon a formal judgment of the court that tried him, and must also have been ratified by the Roman governor, as was required for a capital penalty, though this may have been done in retrospect to cover the invalidity (Acts 7:54–60). But a lynching must be ruled out, partly in view of the terms in which the witnesses are referred to (Acts 8:1; 22:20), and partly because a proper judgment must have been necessary as a basis for the arrests which followed (Acts 8:3; 9:2; 22:5), particularly as the operation extended to Jewish communities in foreign territory (cf. above, p. 14). These arrests were also the prelude to executions, but apparently while a judgment obtained against one member of a group could be used as a warrant for arresting the others, individual guilt still had to be established before condemnation. The means to this end was the extorting of the assertion that Jesus was the Son of God. This had constituted blasphemy in the original case (Acts 7:56), and this surely is what must be meant by Paul's saying he 'compelled them to blaspheme' (Acts 26:10, 11). This is written from the Jewish point of view, not the Christian.

The legal charges that secured the condemnation of James are not clear (Acts 12:1–4). An extension of the blasphemy ruling is unlikely, as interest in that series of actions must have lapsed when it was discredited by the defection of its principal sponsor to the criminal group concerned (Acts 9:21–24). In any case James' prosecution was not arranged by the priestly council at all, but by the supervisory civil power, Herod. It is equally uncertain what action he contemplated against Peter. The technical term used ('to bring him forth to the people') is familiar in the Greek republics for a prosecution before the public assembly (cf. Acts 17:5), but may not be significant in this context. However the fact that Peter was arrested at the beginning of a festival period, and his trial delayed until after it was over, suggests that considerations of public order were involved. This is supported by the very heavy guard placed over him. Peter after all had a reputation as a crowd raiser, and as a jail breaker (Acts 5:19), a feat which was duly repeated (Acts 12:7). Relations between the new sect and traditionalists had been poisoned by the affair of Stephen, and can hardly have been helped by the news now arriving from the north (Acts 11:22), that non-Jews were becoming involved. Peter's arrest 'pleased the Jews' (Acts 12:3), or rather James' execution did, which all goes to suggest that the orthodox were now learning to turn their theological odium to good account by playing on the nervousness of the authorities about public order.

The need for keeping the peace at all costs also offered the Jews in foreign republics a handy weapon against their deviationist rivals. A riot was fairly easily organized, and the good connections of the resident Jews ensured that it was turned to the disadvantage of the newcomers (cf. above, pp. 28–31). At Pisidian Antioch (Acts 13:50) an official deportation was apparently secured, but at Iconium (Acts 14:5) it must have been a case of illegal assault, since the government can hardly have authorized a stoning in which non-Jews would have participated, though there was plainly an official act of the Jewish community behind it ('the Jews with their rulers'). At Lystra (Acts 14:19) the phraseology seems to rule out a public act, though it may be consciously pejorative, for one would certainly think approval was necessary for the Jewish execution that was actually carried through.

There was no organized Jewish community at Philippi (cf. above, p. 29). The Jews presumably found the restrictions imposed by the Roman citizen body made regular settlement not worth their while. It was these restrictions that were invoked when Paul and Silas were denounced before the magistrates. This, together with the usual accusation of disturbing the peace, sufficed to bring the disciplinary powers of the magistrates into play without a formal trial, though again the writer's derogatory term for the crowd may conceal some form of public approval (Acts 16:22). These proceedings, which were proper against foreigners, nevertheless constituted a breach of citizen rights (cf. above, pp. 18–19) which seriously embarrassed the officials concerned when their error was discovered (Acts 16:37).

The grounds on which a public prosecution was proposed at Thessalonica (Acts 17:5–9) are difficult to interpret precisely, which may be the reason why the action was never brought (cf. above, p. 18). The charges probably did not come under public law at all, but were concerned with the personal duty of the inhabitants to the Caesar (cf. above, p. 24). Together with the threat to public order created by the mob action (cf. above, p. 29), this insinuation of disloyalty to the imperial house was sufficient to persuade the authorities to take security from the patron of the Christian preachers for their prompt removal. They were apparently surprised to come out of it so lightly, and complied with the order under cover of darkness, fearing lest worse should happen. This was thoroughly justified in the event, since it was the Jews of Thessalonica who later made it impossible for them to stay in Berea (Acts 17:13, 14). At Athens Paul was left untouched, apart from an inconclusive enquiry into the theological content of his preaching by the court of the Areopagus (Acts 17:19; above, p. 17).

In all the encounters with authority up to this point, with the exception of the trial of Jesus himself, the officials of the central Roman government had not been involved. At Corinth however the differences between Jews and Christians were for the first time submitted to the jurisdiction of a Roman magistrate, with the result that several important points were clarified (Acts 18:12–17).

The Jews, recognizing that the blackmailing tactics that worked well with authorities not ultimately independent (cf. above, pp. 23–24) were out of the question with a fully competent authority (the proconsul at Corinth, unlike the procurator at Caesarea above, p. 14, held his powers in his own right), now at last attempted to proceed on their real objections, relying on the official recognition their association enjoyed (cf. *supra* p. 29) to obtain a ruling on its internal affairs. The proconsul however rejected the suit without opening the hearing. Offences against the laws of a Jewish association were not actionable in the civil courts. Only prosecutions within the terms of the civil law would be admitted. Judaism was autonomous. This definition was of cardinal importance to the Christian groups.

Gallio's judgment meant that provided the Christians could avoid inculpation on criminal grounds, their opponents were powerless at law. Conversely the possibility of an intensified campaign of slander with a view to prejudicing the courts was opened up. Nevertheless while an atmosphere of suspicion would obviously assist criminal suits, specific acts must be attested if the informer was to avoid the penalties for calumnious prosecution. This device was the essential check in a system of criminal jurisdiction that was set in motion not by the crown but by private prosecution. It may well provide the explanation of the surprising action taken against the leader of the unsuccessful suit in this instance (cf. above, pp. 28–29). It has always been a puzzle how so meticulous a lawyer as Gallio could have regarded an assault of this kind with such apparent equanimity. It cannot admittedly be said that Sosthenes was in any way legally penalized. After all, he had not lost his suit; it had merely been disallowed. But the suspicion that accrued to unsuccessful litigation may have created the atmosphere in which an outrage of the present kind could be ignored.

The incident at Ephesus where hostility towards the Christians led to an irregular public assembly's attempting to take the law into its own hands offered another important clarification (Acts 19:37–39). When order was restored, the authorities insisted that action of this kind only involved the republic itself in trouble with the Romans (cf. above, pp. 15–16); that complaints should be laid before one of the regular meetings; but that in any case criminal charges must go before the Roman proconsul, who, as at Corinth, was a fully competent governor. This meant that the possibilities of bringing an action against Christians were limited not only by legal safeguards, but much more severely by the problems of access. Men of proconsular status were few and far between. The assizes were busy, and long and expensive delays might be involved in bringing a case forward.

The difficulties are extensively illustrated by the long series of hearings to which Paul was subjected as a result of his final visit to Jerusalem (Acts 20–26), complicated in addition by the fact of his dual rights, and the common situation where the proconsular authority was that of the Caesar in the capital, being exercised on the spot solely by delegation, and therefore not inappellable (cf. above, p. 14). One of the most interesting features of these hearings is the shift of ground on the part of the prosecution as the trial was shifted from one court to another. As long as it remained within the competence of the Jerusalem authorities, the religious grievances were the substance of the charges (Acts 23:29). But once it was transferred to Roman jurisdiction political charges became prominent (Acts 24:5). The affair was prolonged not only by its legal complication, but by the venality and time-serving of one Roman deputy (Acts 24:26, 27), and the attempted compromise of another (Acts 25:9–12), which led to its being remitted to the titular governor in the capital. Such irresponsibility was probably unusual.

In the equally uncommon event of the central government itself behaving erratically, the situation of course became unpredictable. The action of Nero, though presumably exceptional, nevertheless has some significant aspects (Tacitus, *Ann.* 15.44). In view of the popular odium towards the Christians, it was found convenient to divert the responsibility for a disastrous fire on to them. A select number were arrested on admission of membership in Christian societies, charged, and convicted of arson. This judgment was then used as the basis for mass arrests, membership now being accepted as sufficient evidence of guilt. This was presumably only a short-lived and localized excess, but the regrettable precedent remained.

It is not known from Roman sources how Christians were dealt with during the fifty years between Nero and Pliny. But Pliny's letter on the situation in Bithynia shows the difficulties the government was having in unravelling the complicated situation that had resulted. It was now possible for persons to be incriminated through the normal channels on the grounds that they were Christians. Pliny had no hesitation in accepting the actions, but did not know whether individual crimes had to be proved, or whether proof of membership in itself justified condemnation. Trajan's reply was clear. If an action was brought and membership proved, Christians must be punished. In other words, the government had resigned itself to the impossibility of ascertaining the truth about the charges made against these persons, and regretfully admitted the long history of complaints about them as warranting penalization. Every possible means of avoiding the issue was to be taken. There were to be no official searches made. Anonymous information was to be ignored. Finally any person inculpated by the proper method was nevertheless to be acquitted if he made a token act of renunciation by an offering to the official gods.

Unfortunately this was the last thing many of the Christians were prepared to do. Pliny had already offered them this way out, and upon their refusing to accept it three times over, although they were warned of the consequences, had executed them in disgust for their insubordination. This is the essential point. From the official point of view, no-one was punished simply for being a Christian or for not honouring the official gods. This was naturally how the Christians saw it, but to the government the problem was not one of religion, but of administration and public order. If the Christians would not co-operate in getting themselves out of an awkward legal situation, they would simply have to suffer for it.

It must be remembered that this policy was developed from precedent to precedent as the particular situation demanded. There are no grounds for assuming that it was either universally or continuously applied. Pliny was completely unfamiliar with the business, and amazed to find it so prominent a problem in his administration. Action depended on informers, and informing was only safe where there was public antipathy to back it up. The basic problem for the Christians was thus not their relations with the government, but with the communities within which they lived.[56]

VII. IDEAS OF SOCIAL OBLIGATION

The foregoing pages offer some prolegomena to the study of the ideas of social obligation held by Christians in the first century. The defining of the ideas themselves is better left to students of theology. In writing this essay the intention has been to avoid working from any particular assumption about the content of New Testament social thought saving only the axiom that it cannot be properly understood except in the light of the situation to which it was addressed. If this view is correct the situation must first be defined as independently of the ideas as possible. Otherwise one may read the situation in terms of the ideas, and not the ideas in terms of the situation. It is hoped that as a result of the present study the situation will prove to be clearer than it has been, and that its description may be found useful in clarifying the ideas. There follow by way of conclusion a few general and very tentative observations on this matter; they may at least provoke others to reply.

It may be noted first of all that although there is no systematic theory of social obligation expounded, or at any rate none that is obviously

---

56 Cf. A. N. Sherwin-White, 'The Early Persecutions and Roman Law Again', in *Journal of Theological Studies*, 1952; L. de Regibus, *Politica e Religione da Augusto a Costantino*, 1953; H. Last, 'Christenverfolgung II', in *Reallexikon für Antike und Christentum*, 2 Bd., 1954; H. Mattingly, *Christianity in the Roman Empire*, 1955; J. Moreau, *La Persécution du Christianisme dans l'Empire Romain*, 1956.

consistent from one writer to another, the subject is of very great concern to most of them. Apart from theological exposition, it is with the problems raised in social relationships that the didactic and paraenetic passages in the New Testament seem to be principally concerned. Much less attention is paid for instance to religious duties or the cultivation of piety. The attempt to extract a theory of social obligation from these writings is therefore not necessarily foredoomed to failure as anachronistic. The New Testament is a veritable case-book of social precept and practice.

Another point of some importance is that there was usually a disconcerting gap between precept and practice. The social behaviour implied by the vigour of the criticism often contrasts strangely with the tenets of the faith. All sorts of delinquencies, particularly disunity among the members and lack of regard for social convention are repeatedly attacked, and all on the most compelling theological grounds. But it is apparent that the dangers involved are not merely those of theological irregularity. The acute sensitivity to public opinion reflects a feeling of insecurity that does not spring only from the eschatological faith. Plainly their security as groups was felt to depend to a large extent on their activities escaping public attention, and any abnormal behaviour would only feed the willing rumours that circulated to their discredit. It is from this preoccupation that much of the social teaching starts. The resultant apologetic character of New Testament social thought must not be lost sight of in attempting to draw positive principles from it; no doubt it has its dogmatic corollaries; but it was formulated primarily for defence rather than attack.

With regard to public obligations, the attitudes change with changing circumstances. They range from acquiescence to ill-concealed defiance. But given the character of the republican community of the times (cf. above, pp. 21–22), the idea of positive responsibility is out of the question in any case. The old community ideals no longer had any political application outside the narrow circles of the governing aristocracy; the only duty of the rest was loyalty to their betters; and in this duty they were for the most part heartily encouraged by the New Testament writers. Three distinct approaches to the question may be noticed, corresponding perhaps to three stages in the relations between the Christians and the Roman government.

There is first the argument that there is a duty of complete obedience to authority on the grounds that it is the instrument of God's will. This plainly does not envisage direct opposition by the authorities to Christianity. The government is assumed to be not inimical to the faith, and may even be counted on for protection. Such passages must therefore be given an early dating. They belong to what we may call the Gallio period, when Roman courts would only accept suits against Christians on criminal charges (cf. above, pp. 49–50). The classic exposition of the principle involved is Romans 13:1–7. Throughout that letter there is no hint at all of public hostility.[57] The same confidence in the goodwill of the authorities is implied naturally enough in the letters to the Corinthians, the original beneficiaries of Gallio's judgment. The revelations made in 1 Corinthians suggest that the rumours circulated about the Christians were not by any means entirely slanderous. Informers of a later generation would certainly have had plenty of material to work on in the Corinthian group, and it was fortunate that their standing in society was sufficiently good to make it a matter of no concern to them. But the Christians to whom Peter wrote could expect prosecution for their sins.

The first Epistle of Peter represents the second approach, belonging clearly to what we may call the Nero period, the stage when the Roman authorities had allowed convictions for criminal offences to serve as a precedent for prosecutions on the ground of membership alone (cf. above, p. 51). This danger is plainly envisaged by the writer. The authorities are still to be respected, but there is little hope held out of just treatment. Consolation is offered in the parallel with the innocent sufferings of Christ, and efforts are to be concentrated on avoiding any criminal act that would warrant prosecution anyway. The same anxiety about public opinion is evident in some of the other later Epistles, such as 1 Timothy and Titus. The tightening up of the ecclesiastical machinery, which in itself can hardly have been calculated to pacify the authorities, is designed largely to stop up the loop-holes in the behaviour of the Christians. Drunkenness, brawling, and bad domestic relations were all likely to attract unwelcome attention. In spite of the provocative attitude of their opponents, nothing must be done that would upset the government.

The transition from loyalty for principle's sake to loyalty for fear of trouble may also be traced in the changing attitudes to Judaism. The question of loyalty to the national religion is for Jewish Christians parallel to that of the loyalty of the citizen to his government. Conformity is de-

---

[57] This incidentally makes it much less likely that the expulsion of the Jews from Rome under Claudius (Acts 18:2) had anything to do with troubles over Christianity there. The Romans of course need not have distinguished Christians from Jews, but the letter equally bears no trace of Jewish hostility towards Christians. The discreet attitude of the Roman Jews on Paul's arrival (Acts 28:21, 22) supports the point; it virtually rules out any history of conflict at Rome.

manded at first out of respect for customs of God's institution, then more for fear of retaliation. This reflects of course the shift in the Jewish polemic from religious to political attacks (cf. above, pp. 50–51).

Throughout these earlier stages the transitory character of the existing institutions had always ultimately been insisted upon, even when the strictest conformity had been demanded. The third approach takes up this idea and presses it to the complete exclusion of any responsibility towards the government. It becomes the basis for an apocalyptic denunciation of the temporal power. This attitude clearly belongs to what we may call the Pliny period, the stage when the Romans themselves, in an endeavour to stop an embarrassing spate of prosecutions, tried to prevail upon Christians to make a formal renunciation of their membership in the incriminating society (cf. above, p. 51). The reaction was wildly defiant, at least as far as the New Testament documents go, and only thinly veiled behind the traditional apocalyptic imagery. It had been temporarily manifested at the very beginning of the movement (cf. above, p. 47). The classic expression of it is seen however in the Revelation, where the honours required by the imperial power turn it into the incarnation of evil. This is the insubordination that Pliny found intolerable. The Christians too had by this time exhausted their patience. The same government that had once been honoured as God's minister, is now denounced, at any rate within the esoteric security of the seer's art, as God's archenemy.

So much for the republic. With regard to the household obligation, the New Testament writers are unanimous: its bonds and conventions must at all costs be maintained. Slavery is admittedly meaningless in the household of faith, but nevertheless one is to stay where put by God. A parallel is drawn between this and the Jewish obligation (1 Cor 7:17–24). Its invalidity is insisted upon at the same time as conformity is demanded. In the case of the Epistle to Philemon, which concerned a notorious breach of the household bond in which Paul had become involved, the apostle not only avoided asking for emancipation as a solution, but ostentatiously offered to meet the damages himself. There is of course no mistaking in this the interest of the patronal class which normally sponsored Christianity to its dependants, but the primary reason no doubt is that the entrenched rights of the household as a religious and social unit offered the Christians the best possible security for their existence as a group. Any weakening here would thus be a potentially devastating blow to their own cohesion, as well as having revolutionary implications from the point of view of the public authorities.

It was only within the intimacy of the Christian associations themselves, untrammelled by past history or ulterior objects, that free expression could be given to the principles of the fraternity. The initial spontaneous communism soon broke down, but it was at least followed by repeated appeals for unity and equality, which found some response at most periods. The programme was always hampered, however, by the need to keep a watchful eye on possible repercussions abroad. It could be disastrous if enthusiastic members failed to contain their principles within the privacy of the association, and were led into political indiscretions or offences against the hierarchy of the household. Hence the growing stress on good order and regular leadership within the associations themselves.

Nevertheless it is in this context that the tradition of frank and uninhibited social criticism of Jesus was maintained. The Epistles are full of this, but James is perhaps the most outspoken. The fact that he is probably addressing the Jewish community in general rather than the Christian societies (cf. above, p. 38) does not rule him out of consideration in this case. As with the others, the autonomy of the Jewish associations in their internal arrangements was freely recognized by the authorities. James openly attacks the snobbery of social rank, and the injustices of wealth. Accumulated wealth, wealth used for luxury, wealth derived from the exploitation of labour, are all fiercely denounced.

The reaction of the Christians to their social situation thus varied from occasion to occasion, depending on the conventions of the particular institution involved. But they certainly did not regard this as simply a matter of expediency. The writers do not justify their attitudes from the situation, but from their theological beliefs.

The idea that gives consistency to their varying social attitudes is the belief which originally marked them out from Israel, that Jesus is the Messiah. His Messiahship was vindicated by the resurrection, which in turn anticipated the imminent judgment. It is in terms of these two events, which were deemed to be, in the fullest sense of the word, epoch-making, that the New Testament writers consistently evaluated their social relationships. The Messiahship of Jesus fixed their historical position unmistakably at the mid-point of the crisis of the ages. Whether socially acquiescent, socially defiant, or socially militant, it is from the belief that the end of all things is realized in Christ's resurrection to power, and from the expectation of the inauguration of the kingdom, that their attitudes are defended.

2

Paul's Boasting in Relation to Contemporary Professional Practice

I. WAS PAUL A LAYMAN IN RHETORIC?

WHEN PAUL ADMITTED that he was only "a layman in speech", ἰδιώτης τῷ λόγῳ (2 Cor 11:6), he may himself in that very phrase have been exhibiting one of the recognized *tropoi* of the rhetorical profession, namely *asteismos* (cf. Lat. *urbanitas*, though the latter was not the name of the equivalent Latin *tropos*) or *prospoiesis* ("affectation", namely, of the worse), being that one of the six distinct forms of irony by which one urbanely displayed one's own skill by affecting the lack of it.[1] Admirers of Paul's rhetoric would certainly be tempted to think this one of his favourite figures, as they would the several forms of irony applied to other people. (Though how one should distinguish, in a letter, between *sarkasmos*, or "flesh-tearing" irony done with bared teeth, *mykterismos*, a "snort" done with visible dilations of the nostrils, and *epikertomesis*, the "jeer" accompanied by *chleuasmos*, or curling of the lip, is an awkward problem if one hopes to do full justice to Paul's candour. The unhappy elders who had to read his letters to their churches must already have been tempted to intone them poker-faced, as we do in ours, if it had indeed been possible for anyone in antiquity to have contemplated so barbaric an impoverishment of speech. But it so happens that we know they

---

NOTE: A paper read to the Tyndale Fellowship in Melbourne on 21 September, and to the Fellowship for Biblical Studies in Sydney on 30 November, 1967. It sets out some of the background material assumed in my article, 'The Conflict of Educational Aims in New Testament Thought', *Journal of Christian Education* IX, 1966, 32–45. It is published through the courtesy of the Tyndale Fellowship.

[1]L. Spengel, *Rhetores Graeci* III, pp. 98.12; 206.11; 214.5; 226.16; 235.26; C. Halm, *Rhetores Latini Minores*, 39.16.

did not, unless we are being taken in by another ironical figure on Paul's part, since his contemporaries actually found his letters, read out by others, more rhetorically effective than anything he was able to put forward in person, "for they say, 'his letters are weighty and strong, but his bodily presence is weak and his speech of no account'" (2 Cor 10:10). Is it possible that his readers, being professionally trained, really could put his work across in a way Paul himself, ἰδιώτης τῷ λόγῳ, could not?)

That it could, however, still all be irony is shown by the featuring of the same term *(idiotes)* in a very similar context in the fragmentary 42nd Oration of Dio Chrysostom, one of the nicest pieces of *asteismos* to come down from antiquity, and a welcome pause for breath amidst the suffocating outpourings of that supremely successful and self-opinionated professional. Moreover, for St Augustine, the master-rhetorician of Latin Christendom, the concessive form of Paul's sentence (*"Even if* I am a layman in speech") allowed a little room for doubt: it was, it seems, not unreasonable to take it as a concession of debate only, and Augustine shows how Paul might have put his meaning beyond doubt had he wanted to (*de Doctrina Christiana* 4.7.15). That the case is clear, however, St Augustine himself does not doubt: Paul was not, he assumes, trained in rhetoric, and hence, not having invested a great deal of expense in the art he does not feel obliged to display it (ib. 14); it would be the mark of an ignorant expert (*imperite peritus,* ib. 11) to contend that he had followed the rules of the art, and would earn the scorn of Christians both learned and unlearned; but he does nevertheless possess the particular eloquence appropriate to an inspired writer (ib. 6.9), and where it corresponds to the classical rules that is not by Paul's device but because eloquence inseparably follows wisdom like her handmaiden, unbidden (*tamquam inseparabilem famulam etiam non vocatam,* ib. 10).

II. DID HE IN FACT USE THE "GRAND STYLE"?

As St Augustine knows, however, the case was somewhat more complicated than that, since it was not every form of rhetoric that was distinguished by the display of the classical ornaments. Where clarity itself might be jeopardized by rhetoric, for instance, "a certain author" (as Augustine discreetly calls Cicero) had specified that one must use "sometimes a careful carelessness" (*quondam diligentem negligentiam, Orat.* 23.77 apud *Doctr. chr.* 4.10.24), of the sort that avoided ornament without reducing itself to squalor. Augustine then applies to the training of the preacher (for that is the subject of his book), and demonstrates from the example of the scriptural writers, the importance of the same anonymous authority's three functions of eloquence, to teach, to delight, and to move to action (*Orat.* 21.69 apud *de Doc. Christ.* 12.27), and of the three styles of oratory respectively appropriate (*Orat.* 29.101 apud 17.34), the subdued, the temperate and the grand. Since ornament was the feature of the temperate style especially, we may well wonder whether Paul was not merely disowning that when he declared, "my speech and my message were not in plausible words of wisdom, but in demonstration of the Spirit and of power" (1 Cor 2:4). This sounds not unlike the distinction which Augustine makes in the following terms:

> The grand style differs from the temperate not so much in that it is adorned with verbal ornaments but in that it is forceful with emotions of the spirit. Although it uses almost all the ornaments, it does not seek them if it does not need them. It is carried along by its own impetus, and if the beauties of eloquence occur they are caught up by the force of the things discussed and not deliberately assumed for decoration. It is enough for the matter being discussed that the appropriateness of the words be determined by the ardour of the heart rather than by careful choice. For if a strong man is armed with a gilded and bejewelled sword, and he is fully intent on the battle, he does what he must with the arms he has, not because they are precious, but because they are arms. (20.42)

Augustine then illustrates this distinction with reference to Galatians 4:10–20:

> Although almost all of the Epistle to the Galatians is written in the subdued style, except the beginning and the end, which are in the temperate style, nevertheless he inserts one passage with such emotion that, without any ornaments like those in the passages quoted heretofore, it cannot be spoken except in the grand style. "You observe," he says "days and months . . . (Augustine quotes the full passage) . . . because I am ashamed for you." Are contrary words set against their contraries here, or are things arranged climactically, or are *caesa* and *membra* and *circuitus* used? Yet not on that account is the grand emotion which we feel in the fervour of this eloquence diminished. (20.44)

The grand style was not infrequently marked off from the other two by the fact that the rhetorical pleasures it afforded were overtaken by more drastic emotions. Augustine illustrates this from his own experience:

> If a speaker is applauded frequently and vigorously, he should not think that for that reason he is speaking in the grand style; for the acumen revealed in the subdued style and the ornaments of the temperate style may produce the same result. For the grand style frequently prevents applauding voices with its own weight, but it may bring forth tears. Thus when I was dissuading the populace of Caesarea in Mauretania from civil war . . .

I pleaded in the grand style. But I did not think that I had done anything when I heard them applauding, but when I saw them weeping. They indicated by applause that they were being taught or pleased, but tears indicated that they were moved to action . . . And behold, by the grace of Christ nothing similar has been attempted there for eight years or more. There are many other experiences through which we have learned what effect the grand style of a wise speaker may have on men. They do not show it through applause but rather through their groans, sometimes even through tears, and finally through a change of their way of life. (24.53)

Paul himself would surely have approved of this test: "I will soon come to you . . . and try out, not the speech of the pretentious, but their power, for the kingdom of God does not lie in speech but in power" (1 Cor 4:19–20). Nevertheless it is difficult to see in Paul a willing exponent of the grand style, nor indeed does Augustine want to go that far. He is ostensibly in conscious reaction against all rhetoric. Yet this very consciousness keeps our question tantalisingly alive. If he knows how to reject it so forcefully, is he not perhaps turning its subtleties against itself, "spoiling the Egyptians", as the great classicising Fathers of the fourth century would have put it?

III. WHAT WAS PAUL'S PERSONAL BACKGROUND?

The historical arguments are inconclusive. An upbringing at Tarsus need not have meant rhetorical training (which was only commenced at tertiary level) for the son of a rigorist Jewish house, as he certainly was. Although he made himself "all things to all men", and boasts of his impeccable title to Jewish orthodoxy, and practised it if need be, he never, unless the disclaimers are ironical, made himself eloquent to win the Greeks; only "weak" to win the weak, or "foolish", that their faith "might not rest in the wisdom of men". But on the other hand he cannot have been ignorant of the art of rhetoric, even if not formally trained. An upbringing at Jerusalem, if that is to be inferred from so conspicuous an instance (Acts 22:3) of his making himself to the Jews a Jew, need still not have exempted him from contact with Hellenic learning, for the Talmud has it that of Gamaliel's thousand pupils five hundred were trained in the wisdom of the Greeks. Eduard Norden sees in this an allusion to the influence on Jerusalem of the hellenised Judaism of Alexandria.[2]

---

[2] *Die Antike Kunstprosa*, Leipzig, 1909, p. 476, n. 1.

It was an Alexandrian rhetorician, Apollos, ἀνὴρ λόγιος (the compliment of the writer of Acts [18:24] is the same as the famous tribute of Augustus to Cicero [Plut. *Cic.* 49.5]), whose powers of persuasion conceivably played a part in arousing the fastidious Corinthians to dissatisfaction with Paul's performance. Yet Paul clearly held Apollos himself in high regard, as he did many others whose names we know and who must from their social station have been rhetorically literate. The rivals, who exploited their talents against him, are regularly damned (and is not this too part of the rhetorical art?) with anonymity (e.g. Rom 16:17–18).

Whatever the circumstances of his upbringing and education, therefore, it is beyond doubt that Paul was, in practice at least, familiar with the rhetorical fashions of the time. As Norden has contended,[3] the rhetoric he fought and by which he was himself found wanting will not have been the classical (Attic) style, but the more florid "Asianic" version, which enjoyed a heady vogue precisely in that age and in those areas through which Paul moved, and which was as far from paying court to the traditional canons of fine speech as was Paul himself.

To return finally to the fourth century, that noble sounding-board of pure and ancient speech, we may now understand why the consensus of learned and devout opinion was to accept (and honour) Paul as ἰδιώτης τῷ λόγῳ, without troubling, as Augustine tended to do, to make him into a kind of professional in spite of himself. John Chrysostom, brightest star of Greek-Christian rhetoric, perceived more clearly than the Latin Augustine that, by the classical standards of the Greeks, Paul was simply no kind of expert, but that his power of speech would still be the marvel of all men until the end of time because in knowledge and penetration of thought he was, in contrast, no layman (*de Sacerdotio* 4.5f.).[4] Paul would surely have approved of this antithesis, as he would also the forthright declaration of Gregory of Nyssa that he had despised the *schemata* (the ornamental figures of speech) and any planned arrangement of his work in order that it might be adorned with the truth alone (*adversus Eunomium* I, 253B, Migne). Of the Latin authors, the compiler of the correspondence between Paul and Seneca makes Seneca regret the poverty of Paul's style (in letter 9 he says he is sending him a manual to improve it), while recognizing the force of Paul's desire not to corrupt his strength by affectation (*ep.* 13). Lastly, although Jerome allows Paul a certain acquaintance with secular learning (e.g. *comm. in ep. ad Gal.* 2.4), he takes the "Hebrew of the Hebrews" theme as the symbol

---

[3] *Op. cit.,* p. 507.
[4] The passages referred to in this paragraph are set out in Norden, *op. cit.,* pp. 501–2.

of weakness in Greek (3.6), but far from finding fault with his solecisms, as the critics did, he vindicates the avoidance of rhetorical polish as the secret of his evangelistic success (*comm. Ephes.* 3.5). In short, then, the verdict of the Fathers would be that Paul used no asteistic irony in admitting he was a layman in speech, but accepted the charge to confound it.

IV. THE PLACE OF RHETORIC IN ANTIQUITY

The study of rhetoric is somewhat neglected even amongst classical philologists, as though artificiality of speech were not a proper object for linguistic study. The historian of the ancient world, however, could hardly exaggerate the importance of rhetoric in shaping antiquity's own understanding of itself. Arising in the experiments of the fifth-century sophists in the art of persuasion ("making the worse appear the better reason"), rhetoric established its classical form in the court speeches of supremely litigious fourth-century Athens (represented by the surviving "Attic" orators and above all by Demosthenes). At the same time it was made the principal basis of education through the work of the deliberative orator Isocrates, and finally, as with most things that the Greeks had devised, set out for systematic study by Aristotle (who rejected the not un-Paul-like criticisms of Plato). By this stage the creative impetus was gone from Athenian democracy, and apart from the grafting in of an indigenous and more pragmatic Roman impulse during the second and first centuries before Christ (important for the thesis of this paper), the tradition settled down to a millennium of ever more unrealistic reaction and counter-reaction to the old style. Gorgias was only the first of many of whom it might be said[5] that, "having nothing in particular to say, he was able to concentrate all his energies upon saying it".

We possess in the collections of Spengel and Halm the many minor surviving manuals of the rhetorical schools. Spengel, in a somewhat selective index to his Greek rhetoricians, lists about 500 technical terms of the art. Halm, whose index is fuller and includes many of the Greek terms in use in Latin, lists close to 2500 technical terms. Such was the repertoire of the professional speaker of antiquity. By contrast, Fowler's *Modern English Usage*, confining itself to terms seriously in use but not so common as to need no definition, finds not more than forty technical terms of rhetoric worth explaining.[6] So far have we

---

[5] J. D. Denniston, *Greek Prose Style*, Oxford, 1952, p. 12.
[6] H. W. Fowler, *A Dictionary of Modern English Usage*, Oxford, corrected reprint of 1937, pp. 597–627, confining himself to terms that are neither obvi-

fallen away from the classical eloquence. And who is to blame for this more than St Paul? No other writer of antiquity so radically defied the rules of civilized speech and yet found readers to admire him, and none tapped so full a fountain of fresh eloquence such as had the power to bring the old tradition to new flowerings. It is noteworthy that Fowler's examples are typically drawn, of all places, from the Bible. Even the fourth-century Fathers, who gallantly did their best to make Paul respectable, could never have contemplated that he would ever displace their precious classics themselves.

Classical rhetoric was concerned first with selecting the appropriate type for the occasion. Greeks distinguished forensic, deliberative and epideictic oratory, suited respectively to proof, advice and display. Within these classes of oration the Latin scholars applied their distinction between the three styles, and the declamatory schools trained one in *suasoriae*, deliberations upon famous moments of crisis, and *controversiae*, or the resolving of typical legal disputes. Coming to questions of detail, there were three all important topics. First came the pattern of sentences, which had to be balanced to suit the subject matter, as Augustine shows on Paul. Secondly, and pre-eminent in epideictic oratory, was the application of figures, these being defined as any departure from the common sense or order of words, provided it was a matter of art and not merely of solecism (though a bold orator could even make figures out of solecisms, such as *antiptosis*, or the conscious use of the wrong case, and *katachresis*, or the use of a word in the wrong sense). Figures were classified into *schemata*, or unusual arrangements of words (further distinguished into figures of speech, which disappeared if the actual words were changed, and figures of thought, not dependent upon any particular words), and *tropoi*, or the turning of words from their normal use (again either literally, as in metaphor, or in the general sense, as in hyperbole). The third point of detailed concern was the rhythm of the words. This feature is more than any other lost to modern ears, for we can no longer master or even calculate that blend of pitch and quantity upon which we know rhythm depended. Yet so finely attuned were ancient ears that Cicero can show how words arranged to make a favourite *clausula*, or "end-pattern", would rouse the audience to applause, while exactly the same words in a different order would have left them unmoved.[7] We know of that mighty political orator, Gaius Gracchus, lost except for fragments, that he employed a servant to stand beside him

---

ous nor so recondite that they would not be used by any 'sensible writer . . . unless he were addressing experts or students'.

[7] Cic. *Orator* 63.214.

with a pitch-pipe to control the modulation of his voice, so fastidious was the taste even of the riotous Roman mobs.[8]

Not only did the mastery of rhetoric provide the necessary training for all public work, but because it was learned only at the tertiary stage of education it formed a peculiarly conspicuous social dividing line between those who belonged to the leisured circles for whom such education was possible and those who could only afford the common literacy necessary to earning one's living. It is important to grasp the importance of this boundary, for Paul, whose calling set him in close relations with those who were established above it,[9] made it his peculiar boast (surely rhetorical) that he fell below it in both respects. He could not speak, and he had to work.[10, 11]

V. Rhetoric in the New Testament

In spite of the fact that, in the last resort, the Fathers were content to take Paul's disclaimers of professional competence at their face value and to appeal to the Spirit, as Paul himself does, as the source of his eloquence, the problem of defining Paul's rhetoric remains. If we leave it at this, we are in the same case as those scholars of an earlier age who thought the *koine* was "the language of the Holy Ghost". But the discoveries of papyrology revealed how the Spirit had used "the instrument at hand".[12] In the fields of vocabulary and syntax the dislocation of New Testament speech from the standards of classical Greek has now been thoroughly explored, so that we may safely say that we have a more exact

---

[8] Plut. *Ti. Gracchus* 2.6.

[9] E. A. Judge, 'The Early Christians as a Scholastic Community', *Journal of Religious History* I, 1961, pp. 127–31.

[10] E.g. 2 Cor 11:6–9. The theme is basic to the Corinthian epistles.

[11] In English one may best appreciate the rhetorical system of Paul's age by reading the anonymous Roman writer (pseudo-Cicero) *ad Herennium,* the several rhetorical works of Cicero and the work of Quintilian on the training of the orator. The effects of this system on the work of other types of prose writer in Latin have been analysed by A. D. Leeman, *Orationis Ratio,* Amsterdam, 1963, and a detailed study of its bearing on the great poet contemporary with Paul will be found in the introduction to R. J. Getty's edition of Lucan I. Modern surveys will be found in G. Kennedy, *The Art of Persuasion in Greece,* Princeton, 1963, and M. L. Clarke, *Rhetoric at Rome,* London, 1953. For the role of Rhetoric in education see D. L. Clark, *Rhetoric in Greco-Roman Education,* New York, 1957 (though his judgement on Paul on p. 142 is too bold), and S. F. Bonner, *Roman Declamation in the Late Republic and Early Empire,* Liverpool, 1949.

[12] See the article of this title by F. I. Andersen, *Interchange* 1.2, 1967, 67–70.

control over the formal sense of the New Testament than did the classically educated Fathers. But in the field of rhetoric itself virtually nothing has been done, so that in this vital point of sense-control we are certainly worse off than they.

It will illustrate the task ahead of New Testament philology if I draw attention to the points at which Augustine himself felt at a loss with Paul's rhetoric. First and most alarming is that Augustine admits, positively gaily, that the lack of traditional rhetorical standards leaves him often in doubt as to the meaning of Scripture (ib. 6.9; 8.22; 9.23). He is prepared, paradoxically, to accept this as a mark of revelation, since it constitutes a test of skill in exegesis. But a modern exegete cannot surely take so sporting an approach to the matter, when it seems certain that it is the difference in rhetorical convention which is the source of Augustine's problem (though? was rhetoric the problem in 2 Pet 3:16?). The second point outstanding in Augustine's treatment is the question of figures. He gives one example of how to detect them in Paul (7.11) and with reference to 2 Cor 11:16–33, of which he gives a structural analysis (reproduced below), he implies that he might easily have gone through it pointing out the figures. Those who have tried to do it may well regret his easy confidence, especially when they recall that Gregory of Nyssa (who was, after all, unlike Augustine, a Greek) says Paul ignored the *schemata* (p. 61 above). The last work in Halm's collection is a pathetic reminder of how feeble our control of this subject has become since classical learning faded: a little manual on the figures of Scripture by the Venerable Bede. Augustine's third point of weakness is on the question of rhythm. He gives an example of how Paul might have improved his rhythms (in Latin!) by slightly rearranging the order of words, and suggests that it would be no great problem to a specialist to put the rhythms in order throughout. The daunting fact is, however, that Augustine is unable to say *(me fateor ignorare)* what the rhythmical properties of Paul's Greek were (20.40–41).

If New Testament scholars regard as essential the definitive handbooks of lexicography (e.g. Bauer/Arndt/Gingrich) and of grammar (e.g. Blass/Debrunner), they must equally demand a complete analysis of New Testament rhetoric. Blass himself, author of standard works on both Attic and Hellenistic rhetoric and of a special study of rhythm in the New Testament period[13] was equipped to do it, but necessarily and rightly confined himself in his *Grammatik des neutestamentlichen Griechisch* to a few closing sections on the subject—to have done more

[13] *Die Rhythmen der asianischen und römischen Kunstprosa,* Leipzig, 1905.

would, by ancient standards, have been to put the university work into the secondary school textbook.[14] Norden similarly was keenly interested in New Testament rhetoric, as the specialist studies collected as *Agnostos Theos* show, but his masterly survey of rhetorical prose from the sixth century B.C. to the Renaissance *(Die Antike Kunstprosa)* is all too brief if the best we have on the New Testament. For English readers the opening chapter of N. W. Lund[15] gives a brief review of the older work in German and also of Bultmann[16] and of J. Weiss.[17] The work of A. N. Wilder[18] is unfortunately affected by the curious modern fixation that the New Testament is a Hebraic work. While the classical scholars of a century or two ago certainly committed absurdities in trying to identify it with the classical tradition and the *religionsgeschichtliche Schule* of this century took it too close to Hellenistic ideas, the fact remains that it was written in Greek, if not *by* rhetorically literate Greeks at least partly *for* them. We must hold tenaciously both to the Hebrew sources of the thought and the Greek influence on its form. Norden criticizes those who confuse Hebrew parallelism of thought with Greek rhetorical antithesis.[19] The New Testament has both, in a bewilderingly unsystematic synthesis, which is only one reason why we must urgently look for the scholars who will be able to give us control of the New Testament art of speech.[20]

VI. PAUL AND HIS PROFESSIONAL COMPETITORS

Those who do not know the (much neglected) rhetorical literature of the time might be tempted to think, after reading the Corinthian letters especially, that Paul was pathologically concerned about his own status. As a quick antidote to this view I urge the reading of Oration 37 of Dio Chrysostom, thought to be the work of his pupil Favorinus, friend of Plutarch and teacher of Herodes Atticus. Like Paul, he had been treated with contempt by the Corinthians, after initially being lionised, and his speech is an elegantly self-centred reprimand to them after

---

[14] Eleventh edition, revised by A. Debrunner, Göttingen, 1961, pp. 310–18.

[15] *Chiasmus in the New Testament,* Chapel Hill, 1942.

[16] *Der Stil der paulinischen Predigt und die kynisch-stoische Diatribe,* Göttingen, 1910.

[17] *Beiträge zur paulinischen Rhetorik,* Göttingen, 1897.

[18] *Early Christian Rhetoric,* London, 1964.

[19] *Die Antike Kunstprosa,* pp. 507–9.

[20] C. F. D. Moule, *An Idiom Book of New Testament Greek,* Cambridge, 1953, pp. 193–201, confines himself to 'miscellaneous notes on style'.

he was restored to favour. (Similarly those tempted to think Paul was morbid should read the hypochondriac literature of the Younger Seneca, Aelius Aristides and Marcus Aurelius.) The important thing to grasp is that at this level of society self-admiration, including of course its deceptive asteistic refinements, was absolutely *de rigueur.* As Paul himself complains, he was despised for *not* indulging in it (2 Cor 11:20–21). I have suggested elsewhere that Paul found himself a reluctant and unwelcomed competitor in the field of professional "sophistry"[21] and that he promoted a deliberate collision with its standards of value.[22] It would be hard to find a more momentous or conscious upheaval in all the cultural history of the West. The historian will surely concede Paul all his sense of destiny in the matter.

VII. THE RHETORIC OF PAUL'S BOASTING PASSAGES

It is striking that Paul's attacks on boasting repeatedly take the form of a passage composed distinctly from the general flow of his writing.[23] They are usually amphidiorthotic, for example, that is, they are marked off from the context by the figures prodiorthosis (e.g. 1 Cor 4:6–7) and epidiorthosis (14–15). Their contents consist of highly schematic contrasts between the boasting of others and of himself, and secondly of elaborate presentations of his own claims to glory, which are always the opposite of what is normally boasted of. In the appendix of my article I give evidence for thinking them a parody of conventional norms.[24] The difficulty I now see with this, however, is that Paul takes his "foolish" boasting with too much anguish for us to assume it was merely a mockery, unless of course the interjections are themselves part of the irony. My interpretation of the basket passage is strengthened by Augustine's judgement, though he does not apparently see the contrast with the mural crown (which was still known in the fourth century, Scriptores Historiae Augustae, Probus 6.1), and also by the fact that the oath, which has

---

[21] *J. Rel. Hist.* I, 1961, 125–37.

[22] *J. Chr. Ed.* IX, 1966, 37–40.

[23] 1 Cor 4:8–13; 2 Cor 4:3–10; 11:21–33; Phil 3:4–11; cf. 1 Cor 9:19–33; 2 Cor 4:7–12.

[24] *J. Chr. Ed.* IX, 1966, 44–45. Unfortunately neither Menander on epideictic (Spengel) nor Priscian on praising (Halm) treats the conventions of *self*-laudation. Apparently they escaped the usual analysis due to their unfamiliarity to Greeks before the Roman conquest, but they can be clearly reconstructed from Roman examples.

always been the stumbling-block of commentators, may be read as an example of the *horkou schema* or *figura iusiurandi,* a recognized rhetorical ornament. Of one thing we may be sure, that such is the subtlety of the lost rhetorical art, that until we have it back under control we can hardly think we know how to read passages which both by style and content belong to Paul's struggle with rhetorically trained opponents for the support of his rhetorically fastidious converts.

VIII. Appendix

Augustine, *de Doctrina Christiana* 4.7.12 (based on translation of D. W. Robertson).

Writing to the Corinthians in the second Epistle he refutes certain persons, pseudo-apostles from among the Jews, who had attacked him. And since he was forced to praise himself, attributing this praise to a kind of folly of his own, how wisely and how eloquently he speaks. Companion to wisdom and leader of eloquence, following the first and not scorning the second, he says: "I say again . . . [quoting the whole passage 2 Cor 11:16–30] . . . I will glory of the things that concern my infirmity." Those who are awake will see how much wisdom lies in these words. With what a river of eloquence they flow even he who snores must notice.

Moreover, the informed will recognize that those *caesa* which the Greeks call *kommata,* and *membra* and *circuitus* which I mentioned a short time ago, since they are intermixed with a pleasing variety, lend all that fair appearance to the diction, its good looks as it were, by which even the uneducated are delighted and moved to action. From the point at which we introduced the passage there are periods,

16 Πάλιν λέγω, μή τίς με δόξῃ ἄφρονα εἶναι.	The first of which is the least since it contains two *membra,* and a period may not have less than two *membra,* although it may have more.
εἰ δὲ μή γε, κἂν ὡς ἄφρονα δέξασθέ με, ἵνα κἀγὼ μικρόν τι καυχήσωμαι.	There follows another which is tricolic (containing three *membra*).

17 ὃ λαλῶ,	The third which follows
οὐ κατὰ κύριον λαλῶ,	has four *membra*.
ἀλλ' ὡς ἐν ἀφροσύνῃ,	
ἐν ταύτῃ τῇ ὑποστάσει τῆς	
καυχήσεως.	
18 ἐπεὶ πολλοὶ καυχῶνται κατὰ	The fourth has two,
σάρκα, κἀγὼ καυχήσομαι.	
19 ἡδέως γὰρ ἀνέχεσθε τῶν ἀφρόνων	and the fifth has two.
φρόνιμοι ὄντες.	
20 ἀνέχεσθε γὰρ	The sixth is also bicolic.
εἴ τις ὑμᾶς καταδουλοῖ,	
εἴ τις κατεσθίει,	There follow three *caesa*.
εἴ τις λαμβάνει,	
εἴ τις ἐπαίρεται,	
εἴ τις εἰς πρόσωπον ὑμᾶς δέρει.	Then there are three
21 κατὰ ἀτιμίαν λέγω,	*membra*.
ὡς ὅτι ἡμεῖς ἠσθενήκαμεν.	
ἐν ᾧ δ' ἄν τις τολμᾷ,	There is added a tricolic
ἐν ἀφροσύνῃ λέγω,	period.
τολμῶ κἀγώ.	

22 Ἑβραῖοί εἰσιν;	κἀγώ.	Then three times *caesa* are
Ἰσραηλῖταί εἰσιν;	κἀγώ.	put as questions answered
σπέρμα Ἀβραάμ εἰσιν;	κἀγώ.	by three *caesa* used as
		answers.

23 διάκονοι Χριστοῦ εἰσιν;	The fourth of these *caesa* is
παραφρονῶν λαλῶ, ὑπὲρ ἐγώ.	then put as a question and
	answered by a *membrum*.
ἐν κόποις περισσοτέρως,	Then, the interrogatory
ἐν φυλακαῖς περισσοτέρως,	form having been grace-
ἐν πληγαῖς ὑπερβαλλόντως,	fully abandoned, the four
ἐν θανάτοις πολλάκις.	following *caesa* are poured
	forth.

24 ὑπὸ Ἰουδαίων πεντάκις
   τεσσεράκοντα παρὰ μίαν ἔλαβον,

Then a brief period is
introduced, since by the
elevation of the voice two
membra are distinguished.

25 τρὶς ἐρραβδίσθην,
   ἅπαξ ἐλιθάσθην,
   τρὶς ἐναυάγησα,

Then the voice returns to a
series of *caesa* of which
there are three.

νυχθήμερον ἐν τῷ βυθῷ πεποίηκα.

There follows a *membrum*.

26 ὁδοιπορίαις πολλάκις,
   κινδύνοις ποταμῶν,
   κινδύνοις λῃστῶν,
      κινδύνοις ἐκ γένους,
      κινδύνοις ἐξ ἐθνῶν,
      κινδύνοις ἐν πόλει,
      κινδύνοις ἐν ἐρημίᾳ,
      κινδύνοις ἐν θαλάσσῃ,
      κινδύνοις ἐν ψευδαδέλφοις,

Then fourteen *caesa* are
poured forth with a most
pleasing vigour.

27 κόπῳ καὶ μόχθῳ,
   ἐν ἀγρυπνίαις πολλάκις,
   ἐν λιμῷ καὶ δίψει,
   ἐν νηστείαις πολλάκις,
   ἐν ψύχει καὶ γυμνότητι.

28 χωρὶς τῶν παρεκτὸς
   ἡ ἐπίστασίς μοι ἡ καθ᾽ ἡμέραν,
   ἡ μέριμνα πασῶν τῶν ἐκκλησιῶν.

After these there is a
tricolic period.

29 τίς ἀσθενεῖ, καὶ οὐκ ἀσθενῶ;
   τίς σκανδαλίζεται, καὶ οὐκ ἐγὼ
   πυροῦμαι;

To this two *membra* are
joined as questions.

30 εἰ καυχᾶσθαι δεῖ,
   τὰ τῆς ἀσθενείας μου
   καυχήσομαι.

Finally, this whole almost
breathless passage is ended
with a bicolic period.

31 ὁ Θεὸς καὶ πατὴρ τοῦ κυρίου
   Ἰησοῦ οἶδεν, ὁ ὢν εὐλογητὸς εἰς
   τοὺς αἰῶνας, ὅτι οὐ ψεύδομαι.

After this burst of force he
rests, as it were, and lets
his reader rest, by
interposing a vignette

32 ἐν Δαμασκῷ ὁ ἐθνάρχης Ἀρέτα
τοῦ βασιλέως ἐφρούρει τὴν πόλιν
Δαμασκηνῶν
33 πιάσαι με, καὶ διὰ θυρίδος ἐν
σαργάνῃ ἐχαλάσθην διὰ τοῦ τεί
χους καὶ ἐξέφυγον τὰς χεῖρας
αὐτοῦ.

(narratiuncula) of inexpressible charm and delight. For he goes on, after saying "The God and Father [etc.]", with the briefest account of his peril and his escape.

3

St Paul and Classical Society

THE TROUBLE WITH Paul has always been to put him in his place.[1] It is not only that it may have been hard to understand or put up with what he was saying (e.g. 2 Cor 6:8; 2 Pet 3:16). People also objected to the way he said it; his personal bearing was unimpressive and his style of speech contemptible (2 Cor 10:10). It is not clear to us precisely what kind of social and literary prejudices inspired these complaints. But a convincing explanation of them would probably do much to open up the

---

NOTE: Revised version of a lecture originally prepared for Tyndale House, Cambridge, and the Universities of Durham, Kiel, Manchester and Oxford. I am grateful to colleagues in these places, and in London and Sheffield, for criticism, and to the Alexander von Humboldt-Stiftung for the opportunity of working at the F. J. Dölger-Institut in Bonn. My purpose is to point out some questions which the career of Paul raises for an ancient historian. Since professional boundaries seem to be a particular handicap to seeing this field as a whole, I have tried to refer to a variety of studies, mostly recent works in monograph form, through which the full literature can be traced.

[1]A comprehensive and up to date introduction to the history of the New Testament in its times is provided by M. Simon-A. Benoit, *Lejudaisme et le christianisme antique d'Antiochus Epiphane à Constantin* (Paris 1968), and in relation to church history by L. Goppelt, *Die apostolische und nach-apostolische Zeit*[2] (Göttingen 1966). For the history of recent research see W. G. Kümmel, *Das Neue Testament im 20. Jahrhundert* (Stuttgart 1970); S. Neill, *The Interpretation of the New Testament 1861–1961* (Oxford 1964). For Paul in particular O. Kuss, *Paulus* (Regensburg 1971); M. Barth et al., *Foi et salut selon s. Paul* (Rome 1970); G. Bornkamm, *Paulus* (Stuttgart 1969, E. t. New York 1971); E. W. Hunt, *Portrait of Paul* (London 1968); D. E. H. Whiteley, *The Theology of St Paul* (Oxford 1964); B. Rigaux, *S. Paul et ses lettres* (Paris 1962, G. t. Munich 1964, E. t. Chicago 1968); E. E. Ellis, *Paul and his Recent Interpreters* (Grand Rapids 1961); A. Schweitzer, *Geschichte der paulinischen For-schung von der Reformation bis auf die Gegenwart* (Tübingen 1911, E. t. [Paul and his Interpreters] London 1912). For a forthcoming volume of H. Temporini (ed.), *Aufstieg und Niedergang der römischen Welt,* is announced M. Simon, *Vingt-cinq années de recherches sur l'Apôtre Paul.* See also B. M. Metzger, *Index to Periodical Literature on the Apostle Paul* (Leiden 1960).

picture of Paul's place in the society of his day. He has been too much at home in modern times for us to appreciate how acute his alienation from his own may have been. But the orthodox fathers, even though they were also willing to give Paul the benefit of the doubt, could not escape the task of explaining it so easily. They had to face it because they still spoke the same language. It was no doubt professional pride that encouraged them to say that the difficulties must have been put there by the Holy Spirit as a test for exegetes. But they could not deny that Paul would have been easier to follow if he had kept to the classical models of expression they themselves accepted.[2] Jewish believers, to judge by the polemical tradition now also retrieved from a Muslim adaptation, complained that it all came of using Greek in the first place.[3]

In modern times people have tried various yardsticks to get the measure of Paul. Theologians disputed whether he should be seen in terms of later orthodoxy or as a more independent figure, perhaps a mystic. Historians of religion have appealed to the hellenistic cults, or more recently to rabbinic Judaism—or especially nowadays to something called hellenistic Judaism which falls between the two, and shares amply in the uncertainties of both. New Testament specialists, for their part, often prefer to hunt between the lines. It all depends upon the identity of Paul's opponents, or upon the practices and beliefs of that very flexible hypothesis, the primitive community.[4] Everyone finds it convenient to postulate a large unknown in terms of which the difficulties of the known can be resolved. It is not for a historian to condemn this very useful method of criticism—you will rightly guess in any case that I am calling for another variation of the same exercise. But it is important to recognise that the need for it arises not from the poorness of the evi-

---

[2] E. Norden, *Die antike Kunstprosa*[2] (Leipzig 1909), 501–2; cf. H. Chadwick, *The Enigma of St Paul* (London 1969), 3–5; M. F. Wiles, *The Divine Apostle: The Interpretation of Paul's Epistles in the Early Church* (Cambridge 1967), 16–18. Wiles is himself less ready to determine the meaning of Paul, and thus more ready to credit the fathers with some understanding, than Eva Aleith, *Das Paulusverständnis in der alten Kirche* (Berlin 1937), which was the first full treatment of the subject.

[3] S. Pines, *The Jewish Christians of the Early Centuries of Christianity according to a New Source*, Proc. Israel Acad. Sci. Hum. 2,13 (1966), 65. The complaint, familiar amongst Jewish Christians, was also raised against Mani by them (the baptist community in which he was brought up now turns out to have been Elchasaites): A. Henrichs and L. Koenen, 'Ein griechischer Mani-Codex (P. Colon, inv. nr. 4780)', *ZsPapEpigr* 5 (1970): 138.

[4] For an outline of the positions alluded to see J. P. Hyatt, ed., *The Bible in Modern Scholarship* (London 1966), esp. J. Munck, 'Pauline Research since Schweitzer', 166–77; W. D. Davies, 'Judaism as the Background to Paul', 178–86; H. H. Koester, 'Paul and Hellenism', 187–95.

dence we have, but from the contrast between its primary quality and the poorness of what we can set beside it. What we lack is not good first-hand sources, but a good secondary tradition and an adequate context. Without such help we find it difficult to cope with the many-sidedness and directness of the way Paul has documented himself, and the severe demands this makes on our powers of analysis and judge-ment. It is akin to the difficulty we have in getting agreement about a controversial figure in our own day.[5] We know him at too close quarters to be confident of our own reaction, until historical classification and interpretation can reduce the fullness of the evidence to a tidy order.

That this has not happened in Paul's case is due to the fact that his subsequent admirers did not wish to treat him according to the classical canons of history and biography. Disputes over orthodoxy, in theology as in law or philosophy, placed a different value upon documents from the past.[6] The proof of a point became more important than illustrating its moral. Authentic documents thus replaced the skills of the writer as the chief means by which history was expected to display the truth it was con-cerned with. 'We may well wonder whether modern political historiog-raphy would ever have changed from rhetoric and pragmatism to footnotes and appendixes without the example of ecclesiastical history'.[7] Certainly the pious manufacture of documents was part of this process. That was already established in the philosophical tradition, and was to enjoy much growth under orthodox care.[8] But the pathology of falsification is itself a response to the demand for autograph documents. Both phenomena de-velop together as part of dogmatic controversy, and that in turn has its roots in the sort of conviction which inspired the letters of St Paul, and se-cured their preservation. Systems of authority, provided they are in dis-pute, may serve to create critical techniques of documentation.[9] The

---

[5] Cf. H. Chadwick, op. cit. (n. 2 above) 18.

[6] Cf. A. Dempf, *Geistesgeschichte der altchristlichen Kultur* (Stuttgart 1964), 276.

[7] A. Momigliano, *The Conflict between Paganism and Christianity in the Fourth Century* (Oxford 1963), 92.

[8] The whole subject has now for the first time been systematically treated by W. Speyer, *Die literarische Fälschung im heidnischen und christlichen Alter-tum: Ein Versuch ihrer Deutung,* HdbAlt-Wiss 1,2 (Munich 1971). For a shorter version see id., 'Fälschung, literarische', *RAC* 7 (1969), and for the notion of 'genuine' religious pseudepigraphy see further W. Speyer, 'Religiöse Pseudepig-raphie und literarische Fälschung im Altertum', *JbAC* 8/9 (1965/1966): 88–125; id., 'Fälschung, pseudepigraphische freie Erfindung und "echte religiöse Pseu-depigraphie"', *EntrFondHardt* 18 (1972): 333–66.

[9] Cf. J. G. A. Pocock, 'The Origins of the Study of the Past', *CompStSocHist* 4 (1962): 209–46.

unprocessed survival of Paul's letters, or parts of them, in spite of and indeed because of the difficulties they presented, may thus be not unrelated to the shift from classical to modern criteria of documentation in history. It would certainly be perverse to think that we might have done better if a good biographer or historian had ironed out the problems for us. Admittedly Paul might have been easier to put in his place, but we should then have faced the question, was it the authentic Paul we had put there. Nor has Paul's self-disclosure been confined within any fixed rules of autobiography—the Greeks had in any case omitted to invent that category of writing.[10] It may be interesting in this respect to compare the semi-autobiographical treatment of Mani preserved in the recently discovered codex at Cologne.[11] Paul probably has no equal in laying bare his own complexities before St Augustine. But Augustine too found him a problem,[12] for he had made himself at home with the classicising fashion of writing, then in its hey-day, in a way that Paul, closer to its origins, had refused to do.

Like Augustine we cannot relate Paul accurately to his times because our understanding of them is focussed upon the points at which the classical tradition acquired its clearest definition. The life of the Greek cities of the first centuries is certainly not one of these points. It is not merely a matter of remoteness from classical Athens. Even the hellenistic age is best known to us in terms of its own classical period three centuries before St Paul. By the time of Polybius, moreover, Greek thinkers were already orienting themselves towards Rome, while Latin writers applied the classical Greek models to Roman use. The slow revival of Greek life that began with Augustus was carried forward under a new but archaising banner, as the Greeks too began to canonise their past. The literary success of the Atticism promoted by Dionysius of Halicarnassus inspired cultivated people to resist the free development of the common

---

[10] G. Misch, *Geschichte der Autobiographie*[3] 1,2 (Frankfurt 1950, E.t. Cambridge [Mass.] 1951), 541–44, notices the importance of Paul in this respect, but it is not mentioned in A. Sizoo, 'Autobiographie', *RAC* 1 (1950) or H. Gerstinger, 'Biographie', *RAC* 2 (1954). On Misch see now A. Momigliano, *The Development of Greek Biography* (Cambridge [Mass.] 1971), 16–17.

[11] A. Henrichs and L. Koenen, op. cit. (n. 3 above), 97–216. For an attempt to tackle the question prior to the announcement of the new material see L. J. R. Ort, *Mani: A Religio-Historical Description of His Personality* (Leiden 1967). For another case see V. Nutton, 'Galen and Medical Autobiography', *ProcCambPhilolSoc* 198 (1972): 50–62.

[12] *Doctr. chr.* 6.9; 8.22; 9.23; 20.40–41. For an outstanding study of Augustine himself, distinguished by its sense of the subtleties of relating a complex figure to changing times, see P. R. L. Brown, *Augustine of Hippo* (London 1967). It is precisely this kind of study we lack for Paul.

language, and its flourishing rhetoric. By the second century, from which we again have a substantial body of extant Greek literature, the classicising movement has prevailed. The barriers of taste, fatal to the comprehension of St Paul, have now been fixed. He is clearly an example of what the new cultivation had not been prepared to tolerate, surviving only thanks to the operation of non-literary interests. But the triumph of classicism must be the major cause of our loss of the main stream of Greek writing in the first century, and thus of any coherent picture of the social and intellectual context to which Paul belonged. It may also be related to some of the troubles in which he was immediately caught up. The only sure way back to the mind of St Paul from the Greek side would be through the reconstruction of first-century conditions. Unless we can do that coherently we cannot even tell how badly handicapped we are working from the clear but different focal point we possess in the second-century literature. After that the position only deteriorates. By the fourth century Christian authors have themselves become leaders in sustaining the classicising rules,[13] and thus imposing a barrier to their own understanding of Paul. By the sixth century, an age of rigid orthodoxy, it was necessary for a respectable author actually to write as though his Christian belief was as alien to the cultural tradition as it would have been in Athens a thousand years before.[14]

It is hardly surprising that our own capacity to grasp the picture of society in Paul's day is limited. It is not merely that much information has been lost, however. A great deal survives, in fragmentary form, and epigraphy in particular is supplying new material faster than anyone manages to digest it. But our attention is distracted by the polarising force of the literary tradition, turning upon other ages and places. We still lack an adequate analysis of Greek (as distinct from Roman) society that is concentrated upon the Julio-Claudian era itself (as distinct from that of Cicero and Augustus or the Flavians and Antonines).[15]

---

[13] Cf. L. Fruchtel, 'Attizismus', *RAC* 1 (1950); C. Fabricius, *Zu den Jugendschriften des Johannes Chrysostomus: Untersuchungen zum Klassizismus des vierten Jahrhunderts* (Lund 1962); id., 'Der sprachliche Klassizismus der griechischen Kirchenväter: Ein philologisches und geistesgeschichtliches Problem', *JbAC* 10 (1967): 187–99.

[14] The thesis of Averil Cameron, *Agathias* (Oxford 1970).

[15] It is over a hundred years since L. Friedlaender, *Darstellungen aus der Sittengeschichte Roms,* first organised the material for the whole period from Augustus to the Antonines with due regard for regional and chronological variations. Even so the weight of the evidence inevitably tipped the balance towards the latter part of the period, as also with S. Dill, *Roman Society from Nero to Marcus Aurelius*[2] (London 1905) [though this remains as good an introduction

A similar gap exists in the modern treatment of the Jews in relation to the Graeco-Roman society of that period. The cultural conflict in Palestine at the time of the Maccabees has exercised a magnetic attraction both in antiquity and in modern times, so that we possess very thorough, coherent and convincing treatments of it.[16] But the triumph of classicising rabbinism from the second century onwards, like its counterpart in the Greek cultural tradition, has cast a shadow back across the position of the Jews in the Greek cities of the first century.[17] We have become increasingly aware of 'the extraordinary variety, complexity and creativeness of Judaism in the Graeco-Roman period',[18] but this has also sharpened our sense of the degree to which the life of the Diaspora communities especially has been lost to view.[19]

In either case, Greeks and Jews, the New Testament itself offers a focal point around which the missing picture could be reconstructed, for it constitutes one of our most coherent sets of documents for them both. But here we are handicapped by disciplinary boundaries. Selective

---

as any to the intellectual world of St Paul], and T. G. Tucker, *Life in the Roman World of Nero and St Paul* (London 1910). With the double projects of M. Rostovtzeff, *Social and Economic History of the Hellenistic World* (Oxford 1941) and *Social and Economic History of the Roman Empire*[2] (Oxford 1957), and of C. Schneider, *Kulturgeschichte des Hellenismus* (Munich 1967) and *Geistesgeschichte des antiken Christentums* (Munich 1954), the middle ground of the Julio-Claudian period largely falls out of view between the two points of concentration. Works such as H. Mattingly, *Roman Imperial Civilisation* (London 1957) and U. Kahrstedt, *Kulturgeschichte der römischen Kaiserzeit*[2] (Bern 1958) are too general for our purpose. We need an analysis of life in the Greek world of St Paul of the type frequently provided for Rome itself at different periods.

[16] Notably V. Tcherikover, *Hellenistic Civilization and the Jews* (Philadelphia 1959) and M. Hengel, *Judentum und Hellenismus* (Tübingen 1969).

[17] The subsequent rivalry of synagogue and church provides a clearer focus for study: M. Avi-Yonah, *Geschichte der Juden im Zeitalter des Talmud* (Berlin 1962); M. Simon, *Verus Israel*[2] (Paris 1964); K. Hruby, *Die Stellung der jüdischen Gesetzeslehrer zur werdenden Kirche* (Zurich 1971).

[18] F. Millar, *JournTheolStud* 23 (1972): 223. For modern work see G. Delling, *Bibliographie zur jüdisch-hellenistischen und intertestamentarischen Literatur 1900–1965*, TU 106 (Berlin 1969).

[19] 'Vom vielfältigen und reichen Leben der D(iaspora) in Geschichte, Gemeindeorganisation, Theologie und Liturgie ist fast nichts erhalten', A. Stuiber, 'Diaspora', *RAC* 3 (1957). The juridical, economic and social position of the Jews has been thoroughly studied by J. Juster, *Les Juifs dans l'empire romain* (Paris 1914), and the documents are assembled: J. B. Frey, *Corpus Inscriptionum Judaicarum* (Rome 1936–1952); A. Fuks, V. Tcherikover and M. Stern, *Corpus Papyrorum Judaicarum* (Cambridge [Mass.] 1957, 1960, 1964). But we need more comprehensive local studies to compare with H. J. Leon, *The Jews of Ancient Rome* (Philadelphia 1960).

import policies may give only a very inadequate contact with the economy that prevails on the other side. In order to make clearer the kind of interchange I am looking for I distinguish it from two well-known exercises which are of far too restricted a type. The History of Religions School confined itself to the supposed traffic of ideas within the history of religions, as though that were essentially where the phenomenon of the New Testament belonged. Too many questions were begged about the nature of religion, and the New Testament tended to be consigned in advance to a place defined according to the conventions of comparative religion, without sufficient regard to its historical singularity. The classic stereotype here was the myth of the redeemed redeemer, studied especially in the earlier decades of this century, which broke down in any case on the problem of anachronism which besets our whole question. It tried to explain too much in terms of too few ideas brought in from too far away.[20]

---

[20] For the history of the modern study of the gnostic redeemer myth see C. Colpe, *Die Religionsgeschichtliche Schule* (Göttingen 1961); for a stock-taking in respect of the mystery cults see B. M. Metzger, 'Methodology in the Study of the Mystery Religions and Early Christianity', *Historical and Literary Studies. Pagan, Jewish and Christian* (Leiden 1968), 1–24; and for the differences in belief between the mysteries and gnosis see K.-W. Tröger, *Mysterienglaube und Gnosis in Corpus Hermeticum XIII* = TU 110 (Berlin 1971), 1–8, 166–70. For examples of the modern use of History of Religions material in the study of Paul see G. Wagner, *Das religionsgeschichtliche Problem von Römer 6, 1–11* (Zurich 1962, ET *Pauline Baptism and the Pagan Mysteries,* London 1967); H.-M. Schenke, *Der Gottmensch in der Gnosis* (Göttingen 1962) [on the church as the Body of Christ]; P. Hoffmann, *Die Toten in Christus* (Münster 1966) [on eschatology]. For comprehensive and detailed criticism of the whole subject-area see K. Prümm, *Religionsgeschichtliches Handbuch für den Raum der altchristlichen Umwelt* (Rome 1954), and A. D. Nock, *Essays on Religion and the Ancient World* (Oxford 1972). The latter, a masterpiece of editing by Zeph Stewart, reprints extracts from 58 of Nock's 414 studies published between 1922 and 1965, and supplies a remarkable series of indexes which enable Nock's views on all important topics to be traced through his whole life's work, including what is not reprinted here. The value of this can be appreciated from the remarks in the introduction about Nock's reluctance to engage either in polemics or in generalisation. He did draw his views together in 1928 in 'Early Gentile Christianity and its Hellenistic Background', *Essays* 49–133 (note too the introduction on recent work provided by Nock for the edition New York 1961), and in 1952 'Hellenistic Mysteries and Christian Sacraments', *Essays* 791–820. His detailed work inspired a strict sense of proportion and of the chronological limits of evidence.

It is argued on the other hand that the History of Religions School has in fact established the radical hellenisation of Christianity even prior to St Paul. See the stocktaking by R. Bultmann in his foreword to ·W. Bousset, *Kyrios Christos*[5] (Gottingen 1965, E. t. Nashville 1970); J. Leipoldt, *Von den Mysterien zur Kirche* (Leipzig 1961); id., *Religionsgeschichtliches zur Entstchung des*

The History of New Testament Times, on the other hand, is a discipline which attempts too little. In particular it tends to drop the heart of the New Testament out of history altogether. This partly arises because the textbooks which are produced under this heading are generally written for students of the New Testament, who are assumed to know in advance what it is about. But this is sometimes reinforced by the conceit that whatever it is about, is something not accessible to historical study anyway.[21] Some escape the issue by turning New Testament history into the history of the origin of the church.[22] By adopting this essentially anachronistic point of reference the question can be reduced to the familiar terms of the rise and development of a social institution. Other-

Christentums: Neue Beiträge zur Geschichte der alten Welt (Berlin 1965) 327/39; J. Irmscher: ib. 317. Academic developments in the United States have led to the revival of such studies there: W. G. Oxtoby, "Religionswissenschaft revisited," in J. Neusner (ed.), *Religions in Antiquity* (Leiden 1968) 590/608. The Society of Biblical Literature initiated a new section on Graeco-Roman Religions in 1970. Amongst others one may note the projects on the Corpus Hermeticum (associated with D. Georgi at Harvard), on the Cynic tradition (associated with A. J. Malherbe at Yale) and on the Corpus Hellenisticum Novi Testamenti, esp. Plutarch (associated with H. D. Betz at Claremont). The Corpus Hellenisticum as a whole is now divided between Halle (see G. Delling: ZNVV 54 [1963] 1/15), Utrecht (see W. Van Unnik: JournBiblLit 83 [1964] 17/33) and Claremont (see H. D. Betz: *Bulletin of the Institute for Antiquity and Christianity* 3 [1972] 4/7), and a series of Studia edited by the three directors has commenced publication: G. Petzke, *Die Traditionen über Apollonius von Tyana und das Neue Testament* (Leiden 1970); G. Mussies, *Dio Chrysostom and the New Testament* (Leiden 1972). Although this new wave of work is not restricted to religious ideas narrowly defined, it faces the same risks of too mechanical a parallelism and the anachronism inherent in working from mainly second-century sources that dogged the earlier enterprises. The great variety of work now being done on the oriental religions in the Roman empire is represented by the series of Études préliminaires edited by M. J. Vermaseren (Leiden 1961ff, some 25 titles so far). The problems of cross-cultural studies in the religious field of the ancient Mediterranean as a whole are being tackled in a series edited by C. Colpe and H. Dörrie: the first titles are B. Lohse, *Askese und Mönchtum in der Antike und in der alten Kirche* (Munich 1969); W. Helck, *Betrachtungen zur großen Göttin und den ihr verbundenen Gottheiten* (Munich 1971).

[21] So B. Reicke, *The New Testament Era* (London 1969) [= *Neutestamentliche Zeitgeschichte* (Berlin 1965)], 188 speaks of 'realities that are not accessible to secular history, but only to salvation history' and passes over the conversion of St Paul by saying (193) 'it was at Damascus during this period that Paul ceased persecuting the Christians and became their colleague'. But it risks invalidating the whole exercise as history if what is held to be the essential explanation of events is in principle excluded from the study.

[22] This solution is adopted by F. V. Filson, *A New Testament History* (Philadelphia 1964) and R. M. Grant, *A Historical Introduction to the New Testament* (New York 1963).

wise the History of New Testament Times tends to be content with correlation. It is the counterpart of searching for references to the New Testament in classical sources.[23] One accumulates details of matters on the other side of the fence which happen to be touched upon in the New Testament, as though this supplied it with its historical framework; the emphasis tends to fall upon items fairly remote from the heart of the matter, such as political events, because of their tangible character.[24] But while it is certainly useful to have the chronological and antiquarian details correct, one must beware of merely working around the edges of the central historical question: how the main interests and events of the New Testament itself are to be seen in relation to their full context in the society of its own times.

A New Testament history in this sense still eludes us, and not surprisingly it has not been given the benefit of a special name. But it is better left without one, since it belongs to no special category of historical or theological study. It is no more than the task any historian faces when his material happens to be drawn from a variety of more specialised disciplines. In the study of the Reformation, for example, it is taken for granted now that ideas and politics, art history and literature, religion and society must all be given their full due by the historian who hopes to do justice to the subject. The whole body of evidence must be drawn together around the principal interests of the period itself.[25] In the field of patristic studies an extensive reorientation of work along these lines is currently taking place.[26] But in the biblical field the obstacles are greater.[27] One may start from either side of the fence. But

[23] For a recent attempt at this see L. Herrmann, *Chrestos: Témoignages païens et juifs sur le christianisme du premier siècle* (Brussels 1970).

[24] Especially regrettable in the case of Reicke, op. cit. (n. 21 above) when it is linked with the neglect of the social setting, of which he happens to have special understanding. F. F. Bruce, *New Testament History* (London 1969) is the most adequate of the recent books from our present point of view, though it too (in spite of its title) tends to leave the ideas out of history, and is better for Jewish than for Greek material. Where the latter is brought to the fore, as with J. Leipoldt and W. Grundmann, eds., *Umwelt des Urchristentums* (Berlin 1964) and E. Lohse, *Umwelt des Neuen Testaments* (Göttingen 1971), we are back to the unresolved questions that are the subject of this paper.

[25] *The Journal of Religious History* was founded to promote this kind of historical study where religious material was involved, as distinct from the more sharply defined fields of the history of religions (in the comparative sense) or of church history. See the remarks of the editor (B. E. Mansfield) in volumes 1 (1960) and 5 (1970).

[26] H. Kraft, *Gnomon* 44 (1972): 113, on the theme Antike und Christentum.

[27] H. M. Orlinsky, *JournBiblLit* 90 (1971): 8 criticises current work in Old Testament studies as historically inadequate because of the artificial way in

those who work out from the New Testament quickly find themselves off solid ground due to the poor control we have over the strictly contemporary material. In what follows I therefore confine myself to a few examples of ways in which the work of ancient historians in the more conventional sense might improve the position, as they see the New Testament as a focal point for their own studies.

It is simplest to begin with Rome, given the interests of the literary tradition (whether Roman, Greek or Jewish-Hellenistic). But this will only give us an adequate approach to St Paul's world if a deliberate effort is made to get beyond the metropolitan and domestic interests of the Caesars which have always been the main interest of historians. Two ways of doing so have been successfully demonstrated in recent years. We now have a detailed analysis of the policies of Augustus as they affected the Greek states,[28] which could profitably be copied for each of his Julio-Claudian successors in turn: we should then not only be able to see clearly the changing imperial attitudes to the Greek cities in the decades during which St Paul moved through them, but should have the necessary chronological framework for the missing social and intellectual history of the cities during his lifetime. On the other hand, there is a distinct history of Roman-Greek relations to be written for each region in turn. The colonies of southern Anatolia have shown the impressive results that can be won from a full study of the epigraphic material.[29] We now have a flesh-and-blood picture of what Roman status meant in remote places where it might be a declining asset. Some of Paul's more puzzling experiences as a Roman citizen took place in these very colonies; we can now envisage the sort of people with whom he was dealing, and understand his predicament better.

Roman citizenship may not have been so decisive a status factor in the Greek cities of the first century as has been supposed. It has now been argued that the social class ranking system that applied later was already beginning to cut across the distinction between citizens and aliens.[30] It had often been given as one of the arguments against the possibility that

---

which the archaeological discoveries of the last generation have been applied, following upon the decline of linguistic standards. But at least the importance of the historical setting is recognised. Its relative neglect in New Testament studies is surely due in part to the intense specialisation caused by new impulses arising within the field itself, discouraging interchange.

[28] G. W. Bowersock, *Augustus and the Greek World* (Oxford 1965).

[29] B. Levick, *Roman Colonies in Southern Asia Minor* (Oxford 1967).

[30] P. Garnsey, *Social Status and Legal Privilege in the Roman Empire* (Oxford 1970), 266. For social status in the courts see J. M. Kelly, *Roman Litigation* (Oxford 1966). For recent work on citizenship see A. N. Sherwin-White, 'The Roman Citizenship: A Survey of its Development into a World Franchise', in

Paul could have meant literally that he fought with beasts at Ephesus (1 Cor 15:32) that such treatment was impossible for Roman citizens.[31] But there was no law against it, and the best one could hope for was that public reaction to the indecency would protect one, if one was of sufficient importance.[32] The decrees of Caesar at Thessalonica (Acts 17:7) are usually interpreted with reference to the Roman law of treason. Those who have recognised that such laws were hardly intended for people of Paul's rank, and that they should not be operated in an independent city or called decrees in any case, have been tempted to despair of the text.[33] But recently discovered inscriptions have shown that the oath of personal loyalty to Caesar (which stood outside any system of law, and embraced Romans and non-Romans alike) was administered through the cities, and that it was expressed in more prescriptive terms than previously known, so that it might easily have been spoken of as a decree.[34] It would be worth trying to estimate how actively the terms of the oath could be followed up in practice. A better appreciation of the complex of civil obligations and expectations under which Paul and his converts lived would not only give us the framework for defining their social position, but might help us understand the force of Paul's doctrines of subordination.

If the monolith of Roman law needs to be dismantled a little to fit first-century conditions, a positive effort of reconstruction is needed if we are to form any coherent picture of the law of the individual Greek states within the empire.[35] The constant flow of new epigraphic texts

H. Temporini, ed., *Aufstieg und Niedergang der römischen Welt* 1,2 (Berlin 1972), esp. 40–55 for the relaxation in the incompatibility of two citizenships in the Julio-Claudian period. For the origin of Paul's citizenship see G. Kehnscherper, 'Der Apostel Paulus als römischer Bürger', *StudEv* 2 = TU 87 (Berlin 1964), 411–40.

[31] R. E. Osborn, 'Paul and the wild beasts', *JournBiblLit* 85 (1966): 225–30 for a summary of the arguments. See also A. J. Malherbe, 'The beasts at Ephesus', *JournBiblLit* 87 (1968): 71–80 (it is a theme of diatribe). But there are also inscriptions, for which see below, which should be taken into account.

[32] P. Garnsey, op. cit. (n. 30 above), 130. Paul's treatment under Jewish law also implies more flexibility than meets the eye, cf. D. R. A. Hare, *The Theme of Jewish Persecution of Christians in the Gospel according to St Matthew* (Cambridge 1967), 43.

[33] So A. N. Sherwin-White, *Roman Society and Roman Law in the New Testament* (Oxford 1963), 96 and 103.

[34] E. A. Judge, 'The decrees of Caesar at Thessalonica', *RefTheolRev* 30 (1971): 1–7; P. Herrmann, *Der römische Kaisereid* (Göttingen 1968), for the origin and development of the oath.

[35] L. Mitteis, *Reichsrecht und Volksrecht* (Leipzig 1891, repr. Hildesheim 1963) remains basic for the eastern provinces, but there is no modern study for, e.g. Asia Minor, to compare with R. Taubenschlag, *The Law of Greco-Roman*

makes an adequate treatment all the more urgent.[36] Again, it is necessary both for a proper appreciation of the social order within which Paul worked, and in view of his frequent use of legal ideas, usually discussed only with reference to Jewish and to Roman law.[37]

The history and life of the Greek cities in their own right calls for much more study in other respects as well. The general treatment of this subject has probably been carried as far as is now humanly possible in the face of the mounting pile of unassimilated evidence.[38] But there are two clear ways forward. The more important cities deserve a thorough individual treatment, such as exists at present only for Antioch.[39] This is both the most reasonable way to organise the epigraphic resources, and at the same time the natural introduction to the study of St Paul in relation to Greek society.[40] The other approach is through the study of

---

Egypt in the Light of the Papyri[2] (Warsaw 1955). For a recent general study see D. Nörr, Imperium und Polis in der hohen Prinzipatszeit (Munich 1966).

[36] There is neither a comprehensive analysis nor a collection of documents that does justice to the evidence for classical Greek law as a whole, let alone the situation in the Greek states within the Roman empire, with its peculiar difficulties. Legal historians recognise what confronts them: e.g. H. Lewald, 'Gesetzeskollisionen in der griechischen und römischen Welt', in E. Berneker, ed., Zur griechischen Rechtsgeschichte, WdF 45 (Darmstadt 1968), 667. But epigraphists complain that the resources they supply remain unknown and unused: e.g. L. Robert, Hellenica 13 (1965): 235.

[37] L. Wenger, 'Über die erste Berührungen des Christentums mit dem römischen Recht', Misc. Giovanni Mercati 5, Studi e Testi 125 (Vatican 1946), 569–607, pays due attention to the problem of Greek law, yet in his article 'Bürgerrecht', RAC 2 (1954), he explicitly confines himself to Roman law, even though the Pauline language on civil status which he discusses takes many terms from Greek practice. Similarly F. Lyall, though recognising our ignorance of Greek law, moves directly from Jewish to Roman law in his articles, 'Roman Law in the Writings of Paul: Adoption', JournBiblLit 88 (1969): 458–66, and id., 'The Slave and the Freedman', NewTestStud 17 (1970): 73–79.

[38] Note the introduction to A. H. M. Jones, Cities of the Eastern Roman Provinces[2] (Oxford 1971), and see L. Robert, Hellenica 5 (1948): 35–58 for the defects of the first edition. A. H. M. Jones, The Greek City from Alexander to Justinian (Oxford 1940) remains a valuable work of overall interpretation of the intractable evidence. A compromise way forward would be through the history of regions, as in M. Avi-Yonah, The Holy Land from the Persian to the Arab Conquests (Grand Rapids 1966), which pays particular attention to the city structure of Palestine.

[39] G. Downey, A History of Antioch in Syria from Seleucus to the Arab Conquest (Princeton 1961), distinguished both for its thorough study of the evidence and for its attempt to portray the life of the city; but notice, as so often, how thin the record is for the first century in particular.

[40] Apart from Antioch there has been no adequate attempt to display the life of the cities in relation to St Paul since the prolific studies of Sir William

particular institutions, where the analysis of special bodies of source
material offers the prospect of quite fresh insights into the life of the
times.[41] To return to the beasts at Ephesus.

Another traditional reason
for not taking them literally (which I should not want to do either,
though for other reasons) has been the well known distaste of the Greeks
for brutal Roman entertainments, making it unlikely that such facilities
for punishment would have been to hand.[42] But it was demonstrated
over 30 years ago that the gladiatorial profession was far better established amongst the Greeks than had been thought, and that well-to-do
citizens both promoted it and showed a positive appetite for such
sport.[43] Other recent examples of this type of work that are illuminating
for the career of Paul are the study of condemnation by popular acclaim
in the free Greek cities,[44] and of the provincial assemblies which provided the framework for the local ranking system.[45]

Ramsay, whose earlier work has been described as confused, tumultuous and dis-
orderly, reduced to ruins not least by what he himself did later, L. Robert, *Villes
d'Asie Mineure*[2] (Paris 1962), 428. For a more favourable verdict see W. Gasque,
'Sir William Ramsay and the New Testament', *StudEv* 5 = TU 103 (Berlin 1968),
277–80; C. J. Hemer, 'The Later Ramsay: A Supplementary Bibliography of the
Published Writings of Sir William Mitchell Ramsay', *TynBull* 22 (1971): 119–24.

[41] F. Cumont, *L'Égypte des astrologues* (Brussels 1937) reconstructed a
broad picture of Ptolemaic society out of fragmentary documents preserved in
later astrological sources, deliberately invoking the spirit of the Renaissance hu-
manists as they confronted the then unknown world of classical antiquity as a
whole; his point was that there is much more to be won by those who can work
beyond the familiar literary tradition.

[42] See n. 31 above, and V. C. Pfitzner, *Paul and the Agon Motif: Traditional
Athletic Imagery in the Pauline Literature* (Leiden 1967). The fact that such ideas
may have been literary conventions does not make the social facts revealed in
the inscriptions irrelevant; the force of a metaphor may be greatly affected by
the immediacy of the experience.

[43] L. Robert, *Les gladiateurs dans l'orient grec*[2] (Amsterdam 1971) reports
now (2–3,15) about four times as many documents as were given in the 1920
edition of Friedlaender, op. cit. (n. 15 above). For the tastes of the well-to-do,
Robert 254–57. Paul's friends the asiarchs (Acts 19:31) would have been offi-
cially responsible for such displays. For their penal use, Robert 320.

[44] J. Colin, *Les villes libres de l'Orient gréco-romain et l'envoi au supplice
par acclamations populaires* (Brussels 1965) [noting (95) the problem of the
second-century and Roman slant of the evidence].

[45] J. Deininger, *Die Provinziallandtage der römischen Kaiserzeit von Augustus bis zum Ende des 3. Jahrhunderts n. Chr.* (Munich 1965) [conjecturing (49) that
the lack of first-century epigraphic support for the term asiarch is due to its having been displaced for formal purposes in that period by the title chief priests of
Asia]. R. MacMullen, *Enemies of the Roman Order: Treason, Unrest and Alienation
in the Empire* (Cambridge [Mass.] 1966) opens up a number of topics suggestive
for the career of Paul, e.g. urban unrest, famines and brigandage.

A full analysis of the social order within the Greek states, which can only be attempted on the basis of such studies, remains one of the most fundamental requirements for the understanding of St Paul. The Roman ranking system, headed by the senatorial and equestrian orders, has been extensively studied, and dominates our picture of the provinces, faute de mieux.[46] The Roman slave and freedman society has also become quite clear to us as a class world of its own.[47] The fact that New Testament writers address themselves directly to persons held in slavery in a way unparalleled in other homiletic traditions[48] is certainly of remarkable value to the social historian. But in order to appreciate its force we need to identify the status of the other sorts of persons being addressed. Until we can do so, the largely irrelevant picture we have of the metropolitan aristocracy will continue to lead to facile assumptions about the low level of Paul and his society.[49] The worst mistake is to assume that it did not matter to St Paul. His constant use of status terms and dwelling upon humiliations is the mark of a man caught up in serious conflicts of rank, and entitled in the normal course of events to considerable respect himself. The same applies to many of his followers and rivals—we must not be misled by his attempts to keep them humble either, which in fact prove my point. We are confused simply because we do not understand the conventions by which social position was regulated in the Greek cities. The status of the women who patronised St Paul would particularly repay attention. They are clearly persons of some independence and eminence in their own circles, used to entertaining and to running their salons, if that is what Paul's meetings were, as they saw best. Much effort has been spent on the question of Paul's attitude to women in general,[50] but the matter might be clearer if we

---

[46] J. Gagé, *Les classes sociales dans l'empire romain* (Paris 1964) deliberately set his whole picture in relation to the imperial power (7), and stresses our lack of information on the city bourgeoisie in general, but especially for the early (as opposed to the later) empire, and for the Greek-speaking cities where the more familiar Latin model of the West did not necessarily apply (10,19,154).

[47] See especially now P. R. C. Weaver, *Familia Caesaris: A Social Study of the Emperor's Freedmen and Slaves* (Cambridge 1972).

[48] H. Gülzow, *Christentum und Sklaverei in den ersten drei Jahrhunderten* (Bonn 1969), 69–72.

[49] Cf. O. Gigon, *Die antike Kultur und das Christentum* (Gütersloh 1966), 16–17.

[50] E.g. P. L. Hick, *Stellung des Hl. Paulus zur Frau im Rahmen seiner Zeit* (Cologne 1957); E. Kähler, *Die Frau in den paulinischen Briefen unter besonderer Berücksichtigung des Begriffes der Unterordnung* (Zurich 1960); J. Leipoldt, *Die Frau in der antiken Welt und im Urchristentum* (Gütersloh 1962). For pointers to the fact that classical Greek and later rabbinic practice (respectively) may not explain the position in the first-century Diaspora communities see C. Vatin,

knew what sort of women it was he had to deal with. Related to this is the question of the way they lived, in what sort of houses, and at what level of wealth. It would be a mistake to think that they were not well-to-do. The free flow of hospitality, gifts and travel facilities implies not only a generous spirit, but the means with which to express it.[51]

The question of Paul's educational level is probably less clear-cut than often thought, but the answer simpler. It has traditionally been posed in terms of Tarsus or Jerusalem, with the balance now tipped strongly in favour of the latter.[52] But this choice may have set a false trail. To have been brought up in Tarsus need not have committed Paul to a full rhetorical education, let alone a philosophical one (both of which were a matter of tertiary training involving much time and money), while being brought up in Jerusalem need not have excluded him from at least a general acquaintance with the Greek cultural tradition. Half of Gamaliel's pupils are said to have been trained in the wisdom of the Greeks.[53] The Greek language was much more common in Palestine than has usually been assumed, and may have been known, for example, to Jesus.[54] Qumran shows that even in the most reactionary circles there flourished forms of thought that reflect the hellenisation of Judaism.[55]

Recherches sur le mariage et la condition de la femme mariée à l'époque hellénistique (Paris 1970), 274 and T. C. G. Thornton, 'Jewish bachelors in New Testament times', *JournTheolStud* 23 (1972): 444–45.

[51] W. H. Wuellner, *The Meaning of "Fishers of Men"* (Philadelphia 1967) has shown that the Galilean disciples also did not lead as simple a life as traditionally supposed.

[52] W. C. van Unnik, *Tarsus of Jeruzalem: De Stad van Paulus' Jeugd* (Amsterdam 1952, ET London 1962) has found much support for the view that Paul was not brought up in Tarsus after all. But some still maintain a Greek rhetorical education, e.g. H. H. Koester, 'Paul and hellenism', in J. P. Hyatt, ed., *The Bible in Modern Scholarship* (Nashville 1965), 187–95, and stress the poor claims of Paul to belong to any rabbinic tradition, e.g. F. C. Grant, 'The historical Paul', in A. Wikgren, ed., *Early Christian Origins* (Chicago 1961), 48–59. For fuller discussion see N. Hugedé, *Saint Paul et la culture grecque* (Geneva 1966).

[53] E. Norden, *Die antike Kunstprosa*[2] (Leipzig 1909), 476, n. 1. On the formal similarities between Greek and Pharisaic popular philosophy see H. A. Fischel, 'Studies in Cynicism and the Ancient Near East: The transformation of a chria', in J. Neusner, ed., *Religions in Antiquity* (Leiden 1968), 372–411, and id., 'Story and history: Observations on Greco-Roman rhetoric and Pharisaism', in D. Sinor, ed., *American Oriental Society Middle West Branch Semi-Centenary Volume* (Bloomington 1969), 59–88.

[54] J. N. Sevenster, *Do You Know Greek?* (Leiden 1968), 189–90. Semitisms need not indicate translated material, but rather multi-lingualism in the writers, M. Black, *An Aramaic Approach to the Gospels and Acts*[3] (Oxford 1967), 271.

[55] For the common ground between the dualism of Qumran and John see O. Böcher, *Der johanneische Dualismus im Zusammenhang des nachbiblischen*

In both philology[56] and art history[57] the existence of a sharp distinction
between hebraic and hellenic forms of expression has been strongly challenged in recent years. One wonders whether that antithesis between a
supposedly hebraic community at Jerusalem and a supposedly hellenic
one at Antioch, upon which many theories about the New Testament
have leaned,[58] may not also make too much of the cultural distinction.

Judentums (Gütersloh 1965); P. von der Osten-Sacken, *Gott und Belial: Tradi-
tionsgeschichtliche Untersuchungen zum Dualismus in den Texten aus Qumran*
(Göttingen 1969); G. Klinzig, *Die Umdeutung des Kultus in der Qumrange-
meinde und im Neuen Testament* (Göttingen 1971). For comprehensive reference see H. Braun, *Qumran und das Neue Testament* (Tübingen 1966) and id.,
Gesammelte Studien zum Neuen Testament und seiner Umwelt[3] (Tübingen 1971).

[56] The distinction, stimulated by the work on Kittel's *Theologisches Wörterbuch*, has been emphatically summed up by T. Boman, *Das hebräische Denken
im Vergleich mit dem griechischen*[5] (Göttingen 1968, ET [from an earlier edi-
tion] London 1960). For the reaction see J. Barr, *The Semantics of Biblical Language* (Oxford 1961); A. Momigliano, *Terzo contributo alla storia degli studi
classici e del mondo antico* (Rome 1966), 759–64 = *RivStorIt* 74 (1962): 603–7;
D. Hill, *Greek Words and Hebrew Meanings* (Cambridge 1967).

[57] E. R. Goodenough, *Jewish Symbols in the Greco-Roman Period* (12 vols.,
New York 1953–1965) built up a massive argument for the extensive helleni-
sation of Jewish life on the basis of the objects surviving, for example, in graves.
For a stock-taking, and guide to the main reviews, see M. Smith, 'Goodenough's
Jewish Symbols in retrospect', *JournBiblLit* 86 (1967): 53–68. Goodenough had
commenced his work as a means of approaching the question of the helleni-
sation of Christianity. See his posthumous study, 'Paul and the hellenisation of
Christianity', in his memorial volume, ed. J. Neusner, *Religions in Antiquity*
(Leiden 1968), 23–68.

[58] For the attempt to trace the history of a distinctly hebraic movement see
H. J. Schoeps, *Theologie und Geschichte des Judenchristentums* (Tübingen 1949);
J. Daniélou, *Théologie du Judéo-christianisme* (Paris 1957); J. Hessen, *Griechische
oder biblische Theologie? Das Problem der Hellenisierung des Christentums in neuer
Beleuchtung*[2] (Munich 1962); R. N. Longenecker, *The Christology of Early Jewish
Christianity* (London 1970). For a stock-taking, with reference to the work of
Daniélou in particular, see R. A. Kraft, 'In search of "Jewish Christianity" and its
"theology": Problems of definition and methodology', *RechScRel* 60 (1972):
81–92. See also the collected papers of W. D. Davies, *Christian Origins and Judaism* (London 1962) and of J. A. Fitzmeyer, *Essays on the Semitic Background of
the New Testament* (London 1971). For examples of reaction against a sharply hebraic interpretation of Christian origins see A. A. T. Ehrhardt, *Politische Meta-
physik von Solon bis Augustin*, vol. 2 (Tübingen 1959), 5–44; J. B. Skemp, *The
Greeks and the Gospel* (London 1964); R. Scroggs, 'The earliest hellenistic Christianity', in J. Neusner, ed., op. cit. 176–206. For discussion of the issue in relation
to Paul see H. J. Schoeps, *Paulus: Die Theologie des Apostels im Licht der jüdischen
Religionsgeschichte* (Tübingen 1959, ET London 1961); W. D. Davies, *Paul and
Rabbinic Judaism*[2] (London 1955); R. M. Grant, 'Hellenistic elements in 1 Corinthians', in A. Wikgren, ed., *Early Christian Origins* (Chicago 1961), 60–66;
R. Scroggs, *The Last Adam: A Study in Pauline Anthropology* (Oxford 1966).

Certainly the line between Jew and Greek was critical in other ways. The differences between the classical literatures of the two traditions in their view of man, for example, remained important, and it was the New Testament writers and Paul in particular who (in contrast with the hellenising spirit of other first-century Jews writing in Greek) brought the two into a radical confrontation that was eventually to have great cultural consequences. Nor should one underestimate the severity of the social conflicts between Jews and Greeks in the first century. What is not at all clear is whether these tensions oblige us to assume two distinct systems of formal education existing at that time. Even if this were the position at the elementary level, we need not assume that there were conspicuous differences in the intellectual style of educated people using Greek. Paul himself is a tell-tale figure. Although keenly concerned in principle with the distinctions between Jews and Greeks in relation to the law and the gospel,[59] his activities do not suggest any obvious cultural distinction in practice—witness, for example, the struggles of New Testament commentators to determine whether a particular passage is intended for Jews, for Greeks or for both. I suspect Paul would be surprised at our problem, and perfectly happy to allow that just as many Greeks sought after a sign, and just as many Jews after wisdom (1 Cor 1:22). The complete indifference of Paul to questions of formal education (in sharp contrast with his strong feelings on the personal bearing of the adult man) also suggests that this was not itself the arena of conflict.[60] The terminology of pedagogical training interests him only for metaphorical purposes.

Nor should we be confused about the social and literary level of the Greek used by Paul and other well-educated people at the time, whether

---

[59] A question brought to the fore by J. Munck, *Paulus und die Heilsgeschichte* (Aarhus 1954, ET London 1959).

[60] Even if we assume a distinct system of Jewish education for the first century (for which it is hard to find evidence), it seems obvious that it would have had to be confined to instruction in the law and religious duty. That there was no other way apart from the Greek educational system in which other necessary forms of knowledge could be imparted is strongly implied by the continuing disinterest of the churches in founding their own schools until Julian forced the issue on them. This phenomenon, all the more remarkable in view of the inner mistrust of classical education which Julian rightly put his finger on, is discussed in H. I. Marrou, *Histoire de l'éducation dans l'antiquité* (revised and augmented edition, Paris 1965, E.t. London 1956, G.t. Freiburg 1957). Discussion of the subject in English, as for example in my own article, 'The conflict of educational aims in the New Testament', *JournChristEd* 9 (1966): 32–45, is not helped by lack of the distinction between Bildung and Erziehung, for which see respectively the articles of H. Fuchs, *RAC* 2 (1954) and P. Blomenkamp, *RAC* 6 (1966).

Greeks or Jews. The discovery of private letters of ordinary people in the papyri led to the premature assumption that this was the key to Paul's Greek.[61] But the people of Egyptian villages, even though they used Greek, belonged to that peasant world to which Paul and the urbanised elite were strangers. This was the most profound class division of antiquity, and Paul and everyone he was associated with belong securely on the favoured side. The so-called common Greek was much more than popular speech. Although it had been assumed that formal education was given in classical Greek in the first century as it was to be later, papyrus school exercises show that the common Greek was used in the schools.[62] From this it may be taken for granted that, apart from those who consciously adopted the new fashion of classicism, the common Greek served the purposes of people in all positions. It supplied not only conversation, but what has been called professional prose (Fachprosa), the existence of which has been demonstrated with reference to a selection of technical writers from the period Augustus to Hadrian.[63] This was the regular written language of educated people. It was also the language of St Paul.

It is now time for someone to write a full history of the lost Greek literature of the first century.[64] Its neglect is due not only to the forbidding lists of names, titles and fragments which confront the enquirer.[65] Philologists have done wonders with far less if there has been sufficient cause.

---

[61] 'Nothing could be less like the Pauline letters than the majority of the documents in Deissmann's *Light from the Ancient East*', A. D. Nock, *Essays on Religion and the Ancient World* (Oxford 1972), 347 = *JournBiblLit* 52 (1933): 138.

[62] L. Rydbeck, *Fachprosa, vermeintliche Volkssprache und Neues Testament* (Uppsala 1967), 111, n. 8.

[63] Rydbeck's thesis is based upon an analysis of Didymus (philology), Dioscurides (pharmacology), Heron (technology), Nicomachus (mathematics) and Ptolemaeus (astronomy).

[64] Cf. H. Erbse, 'Literatur', *Lex. d. Alten Welt* (Zurich 1965) col. 1739. A. Lesky, *Geschichte der griechischen Literatur*[3] (Bern 1971, E.t. New York 1966), 903–1001 gives the fullest modern discussion, although he explains in the introduction his reasons for neglecting the imperial period in general, and especially philosophy, Wissenschaft and Christianity. A. Dihle, *Griechische Literaturgeschichte* (Stuttgart 1967), 383–93 gives a good introduction to the subject of Fachprosa, but does not attempt to go into the imperial period on the grounds that Greek literature should then be treated jointly with Roman. An exceptionally valuable illustration of what could be done is provided by A. Wifstrand, *Fornkyrkan och den grekiska bildningen* (Lund 1957, F.t. Paris 1962, G.t. Bern 1967); based upon detailed knowledge of the technical and petty literature of the imperial period, it deserves the attention of New Testament students, although directed towards later times.

[65] The fullest lists are in W. v. Christ, W. Schmid, and O. Stählin, *Geschichte der griechischen Literatur*, vol. 2,1[6] (Munich 1920), 308–534. How much life can still be breathed into the dry bones is shown by H. Bardon, *La*

But literary historians have been able to spare no interest for a period seemingly dead to new talent, and taken up with the pedestrian dissemination of learning, or the fad of Atticism. A historian of education and society, however, will find these things of great enough interest in themselves, while the prospect of providing the New Testament writers with their lost intellectual milieu must be regarded as one of much wider importance still. The work needs to be done not only with careful attention to periods, places and types of writing, but with an overall eye to the way the intellectual life of the age as a whole was carried forward.[66] It was clearly a time in which knowledge circulated widely, as the great scientific advances of the hellenistic age, and the cultural tradition as a whole, were reduced for general consumption. We need a living picture of the scholarly industry and of its outworkings in the community at large— the textbooks, manuals, digests, encyclopaedias and libraries through which information was available.[67] Not that St Paul should be thought of as working directly from such resources, let alone from the classical authors themselves. But if these are the effective sources of knowledge at the time, we should begin there before trying to decide how it may have reached him.

Philosophy in particular should be set in relation to St Paul as a phenomenon of education and society. In what way did philosophical ideas generally circulate amongst cultivated people? The formal tradition of the great classical schools is not the answer to this question.[68]

---

littérature latine inconnue, vol. 2 (Paris 1956), which of course omits the literature which does survive.

[66] E. Cizek, *L'Époque de Néron et ses controverses idéologiques* (Leiden 1972) illustrates the possibility, though mainly concerned with the Latin writing associated with metropolitan circles.

[67] Cf. B. Gerhardsson, *Memory and Manuscript: Oral Tradition and Written Transmission in Rabbinic Judaism and Early Christianity* (Lund 1961), 15. An introduction to the desired study is provided by M. P. Nilsson, *Die hellenistische Schule* (Munich 1955), which was inspired by a sense of the social importance of the developing educational system. Much valuable reference material and discussion will be found in H. Fuchs, 'Enkyklios Paideia and Enzyklopädie', *RAC* 5 (1962); I. Opelt, 'Epitome', ibid.; H. Chadwick, 'Florilegium', *RAC* 7 (1969). Examples of other useful lines of work are M. Fuhrmann, *Das systematische Lehrbuch: Ein Beitrag zur Geschichte der Wissenschaften in der Antike* (Göttingen 1960) and H. Blum, *Die antike Mnemotechnik* (Hildesheim 1969).

[68] Nor was there any systematic relation between their ideas and those of Paul. See H. Chadwick, 'Philo and the beginnings of Christian thought', in A. H. Armstrong, ed., *The Cambridge History of Later Greek and Early Medieval Philosophy* (Cambridge 1967), 137–92, esp. 158f. For the cultural importance of Stoicism see M. Pohlenz, *Die Stoa: Geschichte einer geistigen Bewegung*[2] (Göttingen 1959), and for its ideas J. M. Rist, *Stoic Philosophy* (Cambridge 1967);

Philosophy in that strict discipline was a matter for only very few—those with the special interest and ample leisure required to devote years of adult life to such training. Nor does the answer lie in the notorious activities of the Cynic street preachers.[69] They were far too conspicuous and vulgar to do anything but repel people from the well-established circles in which Paul moved. But there must have been some form of intellectual intercourse behind the closed doors of educated people. When Paul withdrew from the synagogue in one city after another he must have carried on his activities under the umbrella of some accepted social convention or institution which made such meetings easy. It does little to help answer this question to examine Paul's enterprise in the light of subsequent ecclesiastical practice, or that of the mystery cults. In these cases we are dealing with religious procedures, in which order and ceremony, decorum and restraint were of the essence of the matter. But Paul belongs to a society of vigorous talk and argument about behaviour and ideas, carried on through privately organised meetings. If we knew more about the antecedents of the sophistic movement that flourished in the second century,[70] we might come closer to the social setting of Paul's mission. But in content what was being talked about certainly has more in common with philosophy, though it lacks altogether the conceptual security of a regular system of thought.

The conception of popular ethics opens a promising way forward in this matter.[71] By this is meant not any systematic propagation of ideas to the public, such as the Cynics undertook, but the way in which a loose body of general principles for life develops amongst thoughtful people in a community. This common stock is not subject to the discipline of the philosophical schools, though it may draw from them and feed ideas into their systems. But it is also just as likely to give and take in connection with other systems, such as religious movements or the social order.

---

for careful comparison with Paul see J. N. Sevenster, *Paul and Seneca* (Leiden 1961) and A. Bonhoeffer, *Epiktet und das Neue Testament*[2] (Berlin 1964).

[69] See in general D. R. Dudley, *A History of Cynicism* (London 1937) and for the various types of Cynic in relation to St Paul A. J. Malherbe, ' "Gentle as a nurse": The Cynic background to 1 Thess. 2', *NovTest* 12 (1970): 203–17.

[70] G. W. Bowersock, *Greek Sophists in the Roman Empire* (Oxford 1969).

[71] The notion of Vulgärethik has been set out in a series of valuable studies, not yet adequately noticed from the New Testament side, by A. Dihle, 'Antike Höflichkeit und christliche Demut', *StudItFilClass* 26 (1952): 169–90; 'Demut', *RAC* 3 (1957); *Die goldene Regel: Eine Einführung in die Geschichte der antiken und frühchristlichen Vulgärethik* (Göttingen 1962); 'Ethik', *RAC* 6 (1966); *Der Kanon der zwei Tugenden* (Cologne 1968). For a summary of Dihle's work see my article, ' "Antike und Christentum". Some recent work from Cologne', in a forthcoming number of *Prudentia*. [Ed.: It appeared in *Prudentia* 5 (1973): 1–13.]

It is not the manufacturer, or even the promoter of ideas, but a bank or market where they are stored and exchanged, and related to the general intellectual currency of the times. If we knew more about the conventions by which it operated in the Greek cities we should be able to say more clearly how Paul was placed in the society of his day. The Cynic-Stoic diatribe has haunted New Testament criticism for too long. It is a ghost summoned up for lack of a more adequate explanation of what confronts us there. It is not at all clear that it has any claim to exist, especially at this period, but the reservations of classical scholars, and the problems of definition and evidence, are not always noticed on the New Testament side.[72] The reason is interesting. Like the myth of the redeemed redeemer, to which it is a kind of literary counterpart, it owed its special lease of life to the History of Religions School.[73] But it seems largely to have escaped the scepticism with which the redeemer myth has been treated in this generation. This is perhaps because it remains out of reach of the new currents in theology which have transformed New Testament scholarship. It has passed into the safe waters of New Testament background. But it is by no means harmless if it tends to reduce the New Testament paraenesis to a formal type. It is to be hoped that the current revival of work will lead to a careful mapping out of the differences.[74] The so-called diatribe, whether in its drastic Bionic form or in the more temperate work of Musonius and Epictetus, deals in commonplaces, delivered as a literary creation against stock targets. It lacks altogether the engagement with actual people, circumstances and disputed ideas that is characteristic of Paul. Obviously the diatribe writers contributed to the bank of ideas and practices that was available in his circles, and one would expect to be able to detect some

---

[72] The appropriate classical term was dialexis (a lecture), diatribe meaning rather the treatment of a theme, and being first attested as a literary label in the subscriptio to the oldest MSS of Epictetus: see A. D. Nock, *Sallustius Concerning the Gods and the Universe* (Cambridge 1926) xxvii–xxxii; W. Capelle and H. I. Marrou, 'Diatribe', *RAC* 3 (1957); H. Cancik, *Untersuchungen zu Senecas epistulae morales* (Hildesheim 1967), 46–48. For illustrations of the flimsy state of the evidence see V. Martin, 'Un recueil de diatribes cyniques: Pap. Genev. inv. 271', *MusHelv* 16 (1959): 77–115, and A. C. van Geytenbeek, *Musonius Rufus and Greek Diatribe* (Assen 1963).

[73] The standard references remain R. Bultmann, *Der Stil der paulinischen Predigt und die kynisch-stoische Diatribe* (Göttingen 1910) and P. Wendland, *Die hellenistisch-römische Kultur in ihren Beziehungen zu Judentum und Christentum* 2/3 (Tübingen 1912). A pupil of Bultmann's claims to have found the missing link, H. Thyen, *Der Stil der jüdisch-hellenistischen Homilie* (Göttingen 1955).

[74] See the articles of A. J. Malherbe and H. A. Fischel cited in nn. 31, 53, 69 above, and H. Funke, 'Antisthenes bei Paulus', *Hermes* 98 (1970): 459–71.

similarities. But we cannot afford to build too much upon them if we are to explore adequately the many-sidedness and singularity of Paul's epistolary technique.[75] The current debate over the last four chapters of 2 Corinthians will illustrate how much is still uncertain.[76] Much attention has been attracted by the hypothesis that Paul's Jewish opponents had set up as their ideal for the apostle the type of the so-called divine man.[77] This suggestion may well fit the fact that Paul was expected to produce more dramatic proofs of his apostleship, and its greatest value could be in opening up the whole question of the religious expectations characteristic of Paul's day.[78] There is a risk, however, that it may now be used to ex-

---

[75] Even under this heading study has been somewhat stagnant since Deissmann, cf. J. Schneider, 'Brief', *RAC* 2 (1954), but one may hope for new leads from K. Thraede, *Grundzüge griechisch-römischer Brieftopik* (Munich 1970) [which apparently embraces his 'Einheit-Gegenwart-Gespräch: Zur Christianisierung antiker Brieftopoi' (Diss. Bonn 1968)]. See also E. Kamlah, *Die Form der katalogischen Paränese im Neuen Testament* (Tübingen 1964) and N. Schneider, *Die rhetorische Eigenart der paulinischen Antithese* (Tübingen 1970). Useful summaries of older work may be found in the studies of B. Rigaux and E. W. Hunt (n. 1 above). E. von Severus, 'Gebet I', *RAC* 8 (1972): 1175–85, stresses the importance of independent elements in Paul's style, but on the other hand A. Brunot, *Le génie littéraire de s. Paul* (Paris 1955) and A. N. Wilder, *Early Christian Rhetoric: The Language of the Gospel* [2] (Cambridge [Mass.] 1971) move too far beyond the historical situation with which we are concerned.

[76] G. Bornkamm, 'Die Vorgeschichte des sogenannten Zweiten Korintherbriefes', *Gesammelte Aufsätze* 4 (Munich 1971): 162–94. For recent discussion of various aspects of the matter see also K. Prümm, *Theologie des Zweiten Korintherbriefes 2* (Rome 1962); W. Schmithals, *Die Gnosis in Korinth*[2] (Göttingen 1965, E.t. Nashville 1971); id., *Paulus und die Gnostiker* (Hamburg 1965, E.t. Nashville 1972); R. Batey, 'Paul's Interaction with the Corinthians', *JournBiblLit* 84 (1965): 139–46; D. W. Oostendorp, *Another Jesus: A Gospel of Jewish-Christian Superiority in 2 Corinthians* (Kampen 1967); R. McL. Wilson, 'How gnostic were the Corinthians?' *NewTestStud* 19 (1972): 65–74.

[77] The thesis of D. Georgi, *Die Gegner des Paulus im 2. Korintherbrief: Studien zur religiösen Propaganda in der Spätantike* (Neukirchen 1964). For discussion see M. Rissi, *Studien zum 2. Korintherbrief* (Zurich 1969); C. K. Barrett, 'Paul's opponents in II Corinthians', *NewTestStud* 17 (1971): 233–54; J. F. Collange, *Énigmes de la deuxième épître de Paul aux Corinthiens* (Cambridge 1972).

[78] While ample efforts have been made to relate the New Testament to gnosticism, the mysteries or the philosophical schools, all of which were relatively discreet and limited as social phenomena, comparatively little has been done to construct an adequate picture of the more confused but much commoner apprehension of the supernatural through such practices as portents, prodigies, dreams, magic and astrology. It would give us a more realistic picture of the world Paul was addressing if we had a comprehensive interpretation of its mentality such as has been provided for the third century by E. R. Dodds, *Pagan and Christian in an Age of Anxiety* (Cambridge 1965). Some recent contribu-

plain too much, and that too solid a structure will again be erected upon uncertain foundations. The divine man as a type is not much better attested than the diatribe, especially for our period.[79] We have a long tradition from previous times of Greek admiration for the divine in man, but it disappears in the first century along with the evidence for many other things. Only in the second century do we have a clear-cut type of religious professional which may justify the use of such a label. But the modern categorisation is in any case adventurous.

The solid ground in the problem of 2 Cor 10–13 is not to be found between the lines. It lies in the actual reaction of Paul as we possess it, especially in its intensity and elaboration. His critics objected to his personal style, both in bearing and speech, and in the way he would not accept support from the community. Whatever it may have been that they would have preferred him to be, it is clear that the breaking point for him was the demand that he boast of his record and rank himself in a competition of honour with his rivals. There has just been published the first full-scale attempt to explain this reaction in relation to hellenistic-Roman materials.[80] Paul had been formally charged, it is claimed, with being a public fraud (because he would not produce the impressive record expected), and in reply is consciously identifying himself with the Socratic refusal to defend himself. In working out this subtle theme a remarkable range of echoes of other familiar literary and social types is invoked by Paul. Many points of detail might be queried. But there are two general weaknesses in the case. In the first place, as with the divine man

---

tions are J. Lindblom, *Gesichte und Offenbarungen, Vorstellungen von göttlichen Weisungen und übernatürlichen Erscheinungen im ältesten Christentum* (Lund 1968); H. G. Gundel, *Weltbild und Astrologie in den griechischen Zauberpapyri* (Munich 1968); W. and H. G. Gundel, *Astrologoumena: Die astrologische Literatur in der Antike und ihre Geschichte* (Wiesbaden 1966); G. Schille, *Die urchristliche Wundertradition* (Stuttgart 1967); G. Delling, *Studien zum Neuen Testament und zum hellenistischen Judentum* (Göttingen 1970), 53–159 (on miracles).

[79] L. Bieler, ΘΕΙΟΣ ΑΝΗΡ: *Das Bild des 'göttlichen Menschen', in Spätantike und Frühchristentum* (Vienna 1935–1936, reprinted in one volume Darmstadt 1967), was responsible for crystallising the notion, building upon earlier work of Norden, Reitzenstein and Weinreich. The current revival of it is linked particularly with the Corpus Hellenisticum Novi Testamenti (on which see n. 20 above). For examples see H. D. Betz, *Lukian von Samosata und das Neue Testament* = TU 76 (Berlin 1961); id., 'Jesus as divine man', in T. F. Trotter, ed., *Jesus and the Historian* (Philadelphia 1968); G. Petzke, *Die Traditionen über Apollonius von Tyana und das Neue Testament* (Leiden 1970). For criticism see M. Smith, 'Prolegomena to a discussion of aretalogies, divine men, the gospels and Jesus', *JournBiblLit* 90 (1971): 174–99.

[80] H. D. Betz, *Der Apostel Paulus und die sokratische Tradition* (Tübingen 1972).

figure which supposedly confronts him, the pattern of Paul's reply is constructed out of materials from the older hellenistic cultural tradition on the grounds that they can be shown to have been alive still in the second century. But this begs the admittedly difficult yet fundamental question of how far and by what means Paul can be assumed to have shared in a cultural tradition attested only for writers whose main interest was to perpetuate it against just such innovators as he was. Secondly, the net effect is to give a picture of Paul's personality that has much more in common with the detached, ironic Socrates, or the scornful Cynics, coolly indifferent to their fate, than with the passionately committed figure of the epistle, tortured by the problem of how to combine his sense of calling and authority over his obstreperous converts with the self-renunciation to which he saw himself also called.

Yet the conflict clearly has cultural overtones, and there are possibilities which have not yet been considered. The complaints against Paul may have had something to do with the new aesthetic fashion of classicism which was presumably imposing itself upon the expression of educated people during this period. A simple identification of the critics with this cause will not do. They still found his letters weighty and strong, and these clearly made no concessions to Atticism. But Paul's spoken style may have been much more banal. A second possibility arises from the structure of 2 Cor 11:22–33 (sic), which I take as a deliberate parody of conventions of self-display to which he refused to conform.[81] The difficulty is that we know these practices principally from the Roman side. The Greek philosophical tradition, after a period of sympathy with Roman eulogistic ideals, had reverted by Plutarch's time to a more hostile opinion.[82] The material in any case has been analysed neither in antiquity nor in modern times. Although the conventions were familiar, they were not brought within the rules of Greek rhetoric.[83]

---

[81] E. A. Judge, 'Paul's boasting in relation to contemporary professional practice', *AustBiblRev* 16 (1968): 37–50. I have not seen J. G. Bosch, *'Gloriarse' según san Pablo: Sentido y teología de 'kauchaomai'* (Rome 1970), which is apparently an extensive study of the boasting theme against its cultural background.

[82] A. D. Leeman, *Gloria: Cicero's waardering van de roem en haar achtergrond in de hellenistische wijsbegeerte en de romeinse samenleving* (Rotterdam 1949) is fundamental. For later developments see A. J. Vermeulen, *The Semantic Development of Gloria in Early Christian Latin* (Nijmegen 1956), and on Plutarch, *De laude ipsius*, see H. G. Ingenkamp, *Plutarchs Schriften über die Heilung der Seele* (Göttingen 1971).

[83] This in spite of the fact that writers on epideictic oratory (e.g. Menander) covered other forms of eulogy. See T. C. Burgess, 'Epideictic literature', *StudClassPhil* 3 (1900): 89–261; G. Kennedy, *The Art of Rhetoric in the Roman World 300 B. C.–A. D. 300* (Princeton 1972), 21–23.

(Has this anything to do with the failure to categorise autobiography?) But the speech of Favorinus to the Corinthians shows clearly that the practice was within the repertoire of a rhetorician.[84] And the inscriptions show that the art of adorning oneself was in vogue in the Greek cities of Paul's day.[85] As an alternative to, or variation upon, the divine-man-versus-Socratic-tradition explanation of the conflict in 2 Corinthians, I therefore urge a more thorough search of the history of changing fashions in fine speech and self-display in the first century.

It is certain that no explanation can get to the heart of Paul's relation to classical society that does not do full justice to his pursuit of radical self-humiliation. This theme runs through all his work, in theology and ethics alike, and on into his practical relations with both followers and rivals, and the way he talked about himself. It is moreover an attitude in violent reaction to much that was central to the classical way of life, not excluding the smooth doctrines of moderation with which it must not be confused.[86] Those particularly who, like myself, are interested in placing Paul accurately in the Greek society of his day must be careful of making him more at home there than he was. He is after all the historical source of the profound self-doubt that has divided the humanistic spirit ever since.

North Ryde, N. S. W.
Edwin A. Judge

[84] Dio Chrysostom 37.
[85] In addition to the inscriptions (too remote from Paul) cited by A. Fridrichsen, 'Zum Stil des paulinischen Peristasenkatalogs, 2 Cor 11,23ff', SymbOsl 7 (1928): 25–29 [who had anticipated me in this point], notice the rich material in L. Robert, Les Gladiateurs dans l'Orient grec² (Amsterdam 1971), 258–62, 302–7, and especially no. 152 (p. 168) an inscription contemporary with Paul from Magnesia on the Meander. People who could read such texts in the public places of their cities would instantly recognise the force of Paul's parody in 2 Cor 11.
[86] In addition to the relevant works of A. Dihle (n. 71 above) see O. Schaffner, Christliche Demut (Würzburg 1959) [partly critical of Dihle]; S. Rehrl, Das Problem der Demut in der profangriechischen Literatur im Vergleich zu Septuaginta und Neuem Testament (Münster 1961) [independent of Dihle]; R. Vischer, Das einfache Leben: Wort- und Motivgeschichtliche Untersuchungen zu einem Wertbegriff der antiken Literatur (Göttingen 1965); W. A. Beardslee, Human Achievement and Divine Vocation in the Message of Paul (London 1961); R. C. Tannehill, Dying and Rising with Christ: A Study in Pauline Theology (Berlin 1967).

4

St Paul as a Radical Critic of Society

YOU MAY VERY reasonably think it stretches the point to speak of St Paul as a radical. Is he not conspicuously the one whose ideas buttress conservative attitudes in our own society? Is it not the case that he attempted no systematic discussion of social theory, but (in a typically conservative manner) insisted on dealing simply with particular cases, and treated contentious issues of social relations, like slavery and the status of women, in a wilfully ambiguous manner? I do not of course wish to imply that the answer to these questions is 'Yes', but at the same time I do not wish my own title to beg too many questions: it is meant simply as an invitation to reconsider the facts, and I recognize that the problems of definition are not easy ones. But there are aspects of the historical situation which I believe could be clarified, and if we can do this we shall be able to say more accurately what Paul's stance as a critic of society was like.

I. PAUL AND JUDAISM

One basic reason for suspecting that Paul was not a conservative person in his ideas on society is that he deliberately abandoned the security of established status in his own life. There is no doubt that he was a person highly placed in every social scale that mattered in the centres where he worked. The Jews were a much more substantial minority in the Graeco-Roman cities of St Paul than they have been in the modern West. The New Testament itself shows that their leaders were often socially integrated with the governing classes, the *élites* in the various

---

NOTE: This is an edited version of the Tenth Annual Lecture of the Baptist Theological College of New South Wales, Board of Graduate Studies, July 1974.

cities, even though the racial situation could be explosive between Jews and Greeks. Amongst this powerful Jewish class St Paul had the *cachet* of a full rabbinical training in Jerusalem, which gave him acceptance with the synagogue leadership wherever he went. At the same time he probably came from a fully Hellenized family in Tarsus. It is my belief that the style of speech and writing that he disposed of was not (as has been supposed) a sub-educated one, but that it placed him easily in the mainstream of educated public figures, although he certainly did not affect the consciously archaic manner and conventional themes of the literary in-group of the times, which is what we mainly know of from the surviving classical literature.[1]

Most decisive is the fact of his Roman citizenship, which lifts him automatically into the internationalized circle from which all effective leadership came. This ensured him acceptance with the most important people wherever he went, and it can be easily shown that he availed himself freely of this advantage. But at the same time there is the quite baffling frequency of occasions when he was at the opposite end of the stick. A man of his standing had no need to suffer the humiliations of direct redress and physical punishment within or without the law which ancient societies accepted as lying behind their legal processes. The law existed to secure the prerogatives of people like himself, and it was normally operated that way. In any case such a person should have had ample resources in both money and attendants to be able to protect himself against the use of force; yet on various occasions he obviously made no attempt to do so. On the other hand, the book of Acts shows that he understood what his rights were in the matter and was sometimes willing to use them to protect himself.

Those dreadful catalogues of personal disaster, which he unleashes on his critics in the epistles, are not the mark of a man who took punishment and humiliation as part of his ordinary lot in society. There was no point in a lowly man's complaining of what he had to put up with. But for a man of St Paul's rank, the formal recital of affronts is itself a deliberate embarrassment to those he is addressing as well as a mark of his own sensitivity to questions of status. The reasons for this preoccupation on his part with the reversal of social rank will concern us a little later. For the moment I wish simply to register the fact as a sign that we are not dealing with someone comfortably entrenched in the conservative security that

[1] For further discussion and literature on the historical background to this article, see E. A. Judge, 'St Paul and Classical Society', *Jahrbuch für Antike und Christentum* XI (1972), 19–36.

was his birthright. The Abraham of the new covenant had left the old homeland. But what was his call, and where was he going?

At first sight it is easy to give an answer to these questions in relation to his status as a Jew. Paul is openly engaged in what appears to be a radical conflict with the Jewish establishment. It is in the synagogues that the terms of the conflict are thrown down as a challenge, and it is the Jewish leaders who are behind many of the attacks on him in the Greek cities. For his own part he constantly grapples with questions of the status of Jews and of their law, and appears to be setting up the freedom of the Gentiles in Christ as a counter-order to the covenant society of Israel. Surely this is extreme radicalism indeed for a Jew, and so it undoubtedly seemed to his synagogue opponents. At one blow he seemed to be demolishing the law and the whole carefully constructed apparatus of distinction between Jew and Gentile. Yet it has been made clear by closer study that Paul remained closely absorbed in the question of the salvation of Israel, and the whole of his mission to the Gentiles was conditioned by its relation to Israel's hope.[2] As for the law, he certainly did not depart seriously from it in practice. It was rather that he had transposed a traditional Jewish obligation to the law into a personal obligation to Christ, who he believed fulfilled it. Most importantly, St Paul did not at all abandon the basic categories of Hebrew thought, and he argued the consequences of Jesus' Messiahship from within that tradition. So that although the breach with Jewish leaders was sharp and the debate vehement, Paul's teaching is rather a development of Hebrew thought than a break with it. He certainly did not go over intellectually to the Hellenic style of analysis of man and society as other Jewish thinkers were prepared to do. Nor did he in any basic sense himself adopt the Greek way of life as reforming Jews had often done.[3]

On second thoughts therefore it is not clear how radical a critic Paul can be said to have been of the Jewish establishment. It is true that one can superficially align his phraseology and individual precepts with Stoic materials in particular, but that is to ignore the cast of the whole, and the total lack of integration of his thought with the Greek intellectual method. In this we see the mark of his true standing in relation to contemporary Greek education. He was familiar in the ordinary educated way with a range of ideas that circulated in Hellenic society. But at the same time he was altogether removed from any tight professional involvement

[2] On this subject see J. Munck, *Paul and the Salvation of Mankind*, London: S.C.M., 1959.
[3] See for examples V. Tcherikover, *Hellenistic Civilisation and the Jews*, Philadelphia: Jewish Publication Society of America, 1961.

with the classical method of discussion, which was very much the special province of philosophy and the literary *élite*. He would never have been recognized as a man of letters or a philosopher in the technical sense within the Greek tradition. Yet he remains very securely placed amongst the ordinary educated classes, the Hellenized rabbi, freely using the full resources of standard, technical Greek for his own purposes.

II. PAUL AND HELLENISM

On the other hand, since he is deliberately throwing open the heritage of Israel to Greeks without the law, he must come to a full confrontation with Greek ideals of life and society. That there is no systematic exposition of his views in relation to the Greek tradition is itself a mark of his total rejection of it. As a Hebrew his thinking simply did not begin with man at all. And it is in that sense radically anti-humanist. He simply does not concede that the condition of man can be explained by the analysis of man in himself. And by extension the analysis of social relations in themselves forms no part of his understanding of human society. But this does not mean that his understanding of man is otherworldly. On the contrary, it may be said that the Greek philosophers are the other-worldly ones. They detached themselves deliberately from the experience of particular people and real situations. They are often locked into an abstract cycle of debate in general terms, driven more by the sheer rationality of the tradition than by reference to any actual social situation. But there is in my view no writer of antiquity who exposes himself so ruthlessly to direct human contact and reveals himself to others with such candour and directness as does St Paul. Certainly he measures himself and others by direct reference to the will of God revealed in Christ, but this goes far beyond a theoretical exercise. Its validity had been tested profoundly in his own experience and that of his colleagues and followers, and to this experience he constantly appeals. The theories of man in himself or of society in itself are simply not subjects which fall within Paul's horizon. Even when he generalizes on social issues, as, for example, on government or slavery or husbands and wives, it is always with reference to Christ as the starting-point, and to the behaviour of the particular individuals he is writing to as the end-point. He has no use for any theory of society as such and in this negative sense at any rate he is an ultra-radical critic indeed.

But, one may say, does that not just make him a non-starter for this subject? I think myself not, because the people he is dealing with are themselves involved culturally in the conventions of the society to which the classical theorizing is the intellectual ornament. The vigour of his arguments over their behaviour constitutes a real rejection at the practical level of the philosophies, which were themselves isolated in the ivory tower which he did not enter. This can be illustrated by noticing two fundamental features of Greek ethical thought which are totally rejected by St Paul: self-cultivation, and the importance of status.

The Abandonment of Self

Greek ethical thought was concentrated upon the individual person. Indeed the modern notion of the person and of personality has its origins in the Hellenistic era, the era to which Paul belonged. It begins in fact with Panaetius, the Greek Stoic philosopher two centuries before St Paul. Many of the notions beloved by educationalists today are in the closest harmony with this Hellenistic concept of the person. Such phraseology as we are now regularly supplied with by our mentors as objectives of education—such themes as personal development, the importance of self-expression and creativity, and the freedom of the individual—were all prominent motifs in Greek ethics. Indeed the principal difference which I can see between the Stoic emphasis on individual development and that of current educational fashion is that the Stoics wished to train up the individual through his personal development to become a private bastion against the threat of change from without, whereas our modern mentors tell us that they wish to develop the individual so that he can adapt to the changes with which he will be confronted. It is certainly a much more precarious position to adopt in advance than that of the Stoics: they at least put themselves in the place where they could resist the changes if they did not like them.

The absence of education as an issue or interest in St Paul's writing is an important phenomenon. Moreover, in the whole tradition that followed the apostles in the subsequent centuries there is little, if any, inclination to develop the principles of the gospel into educational practice. It was only in the fourth century A.D. when the reactionary Roman emperor, Julian, said that the successors of St Paul, whom he contemptuously called Galileans, might not participate any longer in the classical education, that the idea of doing something about education from scriptural materials was reluctantly accepted into the church.[4] Paul seems to have stood

---

[4] See the discussion of H. I. Marrou, *A History of Education in Antiquity* (ET), New York: Sheed and Ward, 1956.

completely apart from the educational preoccupations of the Greeks, in spite of the fact that some of the words he uses are part of the vocabulary which the Stoics also used. That is simply because they were part of the professional vocabulary of the day. When Paul does use educational terminology it is always for metaphorical purposes, and I think that excludes the possibility of his having serious theories about educational matters themselves.

At its best there is much that is attractive about the ideal of the well-developed person: that is one of the objectives of personal development, to make oneself attractive. And in the Greek tradition enormous value was set upon the beauty of the harmonious person. Virtue was seen as a personal quality to be cultivated, like wisdom and beauty. The vice which is also inherent in everyone's experience was met in Greek thought by the division of man's being into body and soul. This is not, as you should know, a Pauline thesis, although the terminology criss-crosses with the terminology of St Paul. The dichotomy of man into body and soul was the device by which the weaknesses of man could be relegated to a temporary part of him, namely the body, the physical encumbrance which would be shaken off when the soul was liberated and returned to be resubmerged in the divine. You will not have to think far into your knowledge of St Paul to recognize that he too saw the body with some horror as the seat of vile things, and yet instead of merely turning from the body and seeking deliverance from it, he set before himself instead the rival conception of the glorified body. The body was to be the place in which God was glorified through the gifts of the Spirit, in anticipation of the ultimate transformation by which it would be changed into the likeness of Christ's glorious body.

One basic feature of the high value placed upon the individual person in Greek thought is that it is self-protective. The wise man (on whom attention was always concentrated rather than upon the ordinary man, or the man with real problems) could elevate himself by training in virtue above the impact of less fortunate persons. He could make himself immune to disturbances of the soul which might be projected by contact with other people. In each of the classic Hellenistic streams of thought there was therefore developed some version of the ideal of indifference to other people. In the case of the Stoics, the key term was 'apathy', an ideal which was held in high regard. It was the goal to which the perfect man strove in order to insulate himself against the shocks of contact with others. Similarly the Epicureans and Cynics in their own way sought this kind of self-protection.

Paul's particular kind of moral fortitude, upon which we are very well informed in his letters, certainly did not run to the insulation of himself against the shocks of personal relations. His own experience of humiliation in society taught him the other side of life in a way that not many philosophers had known it. A feature of St Paul's thought is his fascination with the self-abasement of Christ, and the meaning of that in terms of the atonement. He could see, contrary to all human expectations, a marvellous outcome from the apparent disaster. So in his own career of setbacks and humiliations he was led by the analogy with Christ's suffering to see a quite opposite kind of ideal to that of the ethical philosophers, the ideal of the man who could give himself up for the others. Self-protection was the first aspect of Greek thought which I think St Paul fundamentally rejected.

The Abandonment of Status

The abandonment of self-cultivation and self-preservation as an ideal of the individual person is coupled in Paul with the rejection of another notable aspect of classical ethics, their emphasis on status—the concern with relations between people and the appropriate ordering of them as between greater and lesser. Status systems are a feature of all human society, and even with our scepticism about status we are highly conscious of the subtleties of it and of the intricate ways in which it can be established and observed at the expense of other people, whatever the formal attitude to it may be said to be. Now if that is the case in our own society, it is not hard to appreciate the position in classical society where the quest for status was itself a noble goal of human endeavour, admired even by those who were exploited by it. There is clear evidence of this in the intricacies and elaboration of the technical vocabulary for status in the classical languages. Their richness of terminology attests a degree of approval for the whole notion of status which is entirely different from the kind of attitude which we have inherited in our society.

Let me take a striking example of the absence of this kind of interest from St Paul's thought. One of the more attractive aspects of classical society is no doubt its theory of friendship. It would seem to us that friendship is a kind of escape from the prescriptive character of status systems. We cannot envisage being friends with others if we have to subordinate ourselves to them or pay court to them or whatever it might be. Yet on closer inspection you will find that the classical theories of friendship are themselves an integral part of the whole status apparatus. Even though friendship was an intimate relationship, it was a highly unequal one, and therefore a perilous one for the less than equal friend.

Even Jesus shows this when he says, 'You are my friends if you do what I command you' (John 15:14). One does not nowadays make conditions for friendship. But it would not have seemed odd to anyone in antiquity, because that is what friendship meant. It was a close bond of intimacy which depended upon conformity to the wishes of the more powerful. When they said to Pilate, 'If you let this man go you are not Caesar's friend' (John 19:12), they were issuing a devastating threat to Pilate's security. For him to have his friendship with Caesar renounced, as would happen if there was any suspicion of his integrity, would be the end of him. He would have to follow it perhaps with suicide. So friendship, while an ornament of the status system, was also a very risky bond. There were, however, grades of friendship, and you might be safer in one of the lesser grades. Those who were admitted to the highest grade, and it was a formal admission—you applied to the great man to be counted as his friend and prided yourself upon your attainment—were obviously set a very dangerous path to follow. In a whole variety of ways the powerful people in classical society had developed techniques for creating obligation to themselves amongst lesser individuals, through money or other assistance such as physical protection.

What was Paul's approach to the creation of obligation between people and of status relationships amongst them? He was of course himself intimately caught up as a human being, and particularly in respect of his mission, in the patronal order of the community. I think it would be fair to say that the persons in the Greek cities who protected him and promoted his activities were from the social point of view occupying positions of elevated status and conferring benefits on Paul and upon the others who came to his meetings that should have created obligations. You must watch with great care the way in which St Paul talks about his relations with them and their relations with each other, and watch as he draws the line between what would have been the natural outworking of the status system and the outworking of the quite different principle of relationships which he is promoting.

One peculiarity that has been pointed out in Paul's writings is that the notion of friendship is absent. Did he then have no friends? Obviously he had the most intimate friendships in our sense, and yet apparently he avoided or found no use for the regular social terminology of friendship. Was this because of the status implications that it had? He was involved in relationships where he was in effect under patronage, or where he was himself in a position of patronage over other people, yet (though there is an occasional use of this kind of terminology) he clearly has no value to place upon patronal relations as such. Instead there is a rich terminology of his own with which he describes his relations with other people. The analysis of this language is difficult for us because we do not know how to relate it to the far more familiar vocabulary of the ordinary status structure. He speaks of his associates not as 'friends' but as 'yokefellows'; he speaks of the women, those powerful women under whose protection he worked, as 'fellow-workers'; he speaks of what we should call leaders as 'servants' and 'ministers'. While all these terms now have handsome overtones in our ears, having been read to us for so many centuries from scripture, it would repay the effort of trying to estimate what the overtones would have been as Paul applied them. Surely they are startling terms to the people he was addressing, terms that were deliberately drawn from the language of servitude and subordination, and not from the language of patronage or leadership or friendship in the patronal sense. Paul and his yokefellows work in bonds, not bonds to each other, of course, but in the common bond of allegiance and service to Christ. So that the human relations escape the traps of superiority and inferiority by a total subjection of all to a common master who stands above all.

The rights of the individual are not a leading theme of Paul's thought, though he does refer to them. In 1 Corinthians he talks in some detail about rights, but always in a somewhat detached manner as though to say that though he might have been claiming rights as an apostle, or rights in respect of his personal freedom, he did not care to use them. He thought it more important than his own freedom and rights to subject himself to the needs of those with whom he was dealing. So that though he claimed to be 'free from all men', using a phrase which would have been music in the ears of the Stoics, he says, 'I have made myself a slave to all, that I might win the more' (1 Cor 9:19).

But could Paul seriously maintain that such an approach would work as the basis of any kind of communal relations? Can one live in a community with other people on the basis of total subjection? This is where one might draw attention to a quite different aspect of his view of people's relations with each other—a kind of positive side to his doctrine of self-subjection—that is, his belief that each person was given some gift of the Spirit, some endowment by God. It was given not for edification of the person who received it and not to raise him up above the others, but for the benefit of the others. The figure of the body draws out the picture of a community of persons bound together by the gifts they each receive, for the benefit of the others. The body involves what appears to be an order of status and dignity—the head is more dignified, the eye is more beautiful and so on—but Paul's development of the figure is designed to show how the dignified and undignified members are all equally devoted to the ends of the other members.

Hence in the church as he wished to see it there was no notion of power or of office, however deeply subsequent ecclesiastical practice has become subject to that kind of magisterium, nor surely is there any ideal or notion of leadership. From the social point of view what more re-markable leader of men could there be than St Paul? Yet in all his think-ing about his position in relation to the others, where is the theory of leadership which one would expect to see in his counterparts on the classical side of the fence? Instead the ideal is that of what he calls 'min-istry', meaning again servitude to the interests of others (not leadership, but its opposite), and of 'stewardship'. So all were servants entrusted with gifts to be used for the rest. St Paul himself faced the excruciating demands that he assume the role of leader in the socially acceptable sense. Much of 2 Corinthians is about that problem. His own followers and converts insisted that he adopt a more presentable position in soci-ety than he was willing to do. The many phrases in the letter in which he takes up their complaints (e.g. 2 Cor 10:9) are evidence of this.

If there is only so poor a chance of practising this kind of society within the circle of believers, is it conceivable that Paul could have thought that you could transpose such principles of human relations to the wider society where people were unbelievers? Yet he did venture to think that. It was their obligation to carry through into all their human relations the principle of service. They should be obedient to the civil power because the emperor himself was the minister or servant of God for their good. Though Paul knew the capriciousness of Roman justice, and though he can hardly have imagined that Nero was really going to live up to that humble ideal or be bound to it, he yet boldly prescribed obedience to the civil power on this basis that it too had the obligation to serve God.

So with slavery—slavery was not a status, Paul suggests, which one need bother to avoid if one was held in it. It would not have been very hard to avoid it in the liberal atmosphere that prevailed with regard to ser-vitude at that time. Emancipation was the normal expectation by the age of thirty and it performed indeed a valuable career function which could lead on in certain cases to a prominent place in life. Freedman status could be a rank of importance, so there was no reason why people should not seek emancipation. But Paul suggests there was no particular point in their seeking it. He seems to be rather against those who wanted to use the gospel community to encourage emancipation. It seems very curious to us, but while he does not make a great point of it, the reason is that he thinks it offers the better opportunity for people to fulfil their obligations to other men, as to Christ, by showing what good servants they can be in the literal sense. Conversely the masters have their opportunity to show how they can act fairly towards their servants under the common Master.

It is important to realize that in talking to people in slavery like this, St Paul is probably doing something that no other writer from antiquity has done. The Greek and Roman ethical thinkers are working always within the limits of the cultivated *élite*. But here suddenly is a person not speaking in their style at all, and addressing himself very much more openly to the whole community, directly to people in slavery, directly to women, to all sorts of people at the same time. This strikingly open human situation which his letters reveal is itself a sign of the practical character of the principles which he is advancing. I have often wondered whether Paul himself had slaves. He ought to have had, because I do not really see how he could have travelled as he did without people to do the work. I know he sometimes made a point of doing it himself, but surely this was not possible all the time given the circumstances of travel and accommodation.

Paul's vocabulary of work is also revealing. Labour for him is indifferently the term he uses as a metaphor for the service of the gospel and the actual manual labour which at times he undertook to make a point. Now that is very important because the fellow-labourers with him in the gospel are the people who in their other social capacity as eminent citizens of their states were the patrons and the masters. But he brings them all down to the position he has taken up, of labour. This is far removed from the aspirations of the wise man of Greek thought. The latter certainly withdrew himself from the hardships of work and regarded that as a debasing drag on the development of the soul. Yet again the direct correlation of Paul's metaphor of labour with real labour situations and actual hardship in work shows the integrity of his claims when he tries to redefine his relations with other people. He is talking about something he knows about in its literal sense, as well as in whatever metaphorical sense he may be giving to it.

III. The Position of Women

It is now desirable to spend a little time considering what the Greeks in the classical schools of thought held the position of women to be. My reason for doing this is that many of the things which are loosely thought by some people today to have been St Paul's ideas are in fact what the Greek philosophers propagated. In the era of classical Athens, that is about four or five centuries before St Paul, the Greeks held a view of marriage that was totally masculine.[5] Men gave their daughters in marriage to their husbands. This was a contractual transfer of authority

---

[5] The material in the following section is drawn from C. Vatin, *Recherches sur le mariage et la condition de la femme mariée à l'époque hellénistique*, Paris: B.E.F.A.R., 1970. See also Sarah B. Pomeroy, 'Selected Bibliography on Women in Antiquity', *Arethusa* VI (1973), 127–52.

which the Greeks called *engyesis,* a term quite foreign in that connection to the New Testament. It all sounds familiar to us, being not very different from the way in which marriage is enshrined in our customs, but we should check carefully on what it has in common with Paul's view of marriage before assuming that it has anything to do with him.

No marriage in Athens was valid without transfer of authority, and the woman had no power to dispose of her own person. She was in fact the property that was transferred, in much the same way as was the dowry that went with her. Men had an interest in acquiring wives, partly to supply lawful heirs to themselves and partly for the advantage of the dowry. Fathers on the other hand had an interest in the destruction of newborn daughters by exposure, to avoid the cost of endowing them later when they had to be transferred to a husband, because that would lead to the alienation of family property. One may well marvel at the power of conjugal love which had maintained Greek society over the centuries in spite of these disincentives.

In the fourth century, the two great philosophers, Plato and Aristotle, both made serious efforts to define more adequately the place of women in society. As with everything else, Plato set community interests above those of the individual. He desired to bring the other half of the population to bear on the community's good, and he proposed in his model state that there should be a council of women who would supervise the marital life of private couples and also the training of their children—the prototype no doubt of the ambitions of some of our own social managers. But there is no question of equality of women with men in Plato.

The political role of women is confined to the proposed council and marriage itself retains its contractual masculine-oriented form. It was simply that Plato would have it more carefully planned in the interests of the community. Now Plato's objective was demographic—he was aiming at zero population growth. Like his successors in our day, he could not envisage any progress in the economic and political management of society that would allow for growth, and so he determined to freeze his community within the limits he was familiar with. In short Plato was prepared only to organise women into a more active part in sustaining the *status quo,* which subjected them.

Aristotle, however, the younger contemporary of Plato, saw positive dangers in women, and in order to protect society from them, he proposed to reinforce the authority of men. His concern was based upon a highly rational calculation. Aristotle was the founder of scientific study, including the scientific study of man, and he had discovered from this that women were by nature inferior to men and therefore destined to subjection. In particular he had discovered that women did not possess the power of reason itself by which he had arrived at this conclusion. Consequently one must ensure that the necessary part played by women in family life was insulated against any evil consequences it might have if it spilled over into public life. It was the prominence of women in Spartan life which had caused that state's sad decline. Therefore within the family itself, political power should be exercised by husbands over their wives, and, as he put it, royal power by fathers over children. Wives were to be obliged to remain at home, to rear excellent children, and to avoid the luxury or sensuality which it was feared they might indulge in otherwise. Husbands for their part were also strictly bound to their wives—they must maintain fidelity on pain of loss of civil rights. Like Plato, Aristotle was greatly concerned about over-population. He did not favour contraception because that would weaken the family unit, which he thought important, but he was prepared to advocate abortion on the strength of being able to define the foetus up to a certain point as having no soul—another feat of pure reasoning that matches those of our own day.

After the time of Alexander the Great, however, the philosophers suddenly abandoned the attempt to ensure the regulated place of women within the family unit. The Cynic, Diogenes, declared that marriage, like all social institutions, was artificial, invented only by society, and therefore dangerous because contrary to nature. The life lived according to nature demanded the abandonment of marriage. Sexual feeling should be freely expressed (if you were a man), and both wives and children should be held in common. The Stoic philosopher, Zeno, held that community of wives was itself a law of nature which had been suppressed by civilization imposing monogamous limits on it. However, only the wise, Zeno thought, were capable of realizing in practice the community of wives. The accent lies of course, still on men. The supremely wise individual of the Stoics, who could attain the freedom of nature, was naturally masculine. Subsequent Stoic thinkers however took a more sombre view. To Chrysippus marriage was a duty which was owed to the universal society of man, a kind of biological destiny requiring man to be husband and father, for the sake of the race. Epicurus, the pessimistic prophet of pleasure, regarded love as a dangerous passion, and saw sexual relations as positively harmful to the soul. But marriage was a necessity nevertheless, and the wise man would undertake it in order not to stand out from the crowd and thus make his life more troublesome still.

But by the second century B.C., Greek writers were not so able to embrace the cold comforts of individualism. The easy assumption of Hellenic superiority was shaken by the Roman conquests. Polybius, who wrote the history of the Roman conquest of Greece, picked up again the Aristotelian concern for order in marriage in the interests of civic welfare and the revival of Greek civic life. This time however it was not to restrain population growth, but in order to rebuild the fallen birthrate which had undermined the strength of Greece. The new head of the Stoic school in the next generation, Antipater of Tarsus, also expressed alarm over the decline in population. But Antipater went further. Although the interest is still centred on the superior individual, he must now see that he cannot be perfect without the company of wife and children.

From this conjunction of Aristotelian and Stoic emphasis on the importance of marriage there developed for the first time the attempt to define the mutual relations of husband and wife. Although the man still remains the point of reference, the place of affection on either side was now recognized. From Antipater in the second century B.C. through to Plutarch in the early second century A.D. this idea was extended steadily until it became the common property of most, if not all, Greek and Roman thinkers. This is the era in which St Paul falls. His own younger contemporary amongst the Stoics, the Roman, Musonius Rufus, carried the equalization of men and women to the farthest point it ever reached in antiquity. Women for Musonius Rufus have the same reasoning as men, and they should have the same education in philosophy, although the cardinal virtues in their case took the form of the distinctive contributions which women typically made in marriage and child-bearing. Musonius is here building on Plato's plan to exploit the untapped resources of women. Whereas Plato certainly kept women subordinated, Musonius positively tries to assert their equality. There is no trace in Musonius of the leading part being kept for men. None of his successors ever went as far as he did in this respect. Plutarch, for example, in the next generation, maintained once more the superiority of men, and expected women to subordinate their emotions and ideas to those of their husbands. Musonius also held the idea of total commitment in marriage for better or for worse, and this he grounds in the manifest intention of the creator—manifest because of the mutual desire of man and woman. Unlike many Greek moralists he did not set procreation as the sole purpose of marriage but coupled it as an end with the common life of husband and wife. Should this disappear, however, he favoured divorce. Musonius' work is very poorly preserved, and not well known.[6] It is clear,

---

[6] For the fragments of Musonius, see A. C. van Geytenbeek, *Musonius Rufus and Greek Diatribe*, Assen: Royal Vangorcum, 1963.

however, that he so refined the classical tradition that it approximates in some respects to the position held by St Paul.

The main point I hope to have made clear in this survey is that many of the attitudes to marriage which are regarded nowadays as the regrettable legacy from the past are not Pauline, but have their origins firmly in the doctrines of Greek humanism. I refer to the view held by many of the Greeks that women are by nature inferior to men, that they lack in both intellectual and emotional capacity, that the husband owns the wife in some sense and uses her for the purpose of procreation, and that marriage is to be undertaken as a public duty. In order to show how radically different Paul's approach is from this, he may best be compared with his contemporary Seneca, the Roman Stoic. This comparison has always exercised a powerful attraction. There were those in antiquity who thought Seneca so close to St Paul that it was no offence against historical truth to compose their correspondence; there are those in our own century who have wished to derive aspects of Pauline thought from Stoic philosophy or conversely who find Pauline ideas in Seneca.[7]

Seneca speaks loftily and warmly of the women who were closest to him—his mother and his wife—and he had clearly been greatly enriched by his relationship with such women. Yet implicit in his high praise of them is the assumption that their excellence was unusual for a woman. The superiority of the man which Stoicism had upheld is latent even in his high regard for his own closest companions. The inadequacy of women in general is the basis for the compliment which he pays to the women he knows. When castigating moral deterioration it is women whom he has in mind rather than men, though he certainly expects fidelity in the man. Women, however, for Seneca, are obviously the corruptors of men.

Paul by contrast has no special eye for female vice and spares men nothing in his condemnation of sexual licence; both parties come equally under his fire. In commenting on the problems of whether or not to marry in 1 Cor 7, Paul repeatedly turns the question either way, now to the man, now to the woman; now to the woman and now to the man. He places the onus of decision on man and woman alike—either may decide—and he specifically singles each partner out. Certainly Paul holds that the relations of husband to wife and wife to husband are open to being characterized in different ways, so that different qualities may be singled out as appropriate to each, yet the principle of reciprocity is

---

[7] For a thorough comparison, see J. N. Sevenster, *St Paul and Seneca*, Leiden: Brill, 1961.

fully maintained. He also holds that there is an order of relationships that is rooted in creation and in Christ in which the man is the 'head' of the woman, and this he says should express itself in certain norms of behaviour—in church, for example—which seems also to take account of social conventions. Yet in the very process of arguing for this, he takes trouble to insist that there is no suggestion of masculine independence or domination at all (see 1 Cor 11:11). Nor does he use his favourite metaphor of servitude when setting out the relations of husband and wife.

Unlike Seneca, Paul tells us nothing about the women of his own family; we do not even know whether he was ever married. Yet, also in contrast with Seneca, we know that his life and work were very closely involved with women, with many women. The prominence of women amongst his collaborators—the ones I might call his patrons and he would call his fellow-labourers—makes him a most unusual, if not unique figure in the literature of antiquity. Yet he himself shows no special consciousness of this—he often speaks of his personal relations, yet without usually making any particular point of whether his fellow-workers are men or women. In the lists and greetings which he gives, men and women are mentioned indifferently, in varying order, sometimes the wife first and the husband second. So unimportant for Paul is the maleness or femaleness of his fellow-workers.

It is certain, on the other hand, that women played a prominent part in church life, including praying and prophesying in public (with their heads uncovered, against Paul's wish). The restraints which Paul argues for in women, including covering the head, and keeping silence in some cases in church, are partly inspired by the same principle he applied in relation to other institutions, including slavery. He certainly holds basically to the equality of men and women in Christ, but, as in the other cases, he thinks that one should not only not cause a social upheaval by ostentatiously exercising the liberty one might, but that one should positively fulfil conventional expectations as part of one's devotion to each other in Christ.

Would that mean that if the social expectations had been otherwise Paul would have recommended a different set of outward courtesies between men and women? Certainly it would mean that. But would it mean that in freer social circumstances he would have advocated the identical set of obligations for women and for men? I doubt it. Unlike the case of slavery, which he never attributes of course to divine ordering, except in the limited sense that all social institutions should be utilized as part of one's service in Christ and as the place where God has put one, the difference between men and women goes back to the creation itself. It is like the difference between Jew and Greek, though more fundamental still. Paul fought for equality of Jew and Greek in Christ. But he did not challenge the validity of the covenant by which the Jews had first been called and which created greater expectations in their case. Similarly Paul insists that there is no difference between men and women in their standing in Christ yet there are different expectations which each has of the other in marriage arising from the different way they have been made by God. This is not simply a matter of differing anatomy. Paul deliberately singles out a principle of order or headship in the marital relationship by linking it with the relation between Christ and the church.

If he means this seriously, as surely he does, it must have some expression in outward and social behaviour, however that may intersect with particular conventions of society. But the very tying of the relationship to that between Christ and the church excludes the kind of possessive lordship or mastery that was built into Greek custom and attitudes, for Christ as the head of the church is the one who abandoned all claims of status and privilege to give himself up completely for his bride. Christ and the church however are not conflated. Their unity springs from the full surrender that each makes to the other in their different ways.

The mystery of sacrifice and service therefore, which Paul perceived in the cross, leads him to his fundamental position on all questions of social relations. In the last resort, none matters in the kingdom of Christ, not even the marital relation itself. But for that same reason none needs to be destroyed at all costs, and not even if it could be easily circumvented as slavery could have been, for all such relationships provide an occasion in which one may show the fundamental character of the new life in Christ, which is the complete surrender of one's own interest for the sake of the other. There could be no more radical approach to the problems of status and order in society than this.

Paul is not interested in mere social reform or in replacing one order with another. Nor does he merely ignore society or deny its reality. Indeed he regards it in the case of government as the means by which God executes justice. But knowing that men will in the end be delivered from that bondage of self-interest, to which the bonds of the social order set the temporary limits, he appeals to those who look to this redemption to begin now to surrender their own claims. This was no Utopian ideal. He proved that by putting it to the purest test of integrity and practicality—in his own life.

5

The Social Identity of the First Christians: A Question of Method in Religious History

TWENTY YEARS AGO the *Journal of Religious History* opened with my study of 'The Early Christians as a Scholastic Community'.[1] We knew the title was awkward. It carried overtones of a quite different period of history. Moreover, it failed to indicate some of the main preoccupations of the article—the question of what categories of social description were appropriate to a movement occurring in the Roman world, and the prosopography of the Pauline mission. There was of course a reason for the title, to which I shall return.

At a more serious level, it was a conscious plunge into the dark. The question of the social identity of the early Christians was not then the object of the kind of probing it has since attracted. Instead, well-established assumptions cast an illusion of light over the scene. Primitive Christianity was often seen as the 'religious' vehicle for the aspirations of common people, who lacked any great stake in society; it was in due course to supply the 'internal proletariat' that overthrew the old order of classical civilization.

The *Journal of Religious History* was founded to encourage people to look again at such set pieces. Our object was to explore, if possible without preconceptions, the place of 'religious' affairs in human history in general. We did not want to work either as church historians or as comparative religionists, but as ordinary students of history, looking at a major element in human experience in its full context.

---

[1] Vol. 1, no. 1, June 1960, pp. 4–15; vol. 1, no. 3, June 1961, pp. 125–37, reissued with revised footnotes as 'Die frühen Christen als scholastische Gemeinschaft' in W. A. Meeks, ed., *Zur Soziologie des Urchristentums*, Munich 1979, pp. 131–64. Also reproduced in this collection of 'American' contributions to the subject are papers by a number of authors whose work is referred to below.

The New Testament does not often find a place in the historian's curriculum. It has been enshrined within an exquisite discipline of its own, created to meet the demands of a peculiar corpus of sources. The principles of New Testament criticism are of course conspicuously historical in themselves. Yet the ordinary historian keeps well clear. No adequate bridges have yet been built between the preoccupations of students of the Roman world and those of the New Testament specialists. The gap has become only more obvious from the twenty years' work of this journal. It has not succeeded in drawing biblical studies adequately into its spectrum, and indeed its coverage of antiquity in general is slight. Nevertheless, as a student of Roman history, I am glad to accept the invitation of the present editors to return to its starting-point. Readers may find it useful to have a stocktaking of a key point in religious history that is usually pursued under other auspices. More importantly, I think that the dislocation of New Testament studies from the social and intellectual history of its times represents an acute case of the problem of method which besets 'religious' history in general.

I. Changing Views of the Social Level of the First Christians

The 'scholastic community' article was a by-product of a longer essay, which had been published earlier in the same year, 1960: *The Social Pattern of the Christian Groups in the First Century*.[2] The purpose of this was to help revive interest in the social ideas of the New Testament by attempting a fresh kind of contextual description of the early churches. Instead of using categories of analysis drawn from other periods, such as the social class model, or 'church and state', I traced the pattern of certain contemporary institutions as they were reflected in the New Testament writings.

These were, first, the small republican state, which provided the effective framework of civil life for most people in the Roman Empire, repeated as it was many hundreds of times over throughout the eastern Mediterranean; secondly, the far-reaching organization of life on a household basis, through which even Caesarism itself had been built up; and thirdly, the unofficial associations which provided small-scale community life under religious auspices, for trade or other interest groups.

---

[2] Sub-titled *Some Prolegomena to the Study of New Testament Ideas of Social Obligation*, London 1960, reissued without revision as *Christliche Gruppen in nichtchristlicher Gesellschaft: Die Sozialstruktur christlicher Gruppen im ersten Jahrhundert*, Wuppertal 1964.

The main proposition about the social pattern of the churches was as follows (p. 60):

> Far from being a socially depressed group, then, if the Corinthians are at all typical, the Christians were dominated by a socially pretentious section of the population of the big cities. Beyond that they seem to have drawn on a broad constituency, probably representing the household dependants of the leading members. . . . The interests brought together in this way probably marked the Christians off from the other unofficial associations, which were generally socially and economically as homogeneous as possible.

This, I suggested, helped to explain the stress on not using membership to break down the conventional hierarchy of the household. It was sixty years before Pliny was to discover the surprising fact that Christianity was now making inroads into the countryside, where the most under-privileged classes were to be found. 'Until then however we may safely regard Christianity as a socially well backed movement of the great Hellenistic cities' (p. 61).

This approach to the matter caught the eye of a number of classical or ecclesiastical historians in Britain and France,[3] but passed largely un-noticed by New Testament scholarship—such reviews as there were understandably drew back from an exercise that was not built up from within the critical tradition on which such studies rested.[4] Two Austra-lian historians, moreover, questioned the main proposition. J. J. Nich-olls, in this journal, stressed the evidence of Tacitus, where the penalties imposed by Nero on Christians in Rome do not suggest that they were people of any social consequence.[5] Pliny's reference to the countryside in no way suggested a recent development. Nicholls also thought it dan-gerous to argue from the career of so unusual a figure as Paul. G. Yule, in *Historical Studies,* considered that Acts could not be used as a source for such matters if its author was trying to make Christianity look non-revolutionary, while the exceptional character of Paul should cause us to think twice before generalizing from the status of his converts.[6]

There the matter rested for a few years until it was taken up much more energetically in Germany. A Czech reviewer had welcomed the

---

[3] E. Badian, *Durham University Journal* 53, 1961, pp. 140–42; W. H. C. Frend, *Journal of Roman Studies* 50, 1960, p. 283; R. E. Smith, *Journal of Ecclesi-astical History* 12, 1961, pp. 87–88; H. I. Marrou, *Revue des Etudes Anciennes* 63, 1961, pp. 225–28; M. Simon, *Latomus* 19, 1960, pp. 603–5.

[4] J. D. McCaughey, *Aumla* 16, 1961, pp. 194–96; G. Klein, *Zeitschrift für Kirchengeschichte* 195, 1962, p. 210.

[5] Vol. 1, no. 2, December 1960, pp. 115–17.

[6] Vol. 10, 1961, p. 124.

German version of *The Social Pattern* (in spite of some telling reservations) as 'a healthy corrective to the overwhelmingly ideological cast of German scholarship'.[7] From either side of the intra-German boundary, two scholars who had worked extensively on the history of Judaism in relation to the Greeks and Romans, H. Kreissig and M. Hengel, came to broadly similar conclusions on the socially mixed character of the early Christian communities.[8] H. Gülzow, in a thorough examination of the question of slavery in the early church, also endorsed this finding.[9] He subsequently produced a valuable general study of the social conditions of the early Christian mission,[10] and will shortly publish the early church volume in the new series he is editing, which will explore the theme of 'Christianity and Society' from the beginnings until the twentieth century.[11]

In 1974 G. Theissen launched what was soon to be seen as an important sequence of studies in New Testament sociology with a very thorough exploration of the social levels in the Corinthian congregation.[12] He set out explicitly to put to the test the very different interpre-

---

[7] P. Pokorny, *Communio Viatorum*, nos. 3–4, 1964, pp. 317–18.

[8] H. Kreissig, 'Zur sozialen Zusammensetzung der frühchristlichen Gemeinden im ersten Jahrhundert u.Z.', *Eirene* 6, 1967, pp. 91–100; M. Hengel, *Property and Riches in the Early Church: Aspects of a Social History of Early Christianity,* Philadelphia 1974, pp. 36–39.

[9] *Christentum und Sklaverei in den ersten drei Jahrhunderten,* Bonn 1969, p. 28.

[10] 'Soziale Gegebenheiten der altkirchlichen Mission' in H. Frohnes and U. W. Knorr, eds., *Kirchengeschichte als Missionsgeschichte,* Vol. 1, *Die alte Kirche,* Munich 1974, pp. 189–226.

[11] Vol. 2 in H. Gülzow and H. Lehmann, eds., *Christentum und Gesellschaft,* the series being published in Stuttgart by Kohlhammer. [Ed. Three volumes of this series were published, but the volume mentioned was not.]

[12] 'Soziale Schichtung in der korinthischen Gemeinde: Ein Beitrag zur Soziologie des hellenistischen Urchristentums', *Zeitschrift für die neutestamentliche Wissenschaft* 65, 1974, pp. 232–72. This was followed by a wave of eight other articles, and all of them have now been reprinted, along with a new one on 'Gewaltverzicht und Feindesliebe und deren sozialgeschichtlicher Hintergrund', in *Studien zur Soziologie des Urchristentums,* Tübingen 1979. The series is a remarkable *tour de force,* which succeeds to an unparalleled degree in bringing sociological theories to bear upon some of the cruxes of New Testament interpretation without relaxing exegetical or historical discipline. It quickly attracted attention amongst the 'Social World of Early Christianity' working group in the United States, for whom J. H. Schütz in 1977 prepared an unpublished paper, 'Steps toward a Sociology of Primitive Christianity: A Critique of the Work of Gerd Theissen'. In the collected papers, Theissen has responded to this with an account of the development of his thinking, 'Zur forschungsgeschichtlichen Einordnung der soziologischen Fragestellung', pp. 3–34, and

tations which had been applied to the data by Deissmann, in the early part of the century, and by myself.[13] His conclusion was that both points of view were justified, as differing perspectives on a community that was highly stratified within itself. He held that this was no accident, but reflected basic social structures that permitted us to use the Corinthian case as characteristic of the churches in the Greek cities. A 1974 Munich dissertation by B. Grimm[14] concurrently reviewed the whole question from the position of Jesus through to the post-apostolic period, coming to similar conclusions, and demonstrating, as G. S. R. Thomas in his review in this journal notes, that 'the modern view of early Christianity as a religion of the lower and unprivileged classes of Roman society . . . is . . . derived from ancient, aristocratic polemic'.

In the meantime a wave of study projects bearing on the subject had developed in various universities of North America, some of them long-term team efforts which have yet to show their major results. My impression is that much of this interest has been generated by the shifts of academic style and organization that have often drawn New Testament Studies into comprehensive departments of Religion. Here the comparative method of analysis is to the fore, and sociological models provide the basis for study. At the same time the traditional Divinity Schools have sometimes taken up actively the related task of gathering the contemporary data that can be used to fill out the social or cultural context of the early churches. The recent books of J. G. Gager and A. J. Malherbe respectively may be taken as representative of these trends.

Schütz is expected to give his evaluation by way of introduction to the English version of the papers, to be published in Philadelphia by Fortress Press in 1982. [Ed.: This was published as Gerd Theissen, *The Social Setting of Pauline Christianity* (ed., trans., and with introduction by J. H. Schütz; Philadelphia: Fortress, 1982).]

[13] Inspired by the exhilarating sense of contact with ordinary people in antiquity made possible by the flood of new papyrological evidence, G. A. Deissmann became convinced of 'the fact of the close inward connection between the gospel and the lower classes', *Light from the Ancient East: The New Testament Illustrated by Recently Discovered Texts of the Graeco-Roman World*, London 1910, p. 403. In a lecture given just after the appearance of the first German edition, *Das Urchristentum und die unteren Schichten*, Göttingen 1908, p. 41, he says (my translation): 'A generation later there laboured amongst the lower classes of the populous cities of the Hellenistic Mediterranean Paul, the missionary, himself a man of the people [volkstümlich] through and through.'

[14] *Untersuchungen zur sozialen Stellung der frühen Christen in der römischen Gesellschaft*, Bamberg 1975, reviewed by G. S. R. Thomas, *Journal of Religious History* 9, no. 4, December 1977, pp. 428–30.

In his book, *Kingdom and Community,* sub-titled *The Social World of Early Christianity,*[15] J. G. Gager begins with the question of why the study of early Christianity 'seems so different from the study of more exotic religions in Africa, Australia and Melanesia'—religious movements, as he ingenuously remarks, 'that have flourished . . . in the laboratories of sociologists and anthropologists' (p. xi). Insights drawn from such study, he claims, are not only applicable to Christianity, but hold the promise of a genuinely new understanding of 'this particular religion'. He is aware of the problem of some facts being missing, so that 'the fit between theory and fact is often less than perfect'. But he sees signs of 'a new movement' in the direction which corroborates his efforts.

By introducing the term 'social world' Gager means to direct attention to the ways in which Christianity created a world in relation to its particular 'sacred cosmos'. He is following Peter Berger's theory that religion is the establishing of such a cosmos, without which there can be no social existence whatsoever. The 'social world' in which we live determines our experience of what is real (pp. 9–10).

When it comes to the details, however, Gager deliberately steps beyond the world as early Christians saw it, in that he proposes 'to examine specific problems in terms of theoretical models from recent work in the social sciences' (p. 12). 'In each case the model has been formulated independently of Christian evidence.' Amongst the models he uses is that of the Melanesian cargo cult, noting the curiosity that, though anthropologists use New Testament terminology to characterize millenarian movements, it is not easy to find any reverse application of the resultant model to the explanation of the New Testament communities themselves (p. 20). Another such model is that of 'cognitive dissonance', as defined by L. Festinger and others in *When Prophecy Fails.* This explains missionary activity as an attempt to relieve the contradiction of prophecy by event by persuading others that it was true all the same (p. 39).

It is not possible here to do justice to the extent to which Gager has adapted and qualified such models in applying them to the New Testament. The book was nevertheless severely censured by G. S. R. Thomas in this journal.[16] He claimed that Gager had not escaped the danger that 'we may make our evidence fit the paradigm we are using', and that he had been too

---

[15] Englewood Cliffs, 1975. There is an extensive series of evaluations of Gager's work in *Zygon: Journal of Religion and Science* 13, 1978: D. L. Bartlett, 'John G. Gager's "Kingdom and Community": A Summary and Response', pp. 109–22; J. Z. Smith, 'Too Much Kingdom, Too Little Community', pp. 123–30; D. Tracy, 'A Theological Response to "Kingdom and Community"', pp. 131–35.
[16] Vol. 10, no. 1, June 1978, pp. 95–96.

dependent on unsatisfactory secondary treatments for his picture of religion and society in the Roman Empire. On our topic, Thomas claimed,

> the paradigm said that the social status of members of the early church was low, and, having found sufficient evidence along these lines, Gager ignored the rest . . . or sought to attenuate its effect.

He also stated that 'perhaps the most intractable to Gager's thesis will be the case of the very privileged Paul, whose situation receives most inadequate treatment'.

A. J. Malherbe, in his book *Social Aspects of Early Christianity*,[17] has taken as his starting-point the work that had already been done in relation to the New Testament itself. His is the most comprehensive account of it that is available. He clearly distinguishes his approach from that of Gager (p. 20):

> Sociological description of early Christianity can concentrate either on social facts or on sociological theory as a means of describing the 'sacred cosmos' or 'symbolic universe' of early Christian communities. Even though new historical information may be assimilated within old paradigms, we should strive to know as much as possible about the actual social circumstances of those communities before venturing theoretical descriptions or explanations of them.

Malherbe's own centre of interest is in literary forms. He studies first the social significance of the affinities between Paul's first letter to the Thessalonians and the work of popular philosophers, both Cynic/Stoic and Epicurean. He then deals at length with the question of 'social level and literary culture', including the vexed questions of Paul's educational experience and rhetorical competence, and of the cultural level represented by his letters. In the course of this he evaluates my notion of the Christians as a 'scholastic' community, and provides corrections to it. Then, in order to approach the subject from within, he conducts an extensive exploration of 'house churches and their problems'.

It is striking that both of these authors posit a certain 'consensus' of opinion on our question, though pointing in opposite directions. Gager says (p. 96):

> It is only in recent years, and primarily among such classicists as A. D. Nock, A. H. M. Jones, and E. R. Dodds, that the social constituency of early

---

[17] Baton Rouge and London, 1977. Malherbe's book has been reviewed (along with works of R. M. Grant and G. Theissen) by J. G. Gager in *Religious Studies Review* 5, no. 3, July 1979, pp. 174–80, and (along with Theissen) by R. S. Kraemer in *Journal of Biblical Literature* 98, no. 3, September 1979, pp. 436–38.

Christianity has again come into focus. Among this limited circle, something approaching a consensus has emerged on two aspects of the social question: first that for more than two hundred years Christianity was essentially a movement among disprivileged groups in the Empire; and second, that its appeal among these groups depended on social as much as ideological considerations.

Gager refers to my *Social Pattern* as 'the only notable exception to this pattern' (p. 109, n. 19). He does not perhaps allow for the much more localized focus of my work, and it is significant that his remarks introduce a description of the Roman social order, which I had set aside as being too broad a framework for detecting the inner dynamics of a Greek community. Gager is writing, moreover, just prior to the point at which he could have taken stock of what was being written in Germany.[18] Two years later, Malherbe relocated the 'consensus' (p. 31):

> It appears from the recent concern of scholars with the social level of early Christians, that a new consensus may be emerging. This consensus, if it is not premature to speak of one, is quite different from the one represented by Adolf Deissmann, which has held sway since the beginning of the century. The more recent scholarship has shown that the social status of early Christians may be higher than Deissmann had supposed.

In an article published this year,[19] another American scholar, Robin Scroggs, appears to confirm the existence of this shift of opinion, and

---

[18] In fact the relevant chapter in *Kingdom and Community* essentially resumes Gager's chapter on 'Religion and Social Class in the Early Roman Empire' in S. Benko and J. J. O'Rourke, eds., *The Catacombs and the Colosseum: The Roman Empire as the Setting of Primitive Christianity,* Valley Forge 1971, pp. 99–120. In his review of Malherbe (n. 17 above) Gager appears to have shifted his ground somewhat, suggesting that the view of early Christianity as 'exclusively proletarian' never existed 'apart from a few romantics and early Marxists' and that recent work has shown that 'the social sources of revolution lie higher up in the social order' (p. 179). He then develops the distinction between social class (in the sense of the formal 'orders' of the Roman ranking system) and social status, in order to propose that the dominant figures in the churches were drawn to a 'religion with revolutionary implications precisely because of their frustrated social aspirations' (p. 180). This goes altogether too far in the new direction, since it is beyond historical plausibility that Greeks in the mid-first century could have seriously aspired to senatorial or equestrian enrolment. The discord between formal rank (e.g. Roman citizenship) and social status based on wealth was nevertheless a constant source of tension. For its complexities see P. D. A. Garnsey, *Social Status and Legal Privilege in the Roman Empire,* Oxford 1970, esp. 'The Vocabulary of Privilege', pp. 221–33, and 'Privileged Groups', pp. 234–59.

[19] 'The Social Interpretation of the New Testament: The Present State of Research', *New Testament Studies* 26, 1980, pp. 164–79. A similar stage had been

states that: 'The implications of the "new consensus" for the social interpretation of early Christianity are immense and thus its conclusion must be tested with great care.' Although Scroggs is not in a position to conduct such a test within the limits of his article, he poses five questions to the consentients, and clearly reserves his own judgement. I also believe, for reasons given below, that we are still far from being in a position to attempt final conclusions. To promote the debate, therefore, I offer now a first response to Scroggs's questions.

> (1) Should not the Synoptic material (e.g. the strong protest against wealth) be given more weight, even if it does not reflect the same Hellenistic urban context of the Pauline letters? Surely the Synoptics speak for important segments of the first-century church and in their final form do not necessarily reflect only a rural setting.

This objection rests upon the assumption that the contents of the gospels will have been shaped by the interests of the communities for which they were composed. Therefore if the gospels condemn wealth, this implies a community which does not enjoy it. But one only needs to recall Seneca to recognize the capacity of the well-to-do and cultivated to admire the strictures of philosophy while safely insulated against their consequences. Should one not also allow the possibility of a gospel compiler sharply critical of the use of wealth amongst those for whom he wrote (cf. the epistle of James)?

> (2) Is the Acts material as historically trustworthy as the proponents assume?

The dating of Acts can hardly be regarded as settled (see my review in this journal of J. C. O'Neill's book).[20] But even a late date does not exclude the possibility of early information having been carried forward. The Roman historian, J. J. Nicholls, reviewing A. N. Sherwin-White's

---

reached on our topic by F. W. Norris, 'The Social Status of Early Christianity', *Gospel in Context* 2, no. 1, 1979, pp. 4–14. On the other hand, for J. Z. Smith, 'The Social Description of Early Christianity', *Religious Studies Review* 1, no. 1, 1975, pp. 19–25, most of the work that had been done (of which mine was 'all too typical') had been 'clouded by unquestioned apologetic assumptions and naive theories'. From the historical side, the 'new consensus' appears to be in harmony with the works of R. A. Markus, *Christianity in the Roman World*, London 1974, and R. M. Grant, *Early Christianity and Society*, London 1978, though neither is particularly concerned with the New Testament period, while Averil Cameron, 'Neither Male nor Female', *Greece and Rome* 27, no. 1, April 1980, pp. 60–68, takes exception to certain of its details.

[20] Vol. 2, no. 2, December 1962, pp. 152–54, on *The Theology of Acts in its Historical Setting*, London 1961.

book in the journal,[21] refers to his conclusion that Acts has no knowledge of later stages in the development of Roman appeal procedure. 'Acts is remarkably accurate in its record of the legal, administrative and social background of the Hellenistic and of the superimposed Roman world.' On citizenship, 'the situation in Acts is shown to be characteristic of the first half of the first century when Roman citizenship was comparatively rare in the provinces'. 'It is also clear that Acts contains no reference to the later period in which a distinction of a social kind was becoming more important than the distinction between citizens and non-citizens.' In regard to other aspects, one should test the matter by searching for anachronisms by means of similarly detailed analyses of the institutions concerned. But in any case, could one not argue for the 'new consensus' position from the evidence of the Pauline letters alone? It does not depend upon the Acts material being trustworthy.

(3) Even if it is, and granted the evidence of the epistles, should the presence of a few (is it not a universal tendency to remember and name the upper rather than the lower?) wealthier members be allowed to change, in effect, the social location of the community as a whole? Is this not an élitist definition?

This objection would certainly have seemed justified to the ancient (élitist!) critics of the churches, and one must beware of the counter-exaggeration which Christian writers adopted in defence. The fact that the question was a sensitive one in antiquity points the way forward. As I shall argue below, we are witnessing the beginnings of a process by which the pursuit of ideas, traditionally reserved to an élite, was to be so broadly promoted in the community as to produce in the fourth century a type of common culture more socially pervasive than Hellenism had been. The important point is that the movement, in social class terms, is downward rather than upward. The number of those who think and argue about ethical questions is being expanded, but this does not come from below. It is the work of highly articulate people with social influence.

(4) Should economic alienation be the only alienation considered? Do not all societies have categories of outcast individuals and groups who are not economically deprived?

This opens up the whole question of the degree of conflict and of compromise in the encounter between Christianity and classical culture. It is not clear to me whether there is any basic source of alienation at all apart from the refusal of Christians to participate in cultic ceremonies.

---

[21] Vol. 3, no. 1, June 1964, pp. 92–95, on *Roman Society and Roman Law in the New Testament*, Oxford 1963.

The omnipresence of these of course meant that explosions of feeling could occur at a wider variety of points in community life.

(5) Finally (and here I am perhaps out of place) is there any relation between the 'new consensus' and the change in our society from the more 'revolutionary' period of the 1960s to the more 'conventional' 1970s? Is there a need today to find a more 'respectable' (i.e. middle-class) origin for the church? I am quite aware that the followers of Deissmann can be charged with a counter question: do they want to romanticize poverty?

This can only be answered in terms of the particular people who have embraced the views concerned. The work of those who took the first steps in the new direction of course lies well back in the 'revolutionary' 1960s and beyond.

II. THE SOCIOLOGICAL FALLACY IN NEW TESTAMENT STUDIES

In his recent book, *Paul and Power*,[22] B. Holmberg claims that there is 'a fundamental deficiency in methodology' (p. 205) in the work of a range of New Testament scholars from Bultmann to Schweizer. He calls it 'the fallacy of idealism'. It consists of interpreting the historical phenomena 'as being directly formed by underlying theological structures'. It ignores 'the continuous dialectic between ideas and social structures'. Thus Paul's theology of charisma is assumed to be 'the structuring principle' of the social world instead of being recognized as 'a secondary reaction' to its 'concrete phenomena'.

Similarly, the attempt to reconstruct the conflict between Paul and the church in Corinth 'as being an almost purely theological conflict between different christologies and other theoretical conceptions' (Holmberg cites the work of Georgi, Schmithals and Betz as examples) shows the influence of idealistic methodology (p. 206). This assumes that the collection for Jerusalem cannot rest upon an authoritatively binding relationship between Jerusalem and the Gentile churches unless that is expressed in a positive law or formulated theory. The real Pauline church order is thought to be discovered by analysing 'how Paul motivates and interprets relations of obedience', with express disregard for 'the historical information available on Paul's actual exercise of authority'. The idealistic fallacy lies in analysing 'only part of the historical reality while considering this to be the entire or essential reality'.

---

[22] Sub-titled *The Structure of Authority in the Primitive Church as Reflected in the Pauline Epistles*, Lund 1978.

Holmberg guards his flank against the countervailing error of the 'materialistic fallacy'. In that case 'all ideas are only superstructures of purely social processes determined by economic, political and social forces only'. He proposes to escape both forms of simplification by 'a methodological stance that takes into account the dialectic between ideas and facts, theology and social structure'. But has he succeeded? This is not the place for a review of Holmberg's detailed working. But it appears to me at the best only capable of succeeding by accident. His methodological stance does not bestride ideas and facts in an equally secure manner. In particular he does not have his foot on firm ground on the factual side. The extensive reading list conceals a dangerous gap. It couples with New Testament studies a strong admixture of modern sociology, as though social theories can be safely transposed across the centuries without verification. The basic question remains unasked: What are the social facts of life characteristic of the world to which the New Testament belongs? Until the painstaking field work is better done, the importation of social models that have been defined in terms of other cultures is methodologically no improvement on the 'idealistic fallacy'. We may fairly call it the 'sociological fallacy'.

Holmberg likens his work to that of an anthropologist visiting a hitherto unknown tribe: 'he collects the phenomena as they appear and tries to organize them conceptually in structures of an ordinary social kind' (p. 2). But he assumes that in his case the first stage is done: 'there exists a considerable degree of consensus among scholars on the vast majority of details concerning philological and historical fact'. He then proposes to apply Max Weber's classical sociology of authority to the interpretation of the data (p. 6). The hidden pitfall has already been constructed (p. 10):

> The relation between actors in a power relation can be described as an unbalanced exchange relation. One party gives the orders, makes demands, speaks authoritative words and the other gives in return obedience, service, personal support and money. The subordinate actor has to 'pay' in some way.

But in Graeco-Roman society the reverse applies. Money is continually given by the powerful to their dependants, and this transfer of cash downwards in the social scale is the main instrument by which the status of the powerful is asserted.[23]

---

[23] S. C. Mott, 'The Power of Giving and Receiving: Reciprocity in Hellenistic Benevolence' in G. F. Hawthorne, ed., *Current Issues in Biblical and Patristic Interpretation: Studies in Honor of Merrill C. Tenney*, Grand Rapids 1975, pp. 60–72. Cf. the Homeric pattern in M. I. Finley, *The World of Odysseus*, London 1977, p. 64.

Two articles by G. Theissen have analysed various procedures open to a sociologist of the New Testament communities. In the earlier one[24] he distinguishes three main approaches to the sociology of religion: through the phenomenon of an encounter with the holy, which lies essentially beyond the reach of sociological analysis; the reductionist approach (as in Marxism), which explains religious phenomena in terms of non-religious factors; and the functional approach which combines elements of the first two. The basic purposes of society are given as (a) the provision of order and (b) the suppression of conflict. Religion has four possible functions in relation to these. On the one hand, it may act restrictively, (a) internalizing social pressure or (b) intimidating people into conformity (by compensation), and on the other creatively, (a) socializing the natural human qualities or (b) surmounting conflict by innovations. This last is seen by Theissen as the most characteristic function of primitive Christianity. Failing at the more radical level in the tense conflicts of Palestine, it transposed itself into a 'patriarchalism of love' in the more secure societies of the Hellenistic cities.

In his second article,[25] Theissen turns to the methodologically prior question of how one obtains sociologically relevant data from the texts. He distinguishes three methods: (a) the constructive one, whereby one delineates the social groups or patterns of individual experience that can be detected in the source material—and here he warns especially against the danger of making out the prominent cases to be representative; (b) the analytical method, which attempts to determine the general significance of events (which are essentially untypical), or to define ethical norms, or to interpret the social significance of symbols; and (c) the comparative method, setting primitive Christian phenomena in relation

---

[24] 'Theoretische Probleme religionssoziologischer Forschung und die Analyse des Urchristentums', *Neue Zeitschrift für systematische Theologie und Religionsphilosophie* 16, no. 1, 1974, pp. 35–56 = *Studien* (n. 12 above), pp. 55–76. Theissen gave a practical demonstration of his methods in *Soziologie der Jesusbewegung: Ein Beitrag zur Entstehungsgeschichte des Urchristentums*, Munich 1977 (ET *Sociology of Early Palestinian Christianity*, Philadelphia 1977, or *The First Followers of Jesus: A Sociological Analysis of the Earliest Christianity*, London 1978), but is criticized by R. S. Kraemer (n. 17 above) for 'failure to identify the explicit sociological theories which undergird his work', which 'may reflect Theissen's awareness of and sensitivity to the resistance of many scholars of early Christianity to the use of models derived from data outside the ancient world' (p. 437).

[25] 'Die soziologische Auswertung religiöser Ueberlieferungen: Ihre methodologischen Probleme am Beispiel des Urchristentums', *Kairos: Zeitschrift für Religionswissenschaft und Theologie* 17, nos. 3–4, 1975, pp. 284–99 = *Studien* (n. 12 above), pp. 35–54.

either to their contemporary counterparts (with the accent on contrast) or to comparable phenomena in other cultures (with the accent on analogy).

It is the inadequate attention paid to the former of these two comparative procedures which seems to me to vitiate much of the work that is attempted in New Testament Studies under the banner of sociology. Theissen rightly sees that it is an indispensable step, but his main hope of progress is directed towards the mutual correction that arises from competing methodologies. I should have thought there was no hope of securing historically valid conclusions from sociological exercises except by first thoroughly testing the models themselves for historical validity.

III. IN WHAT TERMS IS THE SOCIAL IDENTITY OF EARLY CHRISTIANITY TO BE DEFINED?

The first model to be discarded is that of 'religion' itself. The crippling ambiguities of the term have been demonstrated by Wilfred Cantwell Smith.[26] Only the establishment of Christendom in the fourth century created the conditions which make the typical modern use of the word historically realistic.[27] It was of course a Roman word before that. But it is hard to see how anyone could seriously have related the phenomenon of Christianity to the practice of religion in its first-century sense. From the social point of view, the talkative, passionate and sometimes quarrelsome circles that met to read Paul's letters over their evening meal in private houses, or the pre-dawn conclaves of ethical rigorists that alarmed Pliny, were a disconcerting novelty. Without temple, cult statue or ritual, they lacked the time-honoured and reassuring routine of sacrifice that would have been necessary to link them with religion. Instead of mislocating them under such an unhistorical rubric,

---

[26] *The Meaning and End of Religion: A New Approach to the Religious Traditions of Mankind,* New York 1964. Curiously enough, the 'sect' model has been successfully detached from its religious matrix, and may be applied in relation to the social organization as a whole, as by R. Scroggs, 'The Earliest Christian Communities as Sectarian Movement' in J. Neusner, ed., *Christianity, Judaism and Other Greco-Roman Cults: Studies for Morton Smith at Sixty,* pt. 2, Leiden 1975, pp. 1–23.

[27] E. A. Judge, ' "Antike und Christentum": Towards a Definition of the Field—A Bibliographical Survey', *Aufstieg und Niedergang der römischen Welt,* pt. 2, vol. 23.1, 1979, pp. 14–15; and *The Conversion of Rome: Ancient Sources of Modern Social Tensions,* North Ryde 1980, p. 6.

then, we must first work out how they would have struck other people, as well as how they would have explained themselves to others.[28]

We already know a striking basic fact. Both sides agreed on the frame of reference within which this identification was to be made. One did not look either to religion, to economics or to social class. The Christians in the last resort were seen, and saw themselves, as a kind of national community.[29] Although they clearly lacked the ethnic or cultural identity of the Jews, it was their distinctive style of life which marked them out, and left them in potential conflict with the public community. There may well be no comparable phenomenon known to history, and it could therefore prove a fundamental error to attempt to explain primitive Christianity by sociological methods which work through analogy and presuppose the repetitiveness of human behaviour. Until the work of mapping out their social identity and behaviour has been developed much further in juxtaposition with the conventions and practices of contemporary society, we are in no position to say who or what the first Christians were.

The most open and far-sighted way of setting the horizons of this exercise known to me is that of L. E. Keck in his study, 'On the Ethos of Early Christians'.[30] My article on 'St Paul and Classical Society' proposes a pattern of work that tends in a similar direction.[31] The most successful and extensive demonstration of what lies ahead is to be seen in the work of Malherbe already referred to. It seems clear that we must encourage a variety of much more detailed exercises of that sort. The huge gains in clarity that can be made by concentrating upon one thing at a time have now been most tellingly shown by R. F. Hock in his new book.[32] By

---

[28] R. A. Markus, 'The Problem of Self-definition: From Sect to Church', R. M. Grant, 'The Social Setting of Second-century Christianity', R. L. Wilken, 'The Christians as the Romans (and Greeks) Saw Them', in E. P. Sanders, ed., *Jewish and Christian Self-definition*, Vol. 1, *The Shaping of Christianity in the Second and Third Centuries*, London 1980, pp. 1–15, 16–29, and 100–25; R. L. Wilken, 'Collegia, Philosophical Schools, and Theology' in Benko and O'Rourke, eds., *The Catacombs and the Colosseum*, pp. 268–91.

[29] R. A. Markus, *Christianity in the Roman World*, London 1974, p. 24.

[30] *Journal of the American Academy of Religion* 42, no. 3, September 1974, pp. 435–52. By 'ethos' Keck means to embrace 'the practices and habits, assumptions, problems, values and hopes of a community's style' (p. 440), or of 'divergent life-styles which may co-exist'. 'The more sharply the actual life-styles of the Christian communities come into focus, the better we can understand the ethical teaching which was produced and refined in them' (p. 451).

[31] *Jahrbuch für Antike und Christentum* 15, 1972, pp. 19–36.

[32] *The Social Context of Paul's Ministry: Tentmaking and Apostleship*, Philadelphia 1980.

working out in every relevant direction from the nodal point indicated by his sub-title, he has detected, and frequently tied up, many loose ends in the patchy fabric of Paul's life. The result includes explicit and important correctives to some of my past formulations (pp. 37, 65).

Paul comes out of it much less comfortably placed in society. His commitment to the leather workshop seems a sustained and conscious act of independence that earned him little admiration, and restricted the degree to which he could profit from the social protection and hospitality in people's houses that he might otherwise have enjoyed. The social consequences of this deliberate downgrading of expectations by Paul are very fully explored through contemporary examples from the papyri and from authors such as Lucian. Hock has established a far firmer grip on Paul as a man of his world than we have had before. I do not think, however, that the 'new consensus' is at stake. Indeed, Hock had already indicated that, in taking up the point that Deissmann had appealed to as the mark of Paul as a man of the people, he would be coming to the opposite conclusion.[33] The status opportunities Paul declined remain the measure of his potential professional standing, and of the expectation of his supporters for him. The extent of his renunciation helps to explain Paul's intense consciousness of debasement. He was stepping firmly down in the world.

Hock's work not only demonstrates how much ground is to be gained by firmly securing one foothold at a time, but points in the direction of other and perhaps larger steps that can be taken. It has long been noted that Paul seems to refrain from using the familiar language of friendship.[34] Instead he develops his own ideal of partnership in labour, surely meant as provocation to a society that considered physical toil demeaning, however splendid it may sound in a culture that has institutionalized the Pauline challenge and reduced it to a cliché. What was wrong with friendship? Behind the equable ideal there lay a rigid protocol of social rank, imposed from above by the prescriptive practice of benefaction. One made friends by money. In accepting it, the beneficiaries acquired also an inescapable train of obligations, enforced by the threat of renunciation of friendship. But to refuse a gift was no easier, for one then incurred the burden of enmity, which would have to be practised with exhausting concentration, as ancient writers complain. It may

---

33 'Paul's Tentmaking and the Problem of His Social Class', *Journal of Biblical Literature* 97, 1978, pp. 555–64.

34 J. N. Sevenster, *St Paul and Seneca*, Leiden 1961; E. A. Judge, 'St Paul as a Radical Critic of Society', *Interchange: Papers on Biblical and Current Questions*, no. 16, 1974, pp. 191–203.

well be that the true framework for understanding Paul's imbroglio with the Corinthians lies here. He refused the benefaction they offered, because he preferred financial and therefore social independence, and found himself caught in the inexorable processes of ritual enmity.[35]

The relations between Paul and his collaborators and rivals, especially in Corinth, constitute a crux of our subject. In spite of an array of detailed analyses, no solution has yet generally commended itself as the key to the matter.[36] What seems inescapable, however, is that Paul is caught in a social trap of some sort. 'Idealistic' explanations seem bound to fail here, if anywhere. But the trouble is to identify the social conventions that marked out the battlefield.

As for the household framework of the Pauline churches, we now have a comprehensive attempt by R. J. Banks to suggest what this would have meant in practical experience.[37] There remains, however, the remarkable fact that this familiar institution was not being used only to carry out its time-honoured functions in society, but for a purpose that must have been at the least highly unusual. The household community

---

[35] The thesis of P. Marshall, to whom I am indebted for permission to give prior notice of work he will submit as a Ph.D. candidate of Macquarie University. The elaborate conventions of social enmity in Graeco-Roman times have apparently never been analysed, then or now, so that Marshall's findings, if sustained, will illustrate the mutual clarification that may be hoped for from the partnership of ancient history and New Testament studies. [Ed.: See now *Enmity in Corinth: Social Conventions in Paul's Relations with the Corinthians* (Tübingen: Mohr, 1987).]

[36] Scroggs (n. 19 above), p. 175, notes the standing crux posed for New Testament scholarship by the indignation of the Corinthians with Paul for not taking their money. E. E. Ellis, 'Paul and His Opponents: Trends in Research' in J. Neusner, ed., *Christianity, Judaism and Other Greco-Roman Cults,* vol. 1, pp. 264–98, comes to the conclusion that there are no clear trends, but does not discuss the possibility of social or cultural explanations of the conflict. On Paul's collaborators see now W. H. Ollrog, *Paulus und seine Mitarbeiter: Untersuchungen zu Theorie und Praxis der paulinischen Mission,* Neukirchen-Vluyn 1979, and J. H. Schütz, *Paul and the Anatomy of Apostolic Authority,* Cambridge 1975. But before one attempts to derive social data from the texts one must take care not to misunderstand the literary conventions they may employ, cf. W. H. Wüllner, 'The Sociological Implications of 1 Corinthians 1. 26–28 Reconsidered', *Studia Evangelica* 6 (= *Texte und Untersuchungen* 112), Berlin 1973, pp. 666–72, and 'Ursprung und Verwendung der sophos-, dynatos-, eugenes-Formel in 1 Kor. 1, 26' in E. Bammel et al., eds., *Donum Gentilicium: New Testament Studies in Honour of David Daube,* Oxford 1978, pp. 165–84.

[37] *Paul's Idea of Community: The Early Housechurches in Their Historical Setting,* Sydney 1979; *Going to Church in the First Century: An Eyewitness Account,* Greenacre, N.S.W. 1980: two attempts to translate the historical questions for a general and a popular audience respectively. For an academic discussion of the problems, see Malherbe, *Social Aspects,* pp. 60–91.

is now called upon to provide both the setting for, and the immediate exemplification of, a sustained argument about the right way to organize one's relations with others. This drastic attempt to put ideas at once to work was safely enough contained for the moment within its discreet home. But time was to tell how it contained the potential for turning the whole of society inside out.

Deissmann objected to the 'scholastic' approach to the study of New Testament ethics because he considered that it prevented modern eyes from recognizing how familiar the early Christians seem in the light of the papyrus evidence for the life of ordinary people. In this he was both right and wrong. Right, in recognizing that the Pauline churches must be seen socially in terms of relevant contemporary community life as documented in the papyri and inscriptions—a task still not far advanced beyond where he left it. Wrong, if he meant that the concentration upon ethical argument and practice was somehow foreign to Pauline church life. It is precisely here that the social innovation lies. By setting powerful new ideas to work within and upon the most familiar relationships of life, Paul created in the church a social force of a unique kind. The domestic framework was soon outstripped, as the movement of thought and belief generated institutions that were to become an alternative society to the civil order as a whole. It was not a 'popular' movement as though it simply sprang up from below. There was too much talented initiative, promotion and sponsorship for that. But it deserves to be called popular in the sense that it broke through social barriers and encompassed people of every level of community life in a way that had never before been the case with any movement of ideas of an organized kind. In this sense perhaps Toynbee's 'internal proletariat' may be justified.

History walks a tightrope between the unique and the typical. If we explain everything by analogy, we deny to our forebears the individuality we take as a basic feature of our own humanity. The New Testament is conspicuously modern, and decidedly unclassical, in favouring the possibility of radical innovation—it is no doubt the prime source of our own attitudes in this matter. But we will never get the true measure of that until we can map out adequately the relationships of similarity and difference between the first churches and other group phenomena of their time.

Judaism provides the obvious framework, yet one not yet sufficiently defined in respect of our immediate question.[38] Once beyond the

---

38 J. Peterson, *Missionary Methods of Judaism in the Early Roman Empire*, Chicago 1946; S. Applebaum, 'The Social and Economic Status of the Jews in the Diaspora' in S. Safrai and M. Stern, eds., *The Jewish People in the First Century*, vol. 2, Assen 1976, pp. 701–27.

pale, however, we are lost in the seemingly endless miscellany of contemporary Gentile documentation. Yet the scattered appearance of the inscriptions and papyri is deceptive. The disarray lies essentially in the lack of modern analysis. We know that the Greek cities deliberately cultivated a common tradition of culture. Yet we cannot focus upon it for the right time and area. Two types of study are wanted: city by city,[39] and institution by institution. The prior requirement, however, is for the systematic reporting of new data as they come to hand.[40]

Only when much more progress has been made along these lines will it be possible to write adequately on the social environment of the New Testament.[41] And only when that is done will it be possible for there to be at last a history of the New Testament in its times.[42] By that I mean a history that will do justice to the central figures and ideas of the New Testament by appraising them in a full comparison with the relevant ideas and institutions of their day. A 'religious' history that settles for a predetermined pattern of explanation, be it ecclesiastical or sociological, disqualifies itself from discovering how things were.[43]

---

[39] W. A. Meeks and R. L. Wilken, *Jews and Christians in Antioch in the First Four Centuries of the Common Era*, Missoula 1978, is the major outcome so far of the joint working group of the American Academy of Religion and the Society of Biblical Literature on 'The Social World of Early Christianity', for the objectives of which see the paper of that title by W. A. Meeks, *Bulletin of the Council on the Study of Religion* 6, no. 1, February 1975, pp. 1–5.

[40] C. J. Hemer is collecting epigraphic evidence for a contribution to the Corpus Hellenisticum Novi Testamenti, and the School of History, Philosophy and Politics at Macquarie University is considering tackling the papyrus evidence. Hundreds of new inscriptions may be published in a year, while the volume of documentary papyri published has probably increased fivefold since the work of Deissmann and of Moulton and Milligan was done early this century, with the rate of new publications currently at a higher level than ever before.

[41] According to B. Thiering, reviewing the book in this journal, vol. 9, no. 3, June 1977, pp. 318–19, the best contemporary introduction to the social and intellectual setting of the New Testament is E. Lohse, *The New Testament Environment*, Nashville 1976, but the work leans so heavily towards Judaism and the religious background generally that only eight pages (of high quality) are devoted to social conditions in the Roman Empire.

[42] See my review of F. F. Bruce, *New Testament History*, London 1969, in this journal, vol. 7, no. 2, December 1972, pp. 163–65.

[43] Only at the point of finishing this article have I been able to see H. C. Kee, *Christian Origins in Sociological Perspective: Methods and Resources*, Philadelphia 1980. It does not require any reconsideration of the point discussed here, and is concerned with a much wider range of questions.

6

Rank and Status in the World of the Caesars and St Paul

FROM THE HISTORIAN'S point of view we should note two basic characteristics of papyrological evidence, which distinguish it from our other sources of information.[1] One is that it documents levels of community life that lie well below those illustrated either by the literary authors of the classical tradition, or by the public record of the coins or inscriptions. The papyri offer us the most direct access we have to the experience of ordinary people in antiquity, including even the illiterate, provided their affairs were of enough consequence to be worth registering in writing at all. The second characteristic limits this large prospect. The vast bulk of the papyri has been preserved in Egypt. While Egypt always occupied a central place in Graeco-Roman history, and the Greek-speaking people shared fully in the common culture of the Mediterranean in that epoch, its land and society were also distinctive in many respects. We must always ask of the papyrus documents whether they are telling us something that was peculiar to Egypt.[2]

The Ancient History Documentary Research Centre at Macquarie holds the only working collection of unpublished papyrus documents in this part of the world—more than 350 of them. The University Library also holds our most complete collection of published editions of

---

[1] For an introduction to papyrology, see E. G. Turner, *Greek Papyri*, 2nd ed., Oxford 1980, and for a classification and lists of the various types of documents preserved on papyrus and the materials conventionally studied with it (e.g. ostraka, wooden tablets), see O. Montevecchi, *La papirologia*, Turin 1973.

[2] For treatments of the institutions of Graeco-Roman Egypt based on papyrus documentation, see J. G. Winter, *Life and Letters in the Papyri*, Ann Arbor 1933, and R. Taubenschlag, *The Law of Greco-Roman Egypt in the Light of the Papyri*, 2nd ed., Warsaw 1955.

papyrus texts.[3] Macquarie has deliberately made this a point of concentration for several reasons. For one thing, it provides a stimulus for students of ancient history to seek training in the use of documentary and other sources in the original. A student beginning Greek may even cut his teeth on the few surviving words of a papyrus fragment, and thus become the first person to read the document since it was dumped in antiquity. Secondly, the comprehensiveness of the papyrus documentation provides some shared ground for those working in diverse sectors of ancient history. This technical foothold may prove useful at almost any point in the history of the Mediterranean over the millennium of Greek ascendancy in Egypt from Alexander to the Arab conquest. Thirdly, papyrology provides, next to archaeology, the most encouraging prospect of new discoveries about the ancient world. Publications of newly edited collections of papyri have been appearing during the last decade more frequently than ever before, and there are scores of thousands of new texts in libraries awaiting an editor.[4] For these reasons, we believe, the papyrological interests of the Macquarie Centre place us in an advantageous position to gain some ground in the understanding of ancient history.

The small miscellany of recently published documents which I have chosen to discuss is selected to illustrate two of our current research programmes. One is the plan to assemble systematically and to re-edit all the papyrus documents which bear on the history of Christianity in Egypt down to about the eighth century. The first task here is to develop criteria for deciding which letters or documents refer to people of Christian beliefs. As you will see from the examples taken here, in the period prior to Constantine this is no simple matter.[5] When we have sorted it all out, we hope to publish a corpus of Christian papyri, which will con-

---

[3] The Ancient History Documentary Research Centre can supply from the computer, and will in due course publish, a third edition by S. R. Pickering of *Papyrus Editions Held in Australian Libraries* (the second edition, by G. S. R. Thomas & S. R. Pickering, North Ryde 1974, is out of print). In his inaugural lecture as Professor of Greek in the University of Sydney (Oxford 1938), J. E. Powell said that 'with the possible exception of papyrology, there is no branch of classical research which either now or at any conceivable future time can be carried on at Sydney'.

[4] During the last decade (1970–1979) 78 volumes of newly edited documentary texts appeared, embracing about 4800 items, and many more were published individually in journal articles, to be collected in due course in further volumes of E. Kiessling, *Sammelbuch griechischer Urkunden aus Ägypten.*

[5] See further E. A. Judge & S. R. Pickering, 'Papyrus Documentation of Church and Community in Egypt to the Mid-Fourth Century', *Jahrbuch für Antike und Christentum* 20 (1977), 47–71.

stitute a basic data bank for historians like the existing corpus of Jewish papyri.[6] The second programme aims to correlate the vocabulary, ideas and institutions used or reflected in the New Testament with the evidence for them in the secular papyri and inscriptions. It is a task which was brilliantly begun early this century by Adolf Deissmann in his *Light from the Ancient East* and by Moulton & Milligan in their *Vocabulary of the Greek Testament Illustrated from the Papyri and Other Non-literary Sources*.[7] Since their time the amount of evidence has multiplied at least five-fold, but students of the New Testament have less and less effective access to it. We expect shortly to commence publication of a bulletin which will report annually on newly published texts that illustrate New Testament matters.[8] My first four examples relate to this second programme, and I shall then discuss four which relate to the first.

By 'rank and status' I allude to an interesting new proposition about the spread of Christianity in the Roman world.[9] 'Rank' is meant to denote any formally defined position in society, while 'status' refers to positions of influence that may not correspond to the official pattern of the social order. Status tends to convert itself into rank, and rank is the fossilised status of the past, defending itself against the aspirations of those who have only status, often newly acquired. The hereditary peerage, if you like, against the *nouveaux riches,* or the party officialdom against the intellectual left, or even the governor-general against the prime minister.

Now, it has been the fashion to say that what was wrong with the early Christians was that they came from the lower classes. That is also

---

[6] V. A. Tcherikover, A. Fuks and M. Stern, *Corpus Papyrorum Judaicarum,* vols. I–III, Cambridge (Mass.) 1957–1964. A folder is available from S. R. Pickering, School of History, Philosophy & Politics, Macquarie University, North Ryde N.S.W. 2113, giving details of the proposed *Corpus Papyrorum Christianarum.*

[7] The first edition of Deissmann's *Licht vom Osten* appeared in 1908, while the work of J. H. Moulton & G. Milligan was basically finished before the former's death in 1917. Of the 315 volumes of papyrus documents published between 1891 and 1981 only 37 had appeared by 1908, and 73 by 1917. On the need for a revision of Moulton & Milligan see C. J. Hemer, *Novum Testamentum* 24.2 (1982), 97–123.

[8] G. H. R. Horsley, *New Documents Illustrating Early Christianity,* North Ryde 1981, reviews the relevant items from the 26 volumes of inscriptions and papyri which appeared in 1976 (embracing some 4000 texts, though not all published for the first time).

[9] Advanced by J. G. Gager (in a review of A. J. Malherbe, *Social Aspects of Early Christianity,* Baton Rouge and London 1977) in *Religious Studies Review* 5.3 (July 1979), 174–80. See further E. A. Judge, 'The Social Identity of the First Christians: A Question of Method in Religious History', *Journal of Religious History* 11.2 (Dec. 1980), 201–17.

what the philosophical critics of the second and third centuries had once said about them. They were people of low rank—plebeians, slaves, women—and therefore not expected to hold serious views on morality or God. Modern observers have liked to turn this around and appeal to these formal disadvantages to explain their positive drive. As with Celsus, Porphyry and the other critics of antiquity, they have not been able to think outside the definitions of Plato or Aristotle. Man was what he was for social reasons; indeed it was in his being a social animal that his humanity consisted. What was never explained, either then or now, about the early Christians was why the inspiration should have seized these particular ones amongst the multitudes of the Roman lower classes.

In the past few years, however, serious attention has been given to the claim that the class (or ranking) categories had been misapplied in any case. The philosophical critics of antiquity had only been grinding an axe, after all, and there was evidence to suggest that not all early Christians were so low. They could even be shown to be people of quite high status within their own world—that of the Greek states under the Roman empire—if not in terms of the orders of the Roman ranking system. But the social explanation of the spread of Christianity could still be saved (and this is the new proposition I have alluded to) by invoking what we may call 'status dissonance': perhaps it is the discord between relatively high status in the home town and low rank in Roman eyes that explains the drive.[10]

Even if one accepts the assumptions of social determinism, the problem with this kind of explanation is that we simply do not know enough about the day-to-day workings of rank and status in the Roman world of the Caesars and St Paul. The theories have usually been hammered out in the laboratory of a South-Seas-island anthropologist, and then transposed half-way around the world, and across two millennia, without adequate testing for applicability in the new setting: so powerful is the assumption of the indelible pattern of human social behaviour. This brings us at last to the papyri. They are the ancient historian's best approximation to a South Seas island. Here he can see the ambiguities of rank and status being played out before his eyes, if not in the flesh, then at least in raw documents, unprocessed

---

[10] S. R. Pickering suggests to me that it may also explain the curious lack of documentary evidence for Christians in Egypt in the second and third centuries (when the quite frequent fragments of biblical texts prove that they were active there): perhaps Christians had learned to keep their heads down from the disastrous consequences of the drive of the Alexandrian Jews to convert their high status into corresponding civil rank.

by the orderly minds of social scientists—or historians. Not that eight papyri can take us very far. They are only samples, and what is needed is a systematic analysis of such material. My hope here is simply to illustrate the possibilities of sharpening historical awareness which lie to hand in such documents.[11]

The following petition nicely registers the conversion of status into rank:

> 'To Gnaeus Vergilius Capito by agency of (her) two sons Claudius Potamon and Claudius Apoll(onius?) from Isidora daughter of Apollonius but, by adoption, of Dionysius alias . . . onius, Alexandrian, householder of a house in the Gamma district . . .'

> P.Oxy. 3271 (*c.* A.D. 47–54)

The prefect, to whom it is addressed, is the effective ruler of Egypt, acting for the titular governor in Rome, Claudius Caesar. Nothing survives of the substance of the claim, but we may assume it sought legal redress on some matter of concern to the owner of what we may take to be the block of flats referred to. This could be Dionysius, or the latter's adoptive daughter, Isidora, who lodges the petition. The editor's preference for the latter has been strengthened by evidence subsequently adduced, so that we may now risk translating 'landlady' rather than 'householder' (5 σταθμούχου).[12] She is presumably a citizen of Alexandria, and thus already privileged amongst the Greeks of Egypt. But she has curiously introduced herself by naming her two sons. The names speak for themselves: they are those of Roman citizens. Although it is generally believed that the Latin names used by some Greeks are an affectation of people who were not Roman citizens, there is no doubt in this case. The Greek name pattern does not provide for double names, at least where, as in this case, they correspond to the Roman *nomen* with accompanying *cognomen*. The *nomen*, Claudius, must in any case be decisive, especially when displayed to a prefect in the time of Claudius Caesar, who had imposters executed for assuming Roman names.[13]

---

[11] For convenience I have selected six examples from *The Oxyrhynchus Papyri* 46 (1978), ed. J. R. Rea, and two (nos. 3057 and 3069) from vol. 42 (1974) ed. P. J. Parsons.

[12] J. R. Rea, P.Oxy. 47 (1980), xix, can now cite parallels for the feminine form of 'Alexandrian' to which he believes the text was altered by the writer after (mistakenly) entering the masculine form.

[13] Suetonius, *Claudius* 25.3, and for discussion of Roman policy and attitudes see A. N. Sherwin-White, *The Roman Citizenship*, 2nd ed., Oxford 1973; J. P. V. D. Balsdon, *Romans and Aliens*, London 1979.

Potamon and Apollonius are Greek names used as Roman *cognomina,* suggesting that the brothers were not born Romans. Although their father is not named, the mother's Greek name makes it unlikely. Roman citizen rank was necessary in both parents if one was to be born into Roman citizenship, and Isidora would surely have exhibited her Roman rank if she had had it, since this must be why she puts her sons' names to the fore. The two routine ways of becoming a Roman citizen were by emancipation from slavery to a Roman, and by enfranchisement upon discharge from the Roman auxiliary forces. In the latter case one almost invariably finds Latin *cognomina,* the soldiers having taken a Latin service name, which is then retained as the *cognomen* upon enfranchisement.[14] Freedmen would normally have been given a Greek name while in slavery, which they retained as the *cognomen* upon emancipation.[15] In this case Potamon and Apollonius could have been imperial freedmen, though that in itself should have been specified and was in any case a ranking of consequence which one would wish to parade. Slaves of course have only owners and mothers, not fathers, but Isidora can hardly be a slave or freedwoman mother, since she herself has a father, or indeed two of them.

Ancient historians, who deal only with fragmentary evidence, have to learn not to jump to conclusions, but in this case there seems after all no reason to hold back from first appearances. Isidora is a respectable property-owner of the Alexandrian citizen-class whose sons have received a personal grant of Roman citizenship in the name of Claudius Caesar himself, as part of his new policy of distributing the Roman franchise to individuals in the East. To attain this honour, they must have been either politically important figures (which in any case implies wealth) or just plain rich, if we can conclude from the case of the tribune in Acts 22:28 that Roman citizenship was for sale if you could pay enough.[16]

The study of nomenclature provides a controlled way forward into the question of social rank and status in the Pauline communities, which belong to these same decades. Of the 91 individuals named in the New Testament in connection with St Paul, a third have Latin names. It is a startlingly high proportion, ten times greater than in the case of an

---

[14] L. R. Dean, *A Study of the Cognomina of the Soldiers in the Roman Legions,* Diss. Princeton 1916.

[15] J. Baumgart, *Die römischen Sklavennamen,* Diss. Breslau 1936.

[16] When Cassius Dio 60.17.5 says that prices fell to bedrock under Claudius, he must be implying that there were officials whose venality outstripped the demand for citizenship. If so, we should have to drop our assumptions about the popularity of Roman citizenship.

extensive control group of non-Romans I have checked.[17] The control group was drawn, however, from epigraphic documents, so that one need only conclude that the affectation of Latin names by Greeks was much higher in St Paul's circle than in the circles whose inscriptions have come down to us, naturally those able to afford the best quality of stone and carving. But one must also consider the more serious possibility, that many of the Latin names in the Pauline connection were not affectations, but the legitimate marks of Roman citizenship. This is certain in the one case where the double name is used, and can be safely assumed in the cases of three or four women who bear a Latin *nomen*.[18] *Praenomina* I should be inclined not to claim as indicating Roman citizenship.[19] They had long been domesticated in Greek usage, and one may guess that most people would scarcely be conscious of their Latin origin. But most of the New Testament Latin names are *cognomina*.[20] While some of these also had currency as Greek names, the high level of correspondence between the Pauline list and that of the popular *cognomina* of Roman soldiers suggests to me that Roman citizenship may have spread from such sources much more extensively in the East by this time than has been assumed from the controversies surrounding the

---

[17] The 1064 Greeks named in V. Ehrenberg and A. H. M. Jones, *Documents Illustrating the Reigns of Augustus and Tiberius*, Oxford 1949; E. M. Smallwood, *Documents Illustrating the Principates of Gaius, Claudius and Nero*, Cambridge 1967; and M. McCrum and A. G. Woodhead, *Select Documents of the Principates of the Flavian Emperors including the Year of Revolution*, Cambridge 1961.

[18] Titius Justus (Acts 18:7); Junia (Rom 16:7—the masculine alternative reading Iunias is not epigraphically attested at Rome); Julia (Rom 16:15); Claudia (2 Tim 4:21); and Maria (Rom 16:6), if this is taken as a Latin rather than a Hebrew name. Lydia is probably a Latin rather than a Greek formation, but it is not the feminine form of a Roman *nomen,* while Priscilla (or Prisca) is the feminine equivalent of a *cognomen*: if these women are of citizen rank they must of course have had a regular *nomen* as well.

[19] Marcus ('Mark'), Lucius (probably two separate people at Acts 13:1 and Rom 16:21), Titus, Gaius (probably three separate people at Acts 19:29, Acts 20:4, and Rom 16:23 with 1 Cor 1:14). Loukas ('Luke') may be a hellenised variation of Lucius.

[20] Using the epigraphically attested frequency of senatorial, veteran and servile usage as a guide, I rate the *cognomina* of the Pauline connection in the following order of how respectable they would have sounded to Roman ears: Paulus ('Paul'), Niger, Crispus, Rufus, Pudens, Silvanus, Aquila, Secundus, Justus (probably two separate people at Acts 18:7 and Col 4:11), Fortunatus, Clement, Crescens, Quartus, Urbanus, Tertius, Ampliatus, Achaicus. If these men are Roman citizens, they must all have had *praenomina* and *nomina* as well. If non-citizens, the '*cognomina*' are simply their (single) Greek names.

Claudian grants, and that the Pauline communities for their part may have drawn extensively upon this class of people with army-derived Roman citizenship.

While this would technically rank them highly in their own Greek cities, they need not have been of high status there, as one may assume Potamon and Apollonius of Alexandria were. Indeed, if one must find a source of social impetus for the Pauline churches, might one not invert the proposition about status dissonance, and instead of positing relatively high-status Christians seeking corresponding rank, ask after the possibility of there having been well-ranked ones who sought corresponding status? May there not have been Roman citizens who had not fallen on their feet? There is of course plenty of evidence of former soldiers who did well financially upon retirement, and became leaders in their own towns. But evidence, by definition, tends to come from those most capable of affording it. The same goes for those discharged from slavery into citizenship, another possible source of the Latin names in the New Testament, though if we admit that we must allow for an even larger number of those with Greek names having been freedman-citizens, since Greek names are commoner than Latin as Roman slave names.

If we find the question of names ambiguous, we should pity the task of Eudaemon, the secretary of a tax officer at Oxyrhynchus, who had to be able to distinguish the financial status of people with the same name:

> 'To Quintus Sanquinius . . . inius Maximus, epistrategus, from Eudae-mon, (slave?) of Marcus Antonius Spendon collector. Among the men nominated to serve as sitologi in the Oxyrhynchite nome was listed by mistake instead of Belles son of Dionysius, financially sound and fit for the service, another man of the same name, Belles son of Patermuthis, unfit for the service and poor. Since they are both from the village of Tacona in the same Oxyrhynchite nome and since the patronymic was mixed up by mistake, as stated above, . . .'

> P.Oxy. 3273 (first century)

In discussion since the publication of this text it has been demonstrated that Eudaemon is indeed the slave of Marcus Antonius Spendon, since the correct way of identifying a Roman slave is by appending his owner's three names.[21] (Upon emancipation the Greek Eudaemon will expect to become, as a new Roman citizen, Marcus Antonius Eudaemon, just as

---

[21] J. A. Straus, 'Notes sur quelques papyrus concernant l'esclavage dans l'Égypte romaine', Zeitschrift für Papyrologie und Epigraphik 32 (1978), 259 62.

his owner, Spendon, had done before.) Spendon, or perhaps his father, may well have been close to Caesar's household, if we assume that he is one of those dependants to whom the younger Antonia, daughter of Augustus' sister Octavia and the defeated Antonius, had passed on the latter's name. Others of them, like Antonius Pallas and his brother Antonius Felix became leading imperial administrators in the time of her son Claudius. It was Felix, as procurator of Judaea, who tried the charges against St Paul (Acts 23:24–24:27).

Eudaemon's problem was that through a clerical error, perhaps on his own part, one man called Belles rather than his namesake had been nominated for the obligatory honour of guaranteeing the grain taxes, though in fact he was disqualified by lack of property. In another document we find a village scribe prosecuted for a similar miscarriage (P.Wisconsin 23). The translator of P.Oxy. 3273 has interpreted the liturgical obligation by introducing the terminology of service, which is not found in the Greek text. While it may not be far from the reality in this period, it is certainly remote from the traditional conception of the liturgy. Wealth created the privilege of endowing public needs, but what had been once a competition for influence became, with the loss of ultimate political freedoms, a kind of tax on the rich. Lists were established of those who were 'financially sound' (εὔποροι), and the central administration of the prefect chose the liturgists by lot.[22] The conversion of status to rank in this case is only a way of ensuring that none escapes paying the price of wealth. Yet poverty is hardly the preferred option. The choice of terms clearly shows the public approbation of one who is 'financially sound and fit' (ὁ εὐπόρου καὶ εὐθετοῦντος) to undertake the liturgy. The stigma of being disqualified is reflected in a number of famous sayings of the New Testament: for example, the man who puts his hand to the plough and looks back is not 'fit' for the kingdom (Luke 9:62), while the salt that has lost its savour is 'fit' neither for the land nor the dunghill: men just throw it out (Luke 14:35).

Wealth was not the only thing needed for establishing one's status. Access to the privilege of Greek education was equally necessary, and this, as with one's property, became a matter of civil record and verification:

'No. 120.'

'From Theon son of Theon grandson of Theon mother Diogenous daughter of Dionysius from the city of the Oxyrhynchi. In accordance with the orders concerning scrutiny of those entering the gymnasial class

_____

[22] Taubenschlag, op. cit., p. 617, and N. Lewis, *Inventory of Compulsory Services in Ptolemaic and Roman Egypt,* New Haven and Toronto 1964.

(to discover) if they are of this stock, my son Paysiris mother Thaesis daughter of Didymus was registered in the Cavalry Camp district as having reached the age of thirteen in the past eleventh year of Antoninus Caesar the lord. Therefore I have presented myself for his scrutiny and declare that in the (scrutiny) which took place in the fifth year of the deified Vespasian under Sutorius Sosibius then strategus and Nicander then royal scribe and the other proper persons my grandfather Theon son of Ammonius was scrutinized in the Pammenes' Garden district in accordance with the evidences which he presented that his grandfather Theon son of Ammonius is in the list of the thirty-fourth year of the deified Caesar, and (I declare) that my father Theon entered and was scrutinized in the eleventh year of Domitian on the aforesaid evidences in the same district, and that I entered and took my place in the gymnasium lists in the same Pammenes' Garden district, and that the great-grandfather of the mother of my son. . . .'

P.Oxy. 3283 (A.D. 148/9)

One had to prove descent from those who had been eligible for the gymnasium in the 34th year of 'the deified Caesar' (15 θεοῦ Καίσαρος) (Augustus), nearly a century and a half before in this case. The *epicrisis*, or verification, that is sought is a kind of state-certified old school tie. For those whose great-great-grandfathers were not in the Augustan list, there was a back-door entry, provided their ancestors had made it by Nero's time (P.Oxy. 3279). The implication of this, of course, is that the tests were stricter now in the Antonine age than they had been under the Julio-Claudians.[23]

Whether this educational establishment was imposed in the same way in other sectors of the Graeco-Roman world we do not know. But it is certain that the whole cultural tradition underwent a process of crystallisation during the first century of our era. Classicism now emerged. The practice of an already remote past was consciously adopted as the norm of excellence. The free development of language and art was suppressed. Only what conformed was to be kept. Hence the loss of the vast bulk of the professional writing of the age, and hence perhaps the false appearance of linguistic isolation which the New Testament gives. It was preserved, through the independent tradition of study it had itself generated, as a source of authority in its own right. But its cultural context has been substantially lost. It is not inconceivable that the conflicts between St Paul and his converts in Corinth were affected by the growing

---

[23] On the *epicrisis* applications see Carroll A. Nelson, *Status Declarations in Roman Egypt*, Amsterdam 1979, esp. pp. 33–35, 66–67.

sense of his cultural non-conformity. Already by the second century his successors were steadily coming to terms with the demands of a classicising system of education.[24]

But the second century can also show its own forms of social mobility:

'. . . (I greet your son and?) his children—may the evil eye not touch them—and Isidora your sister and Athenais; and write to me without fail about Dionysarion, how many months old she is. Gaia greets you and so do her children and her husband. You should know, then, that Herminus went off to Rome and became a freedman of Caesar in order to take up official appointments. Greet all your people by name. All mine greet you too. I pray for your health.'

P.Oxy. 3312 (second century)

In this private letter one might have thought one was witnessing the quiet domestic life of a provincial backwater. (Though since the letter is presumably addressed to Oxyrhynchus, it may have been written from anywhere else in the Empire.) The Latin name Gaia (line 9), as I have indicated, is probably the relic of an old fashion of assuming the Roman *praenomina* as Greek personal names. Dionysarion (line 7), by the way, is almost certainly not a baby. It has been pointed out in discussion since the publication of this document that the other children are not named, and that there is no obvious reason for knowing urgently how many months old a child is.[25] The word 'old' is in fact a gratuitous paraphrase. Take it away, and we have a simple question about a pregnant woman. Their months were certainly counted, as with Elisabeth, for whom it was 'the sixth month with her who was called barren' (Luke 1:36). The writer may even be the father of the expected child, as with the Roman soldier of the same century who writes to find out the month of his *de facto* wife, as he intends to assist at the delivery.[26]

But Herminus in our text is the figure who most concerns us. After three recent major studies of Caesar's household we thought we knew that there was no open entry to the service.[27] You could only become a

---

[24] E. A. Judge, 'St Paul and Classical Society', *Jahrbuch für Antike und Christentum* 15 (1972), 19–36.

[25] O. Montevecchi, *Zeitschrift für Papyrologie und Epigraphik* 34 (1979), 113–17.

[26] R. S. Bagnall, *The Florida Ostraka: Documents from the Roman Army in Upper Egypt,* Durham (Nth. Carolina) 1976, no. 14.

[27] H. Chantraine, *Freigelassene und Sklaven im Dienst der römischen Kaiser: Studien zu ihrer Nomenklatur,* Wiesbaden 1967; G. Boulvert, *Esclaves et*

freedman of Caesar by first becoming Caesar's slave, a decision that would be made for you by your previous owner if you were not born into the service. Yet we seem here to be dealing with a man who belongs to a free domestic circle. Even for an imperial slave to go off to Rome implies substantial funds both for the journey and for buying his manumission. It also implies an influential patron in the administration, both to initiate the exercise, and to secure the career appointments sought in Rome. The letter uses the technical Latin term *officium* (13 ὀπίκια) for these, and there can be no doubt that leverage would be needed to break into the queue for such a post. Of all this the letter seems unaware. Was the career ladder in fact more accessible than we have realised, or are we looking in on a circle of people for whom its workings were so familiar that no comment was needed? Either way one recognises in such a letter that the Roman ranking system presented opportunities to the aspiring as well as obstacles.

Now we take a sequence of four letters that show how people conducted status relationships amongst their own friends and family circle. They also illustrate an initial question that confronts us in the project for a corpus of Christian papyri. How can one tell whether a letter may have been written by a Christian or not?

> 'Ammonius to Apollonius his brother, greetings. I received the crossed letter and the portmanteau and the cloaks and the reeds, not good ones— the cloaks I received not as old ones, but as better than new if that's possible, because of the spirit (in which they were given). But I don't want you, brother, to load me with these continual kindnesses, since I can't repay them—the only thing we suppose ourselves to have offered you is (our) feelings of friendship. Please, brother, don't concern yourself further with the key of the single room: I don't want you, my brothers, to quarrel for my sake or for anyone else's; indeed I pray for concord and mutual affection to maintain itself in you, so that you can be beyond the reach of gossip and not be like us: experience leads me to urge you to live at peace and not to give others a handle against you. So try and do this for my sake too—a favour to me, which in the interim you'll come to recognize as advantageous (to you as well). If you've received the wool from Salvius to the full amount, and if it's satisfactory, write back to me. I wrote you silly things in my previous letter, which you'll discount: the fact is my spirit relaxes when your name is there—and this though it has no habit of tranquillity, because of its pressing troubles. Well, Leonas

---

affranchis impériaux sous le Haut-Empire romain: rôle politique et administratif, Naples 1970; P. R. C. Weaver, *Familia Caesaris: A Social Study of the Emperor's Freedmen and Slaves,* Cambridge 1972. Professor Weaver has kindly given me advice on this point.

bears up (?). My best wishes to you, master, and all your people. Good health, most honoured friend.'

(Address) 'To Apollonius . . . , surveyor, his brother.'

P.Oxy. 3057 (first/second century)

The letter of Ammonius presents a puzzling situation, which the editor has twice now been tempted to interpret as implying Christian beliefs.[28] If he was right, it would be easily the earliest such letter extant in its original form, being dated by the handwriting to the late first or early second century. It is completely lacking in the distinctive patterns of greeting which enable us to identify Christian letters from the third century onwards.[29] The term 'brother' for a colleague is routine in the papyrus letters, implying equality of rank, but a commentator on the text points also to the fact that Apollonius is the 'master' (29 δέσποτα) of Ammonius, yet addressed as 'brother'. This, it is suggested, sounds very much like the practice of breaking rank enjoined upon the Christian brotherhood.[30] What aroused the original editor's curiosity was the implication that there is some kind of community of brothers who are in danger of falling out with each other and getting themselves into trouble with outsiders. This sounds even more suspiciously Christian. But the only vocabulary elements in the letter which have a positively New Testament flavour are in that very sentence, where he urges them 'to live at peace and not to give others a handle against you' (lines 19, 20).[31] It is true, and of great historical importance in understanding the character of early Christianity, that it presented an argumentative and provocative face to the world.[32] But the more positive sections of this letter show little trace

---

[28] In publishing the text in 1974 Parsons said, 'If the hand is rightly dated it would be temerarious to look for a Christian context' (in spite of the possibility he saw in the words 'concord and mutual affection'), but later, citing the parallel of a (Latin) letter of Constantine, he was more willing to allow it: P. J. Parsons, 'The Earliest Christian Letter?', in R. Pintaudi, ed., *Miscellanea Papyrologica*, Florence 1980, 289.

[29] M. Naldini, *Il Cristianesimo in Egitto: Lettere private nei papiri dei secoli II–IV*, Florence 1968.

[30] O. Montevecchi, *Aegyptus* 55 (1975), 302, argues that at this date the title should mean 'patron', and is reminded of the letter of Paul to Philemon.

[31] Colin J. Hemer, 'Ammonius to Apollonius, Greeting', *Buried History* 12 (1976), 84–91.

[32] E. A. Judge, *The Conversion of Rome: Ancient Sources of Modern Social Tensions*, North Ryde 1980, 7. S. R. Pickering (see no. 10 above) envisages the author as a Jewish Christian of Alexandria caught up in the troubles of Judaism there and warning Christians elsewhere to 'not be like us'.

of any distinctively Christian vocabulary. We may like to envisage 'concord and mutual affection' (15, 16 ὁμόνοιαν . . . καὶ φιλαλληλίαν) as Christian ideals, but they are in fact part of the general philosophical currency of the times, and neither of the Greek terms is found at all in the New Testament: the editor can cite 1 Clement for 'concord' (and it is frequent in the Apostolic Fathers) but has to go on into the fourth century for a Christian parallel to the whole phrase, by which time an extensive fusion of traditions had occurred anyway.[33]

At many points in the letter there is a marked divergence of vocabulary and ethical attitudes from the Christian pattern. Some key terms do occur in early Christian literature, but used of the attitudes of God, not men: 'kindnesses' (8 φιλανθρωπίαις); 'repay' (9 ἀμείψασθαι); 'a favour to me' (21 χαρισάμενός μοι). Others are used in senses different from that of the New Testament, most notably 'try and do this' (20, 21 πείρασαι . . . τοῦτο ποιεῖν)—the word is not used of personal moral effort in the New Testament literature. Most significant, however, of the mentality of the writer are certain ideas and terms he uses which are quite foreign to New Testament ways of thinking, especially the term translated as 'the spirit' (7 προαίρεσις, 'intention') and 'the only thing we suppose ourselves to have offered you is (our) feelings of friendship' (lines 9–11, a phrase which incorporates the same term). This reflects the distinctive ethics of contractual friendship, that system of gift and counter-gift which people often felt as a burden, stifling spontaneous affection.[34] This letter indeed is a prime document of its oppressive character. It is probable that St Paul's avoidance of the friendship ideology and its social obligations was one of the sources of his conflict with the Corinthian church. But it was his own distinctive ideas of human relations which stamped themselves on subsequent Christian tradition. The absence of any trace of the ideal of spending for no personal return makes it difficult to put this circle of brothers very close to that tradition.[35]

---

[33] Parsons cites 1 Clement 47.7, and from the fourth century Nilus of Ankara (PG 79.144a) and the letter of Constantine in Optatus, Append. III (p. 204 Ziwsa). Professor G. R. Stanton has kindly given me advice on the philosophical currency of these terms.

[34] S. C. Mott, 'The Power of Giving and Receiving: Reciprocity in Hellenistic Benevolence', in G. F. Hawthorne, ed., Current Issues in Biblical and Patristic Interpretation: Studies in Honor of Merrill C. Tenney, Grand Rapids 1975, 60–72. The matter is extensively explored in P. Marshall, Enmity and Other Social Conventions in Paul's Relations with the Corinthians, Diss. Macquarie 1980.

[35] S. R. Pickering, however, refers me to 2 Clement 19 as an example of how Alexandrian Christianity may have differed from the Pauline tradition in this respect, as it did notably also in others.

The question has been also asked of a somewhat later letter, on the grounds of its containing some words that are at first sight very distinctively Christian.[36]

'Apollonius and Sarapias to Dionysia, greeting. You filled us with joy by announcing the good news of the wedding of the excellent Sarapion and we would have come immediately to serve him on a day greatly longed for by us and to share his joy, but because of the circuit sessions and because we are recovering from illness we could not come.'

'There are not many roses here yet; on the contrary they are in short supply, and from all the estates and from all the garland-weavers we could hardly get together the thousand that we sent you with Sarapas, even by picking the ones that ought to have been picked tomorrow. We had as much narcissus as you wanted, so instead of the 2,000 you wrote we sent 4,000.'

'We wish you did not despise us as misers so far as to laugh at us and write that you have sent the money, when we too regard the young people as our own children and esteem and love them more than our own, and so are as happy as you and their father.'

'Write to us about anything else you want. Give our greetings to the excellent Alexander, and to Sarapion and Theon—may the evil eye not touch them!—and to Aristoclea and to Aristoclea's children.'

'Sarapas will tell you about the roses—that I have made every effort to send you as many as you wanted, but we could not find them.'

(2nd hand) 'We pray for your health, lady.'

Back. (1st hand) 'To Dionysia, wife of Alexander.'

P.Oxy. 3313 (second century)

'Being filled with joy' is a characteristic New Testament phrase, though not in the active form as here (3 χαρᾶς ἡμᾶς ἐπλήρωσας). Yet the phrase is a high-flown one, and not paralleled at all in other papyrus letters. 'Announcing the good news' (3 εὐαγγελισαμένη) also belongs to stately speech, and is correspondingly rare in the papyri. In the romantic novel of Longus, *Daphnis and Chloe* (3.33), it is used as here of announcing the wedding. In the New Testament it soon becomes the technical term for preaching the gospel, though even there it is not uncommon in non-gospel connections. But by the latter part of the second century it seems to me less likely that a person familiar with the distinctively Christian

---

[36] J. E. G. Whitehorne, in a letter to me dated 5 March 1979.

sense of the word would have used it in a private connection, given that
it was in any case hardly an everyday word. It is not found at all in Christian private letters of the third and fourth centuries.

Much the same considerations apply to the idea of 'serving' (5
διακονήσοντες) the bridegroom, which picks up the word that in
Christian usage had become the technical term for the service of dea-
cons, though the *Patristic Greek Lexicon* shows that its general senses also
remained current even in such writers. By contrast 'greatly longed for' or
'prayed for' (5–6 εὐκταιοτάτῃ . . . ἡμέρᾳ) is a term with practically no
Christian currency at all. One must also register a large doubt over all
those flowers. People in antiquity soon recognised that Christians had
reservations about flowers, so that Tertullian and other apologists contemporary with our letter-writer even have to explain that it was not
that they were against flowers as such.[37] The trouble was that crowning
people with flowers implied a kind of divinisation that was repugnant to
the Christian conception of man's relation to God. Another consideration against Christian authorship is the conventional allusion to being
immune from the evil eye (23 ἀβασκάντους), not yet one imagines
taken over into Christian usage.

The letter of Apollonius and Sarapias also nicely illustrates the ritual status-games surrounding the exchange of gifts. Dionysia had not
placed herself under obligation to her correspondents by simply asking
for the flowers. She had made arrangements to pay for them. Apollonius
and Sarapias in turn protest cheerfully at the inferior position this puts
them in (though they don't say whether they are sending the money
back). In the classical tradition of social life one strove to excel in benefaction. Giving money to others was not a mark of subordination but of
superiority.[38]

Self-restraint also became a method of impressing oneself upon
other people:

> 'Aquila to Sarapion, greetings. I was overjoyed to receive your letter. Our
> friend Callinicus was testifying to the utmost about the way of life you
> follow even under such conditions—especially in your not abandoning
> your austerities. Yes, we may deservedly congratulate ourselves, not be-
> cause we do these things, but because we are not diverted from them by
> ourselves. Courage! Carry through what remains like a man! Let not

---

[37] T. Klauser, *Reallexikon für Antike und Christentum 2*, 446–59, s.v.
Blume, cites Minucius Felix 12.6, 38.2–4; Tertullian, *De corona 2, 7*; Clement of
Alexandria, *Paed.* 2.70–76.
[38] Contra B. Holmberg, *Paul and Power: The Structure of Authority in the
Primitive Church as Reflected in the Pauline Epistles*, Lund 1978, 10.

wealth distract you, nor beauty, nor anything else of the same kind: for there is no good in them, if virtue does not join her presence, no, they are vanishing and worthless. Under divine protection, I expect you in Antinoopolis. Send Soteris the puppy, since she now spends her time by herself in the country. Good health to you and yours! Good health!'

(Back) 'To Sarapion the philosopher from his friend Aquila.'

P.Oxy. 3069 (third/fourth century)

The letter of Aquila is certainly not by a Christian. The phrase translated 'under divine protection' invokes gods in the plural (20 θεῶν σωζόντων). But the dedication to ascetic practice which this letter dwells upon was pursued in philosophical and Christian circles alike in the third and fourth centuries.[39] Its main roots lie in the radically dualistic anthropology of the Platonic tradition. By suppressing physical appetites you freed the soul for virtue. Although the editor may be justified in describing this as 'self-abnegation', in that the letter speaks of 'ourselves' (line 13) as the distraction, it is clear that the classical appetite for praise and self-admiration still finds plenty of scope within these sacrifices.

The monastic movement was suddenly projected into the public eye early in the fourth century. Although attempting a much more complete repudiation of the world than the philosophers had done, the monks could not escape it. The more they retreated, the more power people attributed to their prayers, and the more eagerly they were tracked down by the desperate or the curious. The holy man rapidly acquired paramount status in fourth-century society. Within monasticism rank and order, of course, soon made their mark, for even solitaries, as monks were supposed to be, preferred to live in crowds, as a cynical Greek poet of Egypt remarked.[40] We have a good number of papyrus letters, from the same epoch as that of Aquila, which document the rapidly solidifying conventions which propped up the new movement.[41] There are clear differences in practice and ideal between it and the classicising philosophers. For their part, the Hellenes, as Julian called them, were contemptuous of

---

[39] F. E. Morard, 'Monachos, moine: Histoire du terme grec jusqu'au 4ᵉ siècle: Influences bibliques et gnostiques', *Freiburger Zeitschrift für Philosophie und Theologie* 20 (1973), 329–425; E. A. Judge, 'The Earliest Use of *monachos* for "monk" (P.Coll. Youtie 77) and the Origins of Monasticism', *Jahrbuch für Antike und Christentum* 20 (1977), 72–89.

[40] Palladas, in *Anthologia Palladus* 11.384, cited by A. Cameron, 'Palladas and Christian Polemic', *Journal of Roman Studies* 55 (1965), 17–30, at 29.

[41] K. Treu, 'Christliche Empfehlungs-Schemabriefe auf Papyrus', in *Zetesis* (Festschrift E. de Strijcker), Antwerp and Utrecht 1973, 629–36.

the vulgar sacrifices of the monks. It was all done for show, and was a patent device for imposing themselves on others, it was claimed.[42]

The last example, the letter of Judas, deals with one of the genuine hardships of life in the Roman world:

> 'To my lord father, Joses, and to my wife, Maria, Judas. To begin with I pray to the divine providence for the full health of you (both), that I find you well. Make every effort, my lady sister, send me your brother, since I have fallen into sickness as the result of a riding accident. For when I want to turn on to my other side, I cannot do it by myself, unless two other persons turn me over, and I have no one to give me so much as a cup of water. So help me, my lady sister. Let it be your earnest endeavour to send your brother to me quickly, as I said before. For in emergencies of this kind a man's true friends are discovered. So please come yourself as well and help me, since I am truly in a strange place and sick. I searched for a ship to board, but I could not find anyone to search on my behalf. For I am in Babylon. I greet my daughter and all who love us by name.'

> 'And if you have need of cash, get it from Isaac, the cripple, who lodges very close to you.'
> (2nd hand) 'I pray for the health of you both for many years.'
> Address. 'Deliver . . .'

> P.Oxy. 3314 (fourth century)

It is an impressive fact that in a major centre a man could find (or plausibly claim to find) no one to turn to for help in a personal disaster. The Christians had specialised in providing just this kind of protection for strangers, and came under strong criticism for offering help indiscriminately and indeed immorally, without regard to the merits of the victim.[43] The fact that Judas can write home and expect his wife to come to his aid suggests they knew nothing of the church's lifeline which excited the contempt and envy of Julian. The notion of 'the divine providence' occurs in several other letters which could be Christian, but the idea is shared with both Jews and Stoics.[44] The mention of 'the cup of water' (10 ποτηρίου ὕδατος) need not be a reference to Mark 9:41, in spite of the apparent parallel in one of the Abinnaeus papyri.[45] Neither this saying nor its counterpart in Matt 10:42 is at all commonly cited in Chris-

---

[42] Julian (Loeb edition), 2:122 (224B).
[43] Julian (Loeb edition), 2:336 (305C), 490 (363A), 3:390 (238E).
[44] M. Naldini, op. cit. 14.
[45] H. I. Bell et al., *The Abinnaeus Archive: Papers of a Roman Officer in the Reign of Constantine II*, Oxford 1962, no. 19, 8–10.

tian literature of the second and third centuries.[46] Nor does Strack-
Billerbeck have any record of Rabbinic sayings which illustrate the
phrase.[47] It may have been an Egyptian saying (a suggestion of S. R.
Pickering), and can hardly be taken as a plain statement of fact if Judas
expected to survive long enough for help to come down the river from
Oxyrhynchus. Apart from the names, then, there is nothing about this
letter that positively suggests Christianity, and we are not clear about the
stages by which biblical names passed into Christian use during the
fourth century.[48]

There is no hint that Judas has any other connection to which he
can appeal. (Though he has disingenuously omitted to tell us who wrote
the letter for him or who the two people were who had been turning him
over.)[49] A man well enough off to be mounted on horseback, and to have
funds at his disposal with an acquaintance near his home, might have
been expected to have had servants with him, or friends to whose protection he could turn. The remark about discovering one's 'true friends'
is not the sarcastic comment on the friendship system it may seem from
this translation. Literally he says that in such emergencies one discovers
'one's own' (15 οἱ ἴδιοι). Judas may be safely left a Jew. Although the
Jews had been in eclipse in Egypt since their suppression in the early second century, the documentary record continues to attest their presence.
Hospitality to strangers was expected in the synagogue communities.
But there is no trace of Jewish settlement at Babylon, and at earlier
stages the nearest point of concentration was 25 km down the Nile, at
Leontopolis.[50]

The followers of Jesus inherited from Judaism their sense of being a
distinct community, a kind of nation of their own. The singular history
of their confrontation with Graeco-Roman society is not likely to be explained simply in terms of its systems of rank and status. Their aim was
not to find their place in the world as it was. They brought with them

---

[46] *Biblia Patristica: Index des citations et allusions bibliques dans la littérature patristique*, 3 vols., Paris 1975–81.

[47] H. L. Strack and P. Billerbeck, *Kommentar zum Neuen Testament aus
Talmud und Midrasch*, Munich 1926.

[48] V. A. Tcherikover, A. Fuks and M. Stern, *Corpus Papyrorum Judaicarum*, vol. III, Cambridge (Mass.) 1964; A. E. R. Boak and H. C. Youtie, *The Archive of Aurelius Isidorus*, Ann Arbor 1960, 377–78.

[49] The observation of G. J. Cowling.

[50] D. Rokeah, in *Corpus Papyrorum Judaicarum* III, Appendix III, shows
that the most frequently attested places of Jewish habitation in Egypt are Alexandria, Arsinoe, Apollinopolis (Edfu), Euhemereia (Fayum), Leontopolis, Oxyrhynchus, Philadelphia and Thebes.

ideas and practices which undercut the classical order. We are still far from getting the measure of what was happening at the social level, whether at the earliest points of encounter in the days of St Paul or at the stage when the power of the Caesars itself was coupled to the new fountain of authority.[51]

Sociological theory may have its explanatory uses, provided it survives the discipline of documented facts. But ancient history has no particular need to look to other epochs for fresh sources of understanding. In the vivid details of the papyrus documents we have an authentic point of contact with the times, through which we can progressively sharpen our focus on them. The coming generation can look forward to a steady flow of new knowledge from the combined efforts of classicist and historian. Practise well-tested skills and meet the new demands of our times. That was the message of Vergil's first eclogue, from which the University of Canterbury has taken its promise—*ergo tua rura manebunt:* 'then you will keep your heritage for ever'.

NOTE: This is the fourth Broadhead Memorial Lecture of the University of Canterbury. The script was originally published as delivered.

---

[51] E. A. Judge, ' "Antike und Christentum"—Towards a Definition of the Field: A Bibliographical Survey', *Aufstieg und Niedergang der römischen Welt* 2.23.1 (1979), 3–58.

7

Cultural Conformity and Innovation in Paul: Some Clues from Contemporary Documents

I. Paul's Blank Cheque

THE SOCIAL ATTITUDES of the first believers in Christ pose a dilemma for Marxism. Marx took over from Feuerbach the explanation of religion as an ideological projection of man's alienation. It offered an imaginary resolution of the social contradictions experienced in practice. Adopting a conceit from the poets of German romanticism, Marx spoke of religion as the opium of the people. But he later sharpened this slogan to specify that it was opium *for* the people. It was a device by which property-owners might induce those they exploited not to do anything about it.[1]

But how did one then explain the first believers in Christ? Since Marxist theory took them all to be 'proletarians' practising 'communism', why should they have resorted to the illusion that would then be used to reassert the established order over them? Engels eventually saved

NOTE: The British Council, through its Academic Links and Interchange Scheme, supported my visit to Britain to deliver this lecture (The Tyndale Biblical Archaeology Lecture, 1983) and to develop the connections formed in recent years between British scholars and the Ancient History Documentary Research Centre at Macquarie University. I am grateful to Professor C. K. Barrett and others for criticism at the Centre's professional development seminar on 8 April, 1983.
[1]Not that true and false consciousness are set in total opposition to each other. Marxists do not necessarily condemn everything about religion, and admit that Marxism too can be penetrated by ideology. They expect a constant struggle to distinguish science from ideology. For these and other corrections I am grateful to Dr. M. C. Hartwig.

the theory by abandoning the search for explanation altogether. Jesus had not even existed (nor the primitive 'communism'). The gospel was a development from Hellenistic thought in the second century.[2]

It fell however to Karl Kautsky, who had once been Engels' secretary, to produce (in 1908) the classic Marxist analysis of the problem. In terms of production the first believers were no true proletarians after all. They were rather consumers, and their 'communism' meant sharing in other people's bounty. You could not therefore expect them to have led the revolution. The practice of charity only created the dictatorship of the benefactors it had raised up as masters within the community.[3]

The problem of the 'communism' of the primitive apostolic community has consequently been discounted by G. E. M. de Ste Croix.[4] He claims that his new work is the first in English, or in any other language that he can read, 'which begins by explaining the central features of Marx's historical method and defining the concepts and categories involved, and then proceeds to demonstrate how these instruments of analysis may be used in practice to explain the main events, processes, institutions and ideas that prevailed at various times over a long period of history'. He approaches Christianity through 'the transfer of a whole system of ideas from the world of the *chora* to that of the *polis*' and holds that it is in this process of transfer ('necessarily involving the most profound changes in that system of ideas') that 'the most serious problems of "Christian origins" arise'. But unfortunately this leads him simply to assert that the difference between the teaching of Jesus and that of Paul is the direct effect of the class struggle, without giving any detailed attention to the ideas of Paul at all, or even establishing what the difference is, if there is one.

Paul wrote 'a blank cheque' for 'the powers that be', says de Ste Croix, and he would no doubt be happy to extend this to the whole of

---

[2] 'Christianity, Origins of', in *Marxism, Communism and Western Society: A Comparative Encyclopedia* (New York: Herder & Herder, 1972) 409–22; D. Lyon, *Karl Marx: A Christian Appreciation of His Life and Thought* (London: Lion, 1979) 38; K. Bockmuehl, *The Challenge of Marxism: A Christian Response* (Leicester: IVP, 1980) 55–58.

[3] K. Kautsky, *Foundations of Christianity* (ET 1925 from 13th German edition, New York and London: Monthly Review, 1972) 323, 331, 345, 347, 415–17, 422, 464, 467.

[4] *The Class Struggle in the Ancient Greek World from the Archaic Age to the Arab Conquests* (London: Duckworth, 1981); reviewed by P. A. Brunt, 'A Marxist View of Roman History', *Journal of Roman Studies* 72 (1982) 158–63; Oswyn Murray, 'Reasons for Decline', *New Statesman* (1 January, 1983) 24–25; W. Schuller, 'Klassenkampf und Alte Geschichte', *Historische Zeitschrift* 236.2 (April, 1983) 403–13.

what I call the ranking order of society, adding servile, sexual and ethnic rankings to those arising from government. He has not told us, however, that it was a crossed cheque, only to be credited to an account, nor that it was not negotiable, being available only to the order of the appointed parties. Then de Ste Croix also fails to tell us that Paul conducted a head-on personal assault on the status system which supplied the ideology of the established order. For the first time in history, moreover, Paul spelled out what may in a sense be called a structural model of social relations. It does not, however, address itself to what we call structures, which lie rather on the ranking side of the distinction I am developing between rank and status, but it belongs to the latter side, that is to the way people use their rank to assert superiority over each other. Status tends to convert itself into rank, as in the case of the rich Greeks who liked to be granted Roman citizenship, but Paul does not advocate this solution. Conversely rank may seek to escape back into status, as for example in the increasing dislike of the liturgical system the more compulsory it became and the corresponding development of financial corruption. Paul's endorsement of rank is a barrier against this.[5]

But like most ancient observers, Paul does not analyse human affairs in institutional terms. His thinking rather attacks the problems at a personal level. It turns the prevailing status system inside out. What one witnesses here is neither the projection of unfulfilled desires nor the use of religion to defend property, but something much more drastic: the deliberate abandonment of status so as to open the way to a new spirit of human cooperation through mutual service. Both as a principle and in practice it would have appealed greatly to Marx's passionate desire to see man remake himself—though the means would have surprised him. It did not grapple with the question of modes of production and class struggle, but then such issues did not confront people in the way they did in the nineteenth century. The issues it did face, however, arise in all societies. They are the ones to which Marxism for its part has often not found the answer where it has been put to the test of practice in our century.

It would have come as a surprise to Paul, in turn, to find his cause classified by Marxists under 'religion'. Paul would have found much more in common with the restless, argumentative and single-minded apostle of revolution—like him a son of Israel turned to the Gentiles, and committed to showing the whole world its true destiny—than he

---

[5] E. A. Judge, *Rank and Status in the World of the Caesars and St Paul* (Christchurch: University of Canterbury, 1982).

would with those who cultivated what Greeks and Romans called religion. Nor would they have expected to find anything to do with religion in Paul's churches. His only use of a technical term of worship in connection with the church-meeting is to describe the reaction of the hypothetical unbeliever who is stunned to discover, contrary to what would have seemed obvious, that God was actually present there (1 Cor 14:25). In that scene of lively social intercourse there was neither solitude nor mystery, no shrine, no statue, no cult, no ceremony, no offering to ensure that all was well between gods and men. Instead there was talk and argument, disturbing questions about belief and behaviour (two matters of little or no concern to religion in antiquity), conscious changes to accepted ways, and the expectation of a more drastic transformation soon to come. The purpose of classical religion was to secure what was already there against just such an upheaval.[6]

So a worshipper of Isis, delivered from his private suffering, calls upon her to appear to him again to listen while he praises her as the universal guarantor of the established order.[7] This new aretalogy, from Maroneia, is the earliest extant, and differs from the four found previously in being more systematic in content and more classical in its Greek. G. H. R. Horsley suggests that it reflects an early stage in the cult of Isis, before quasi-credal conformity was required to the text on the stele at Memphis (line 3). In spite of the differences in form, the same view of the world emerges. It may be described as naturalistic. The gods derive from the earth (Γῆ lines 15–16) and in turn endorse the existing state of affairs. Equality is justified because, by nature, death makes us all equal (line 25). Even grace is improved by its corresponding to what nature in any case requires (lines 33, 34). In the standard version, e.g. at Kyme, aesthetic discrimination is also grounded in nature.[8]

The marriage of Isis and Sarapis (Maroneia, line 17) provides for the cosmic order. On earth Isis is credited with all the variety of good things, from human love, to physical generation, to social order. The at-

---

[6] R. MacMullen, *Paganism in the Roman Empire* (New Haven and London: Yale University, 1981) 57–59.

[7] Y. Grandjean, *Une nouvelle arétalogie d'Isis à Maronée* (Leiden: Brill, 1975), reproduced with English translation and full discussion by G. H. R. Horsley, *New Documents Illustrating Early Christianity,* Vol. 1, *A Review of the Greek Inscriptions and Papyri Published in 1976* (North Ryde, N.S.W.: The Ancient History Documentary Research Centre, 1981), no. 2, lines 6–7.

[8] H. Engelmann, *Die Inschriften von Kyme* (Bonn: Habelt, 1976), no. 41, reproduced in *New Documents 1976,* no. 2, pp. 18–19, lines 32–33. See also V. F. Vanderlip, *The Four Greek Hymns of Isidorus and the Cult of Isis* (American Studies in Papyrology 12) (Toronto: Hakkert, 1972) for other treatments.

mosphere is harmonious and optimistic, even progressive. Political stability depends on the non-violent rule of law (lines 30–31), reflecting
the overthrow of tyranny (Kyme, lines 26–27), and on an effective and
merciful legal system (lines 34–39). There is even a hint of liberation
theology (line 45).

But Marx would surely not have been satisfied. It does not go far
enough, and too much is taken for granted. Even though the author of
the Maroneia text is only trying to offer a kaleidoscopic overview of life,
which scarcely leaves room for hard questions, that very fact betrays his
commitment to the security of established position (which is what
εὐστάθησαν means in line 30—it is the tranquillity of good order). Certainly he has embraced multi-culturalism rather than Greek chauvinism
(line 26), but amongst so thoroughly Greek a set of ideals that amounts
to little more than a sentimental projection of culture-consciousness. It
does not face the problems of culture-conflict. The conflict of the sexes
is glossed over with a neat ambiguity: 'I compelled women to be loved
by men' (Kyme, line 28)—we still cannot tell to which party the compulsion is applied.[9] The issue of slavery and freedom, the third of St Paul's
great ranking distinctions (Gal 3:28), is probably not even on the horizon. Nor are Marx's fundamental questions about man as worker, and
how he is to make himself by winning the value of his productive labour.

The cult of Isis after all only offers reassurance to those whose way of
life is already secure. But in a strange new glossary Isis is registered as ἡ
μεγάλη [ἐ]λπίς, the first time this title has been attested for her.[10] One
may note also Heliodorus, *Aethiopica* 2.25.1–6, for a priest of Isis who ex-
iled himself for unchaste thoughts, which shows that soul-searching went
on. But the general pragmatism of Isis remains. She gathers into one the
multifarious functions of the ten thousand cults of locality, occupation
or life-cycle by which classical antiquity clung to its cultural heritage.
Graeco-Roman religion is not typically either a projection of frustrated
desires nor an instrument of class oppression. It arises from a basically
unproblematic love of life as it is, and the dread of an unknown future.

Where does this leave the Pauline churches? For them the question
of the future had been decisively solved. But life as it was could never be

---

[9] F. Solmsen, *Isis among the Greeks and Romans* (Martin Classical Lectures
25) (Cambridge, Mass. & London: Harvard University, 1979) 42.

[10] A. K. Bowman et al., *The Oxyrhynchus Papyri*, vol. 45 (London: Egypt
Exploration Society, 1977), no. 3239, col. 2, line 21, cited by G. H. R. Horsley,
New Documents Illustrating Early Christianity, Vol. 2, *A Review of the Greek Inscriptions and Papyri Published in 1977* (North Ryde, N.S.W.: The Ancient History Documentary Research Centre, 1982), no. 30.

the same again. The new orientation threw up an array of problems within the existing order, and exposed moral issues in human culture that had not been seen in the same way before. Hardly anything was taken for granted, or simply accepted on the old terms (though occasionally the conventional wisdom may have been thrown into the argument by way of pleonasm, as when 'nature herself' teaches us that long hair degrades a man', 1 Cor 11:14). Paul grappled with the use of three great ranking distinctions of his era. None arises by nature, as Greek analysis had maintained. All are set aside in Christ (Gal 3:28). Yet each has its purpose for the time being, derived from different phases of God's rule over the world—male and female stemming from the physical creation (1 Cor 11:7–10) and Jew and Gentile from the old covenant, while slave and free are best taken as a facet of the socio-political order by which God provides for mankind's temporary well-being (1 Cor 7:17–22; Eph 6:5–8; 1 Tim 6:1–6). No blank cheques are offered to those with priority of rank; but different commitments are asked of the different parties. The ranking principle is endorsed between men and women (Eph 5:22–24) but its status concomitant rejected (v. 25); God deals with the Jew first (Rom 2:9–11) but Jews are not better off (3:9) nor for that matter worse off (11:1)—it does not matter whether one is Jew or Greek (1 Cor 7:18–20); slaves similarly should accept their rank even if offered manumission, but change the spirit in which they serve (1 Cor 7: 20–24; Eph 6:6–9).

It is the same with the powers that be. Paul is not endorsing such demonic social powers as may oppress mankind any more than Jesus had sold himself to Caesar in conceding the tax-money. Nor is he referring to Caesar in particular. What are the ἐξουσίαι ὑπερεχοῦσαι of Romans 13:1? Notice that the ἀρχαί which often go with them in Paul are not mentioned. 'Principalities and powers' only just catches the difference of nuance between the terms. The ancient terminology of power was more developed than ours. I take ἀρχαί to refer to rulers in the sense of their being fountains of power, while ἐξουσίαι refers rather to those who are empowered to administer that authority: the principals and their delegates. If that is correct, the choice of ἐξουσίαι here on their own points downward in the power-structure to the level at which it was imposed in practice on the individual citizen. Even provincial governors are above that level.[11]

---

[11] I reached this conclusion, which tends in the opposite direction from that of many commentators on the passage, before reading A. Strobel, *ZNW* 47 (1956) 67–93; 55 (1960) 58–62, or E. Käsemann, *Commentary on Romans* (ET from the 4th German edition) (Grand Rapids: Eerdmans, 1980) 353–54. Their

A prefect of Egypt (Vergilius Capito) contemporary with Paul has left his edict (7 December A.D. 48) on the pylon of the temple of Hibis in the Great Oasis.[12] Capito complains of his subordinates who extravagantly and shamelessly abuse their ἐξουσίαι: their authorities, that is, delegated through him. He lists the ones he has in mind: soldiers, cavalrymen, orderlies, centurions, military tribunes. He demands that reports on their expense accounts be forwarded by the local secretaries to the state accountants in Alexandria. The edict of Ti. Julius Alexander, preserved at the same spot from twenty years later, complains in turn about the excessive ἐξουσία of the state accountants.[13] They were impoverishing Egypt by entering many people's dues on the basis of analogy alone.

There has recently been found for the first time a systematic regulation of the transport service designed to curb its exploitation through the πλεονεξία of Roman magnates, whether military or businessmen. Coming from Pisidia in A.D. 18/19, it represents what we may suppose Paul and his colleagues could have read on any Roman road.[14] The frustrations of the provincial governor are very apparent. He is caught between the vested interest of travelling Romans in exploiting the system, and the displeasure of Caesar to whom a stream of petitions flowed from aggrieved individuals and states all over the empire.[15] In a lecture last year at the conference of the Australian Historical Association, R. MacMullen of Yale proposed that official and private corruption was

---

case is rejected by K. Aland, 'Das Verhältnis von Kirche und Staat in der Frühzeit', *Aufstieg und Niedergang der römischen Welt* 2.23.1 (1979) 184, on the grounds that in Rome of all places it would be Caesar himself who was in view. But Paul's horizon is surely that of Corinth, not Rome. W. Carr (*Angels and Principalities: The Background, Meaning and Development of the Pauline Phrase hai archai kai hai exousiai* [Cambridge: CUP, 1981] 121) establishes the case against the angelological interpretation of Rom 13:1, but does not deal with the question of which level of human authority is referred to.

[12] W. Dittenberger, *Orientis Graecae Inscriptiones Selectae*, no. 665 = E. M. Smallwood, *Documents Illustrating the Principates of Gaius, Claudius and Nero* (Cambridge: CUP, 1967), no. 382, line 17.

[13] *OGIS* 669 = Smallwood, *Documents*, no. 391, line 51.

[14] S. Mitchell, *JRS* 66 (1976) 106–31, redated by E. A. Judge, *New Documents 1976*, no. 9.

[15] F. G. B. Millar, *The Emperor in the Roman World (31 B.C.–A.D. 337)* (London: Duckworth, 1977) 213–28, 240–52. It was not till the second century that petitions to local authorities in Egypt show a collapse of confidence in justice (R. L. B. Morris, in R. S. Bagnall et al., *Proceedings of the Sixteenth International Congress of Papyrology* [Chico: Scholars, 1981] 363–70); for examples, see J. L. White, *The Form and Structure of the Official Petition* (Missoula: Society of Biblical Literature, 1972).

the fatal weakness that sapped the Roman empire's capacity to resist invasion in later centuries. The general public clung to a belief in the integrity of the law, but it was always threatened by influence, and there is more than a hint in Paul's treatment that believers too needed to be shocked out of the easy assumption that they could manipulate the service for private advantage. A letter to a slave of Caesar in the time of Augustus appeals to him to prevent profiteering.[16] Faced with a corrupt authority Paul would presumably have brought to bear the sanctions implied in God's appointment, as the writer of Acts suggests he did with Felix (Acts 24:25).

But the fact remains that subject to such qualifications Paul did require believers to accept the duly constituted authorities as the responsible agents of God's government of the world as it was. With that goes by implication a similarly defined acceptance of the formal ranking and class distinctions (normally based on property assessment) that provided the basis for government in classical antiquity. He would presumably come close to the principle of relative righteousness, as Sir Ernest Barker has formulated it in the case of St Augustine.[17] The ἐξουσίαι are delegated powers, and have value because of their origin and purpose under God; their utility may be distinguished from the use to which individual incumbents may put them. Paul must therefore be set firmly in opposition to Marx in that he does not hold the formal structure of society in his day to be systematically oppressive and hostile to man's best hopes, and does not in any way suggest or imply that its violent overthrow could as a matter of principle be in the positive interest of mankind or part of a believer's duty to God. Nor does he deal with how it might be reformed, which presumably is embraced in the system as endorsed. But that by no means brings our question to an end.

II. PAUL AND PATRONAGE

If Paul seems to modern eyes surprisingly detached over the question of conformity to the ranking order of community life, what are we to make of his passionate reaction to certain socio-cultural expectations

---

[16] *P.Oxy.* 44 (1976), no. 3208, reproduced in *New Documents 1976*, no. 14.

[17] Introduction to the Everyman edition of J. Healey's translation of *The City of God* (London: Dent, 1945) xviii; the 'righteousness' *(justitia)* of the civil order stems from the fact that God ordained it, but since this was done as a remedy for sin, the 'righteousness' is 'relative' to that. I am grateful to the paper of H. Elias read at Tyndale House on 1 July, 1983, for drawing my attention to this formulation.

people had of him at a more personal level? My proposition is that while accepting rank he repudiates the status conventions which permitted people to exploit the system to private advantage. I refer in particular to two fault-lines that run through the Corinthian correspondence, and throw up repeated shocks in his relations with his own converts at Corinth.

The first may be called 'cultural' in the more aesthetic sense. They did not like the way he spoke or presented himself in public: 'his bodily presence is weak, and his speech of no account' (2 Cor 10:10). It was un-professional. He spoke like an amateur (2 Cor 11:6). The technical term ἰδιώτης which they applied to him, and which was to be thrown up against his reputation even centuries later, means that he was not quali-fied for the career which he might be thought to have assumed, that of a public lecturer.[18] This would have required university-level training under a recognised sophist (or 'professor'), and would have been in-stantly recognisable in his mastery of the complex arts of platform rhet-oric. Whether Paul might have had such training at Jerusalem is not clear. But it is certain that he refused absolutely to practise it if he did.

One can sympathise with the Corinthians, who felt embarrassed for him, and let down on their own account. There were other lecturers available to them who knew how to display their talents properly—to compare themselves with each other, as Paul puts it (2 Cor 10:12). A let-ter home from a first-century university student at Alexandria makes clear what was at stake.[19] The unsuccessful Didymus is despised for as-piring to the competition (it is the cognate of Paul's word, σύγκρισις, line 28), but to reject the very aspiration, as Paul did, was to be a cata-strophic and bewildering failure. It leads Paul into the strange paroxysm of his boasting 'as a fool' (2 Cor 11:21–29), in which he parodies the proud conventions of self-display by parading his own weaknesses.[20] That this is not itself just a clever literary conceit on Paul's part is clear from the personal anguish it causes him (2 Cor 12:11). For his listeners it would have been intensely shocking. It is a repudiation of one of the

---

[18] *New Documents 1977*, no. 106, offers a translation of the P.Bodmer 20 text of 'The apology of Phileas' as revised by A. Pietersma for his forthcoming re-edition of it along with the new *P. Chester Beatty* 15 text. Col. 10, lines 11ff. read: 'Was he not an untrained individual *(idiotes)*? Surely he was not in the category of Plato?' [Ed.: Now available, *The Acts of Phileas, Bishop of Thmuis* (ed., with intro., trans., and commentary by A. Pietersma; Geneva: P. Cramer, 1984).]

[19] C. H. Roberts, *The Oxyrhynchus Papyri*, vol. 18 (London: Egypt Explo-ration Society, 1941), no. 2190.

[20] C. B. Forbes, 'Comparison, Self-praise and Irony: Hellenistic Rhetoric and the Boasting of Paul', *New Testament Studies* (forthcoming). [Ed.: *New Tes-tament Studies* 32 (1986): 1–30.]

fundamental principles upon which the Greek status-system rested, the belief that fine form is congruent with truth. Cultivation in the literary and artistic sense was thus a means of legitimising the status of those who could afford it. And precisely because it made a conspicuous difference to a person's public appearance it became the means by which the social inferiority of the uncultivated was imposed on them as a felt distinction.

As a convert to the persecuted Jesus, paradoxically discovered from the very depths of that humiliation to be anointed as Israel's Messiah (Acts 2:36), Paul consciously sought the reversal of his own socio-cultural expectations. It was the expression of his identification with Christ in weakness, and he expected his own converts to follow him in it. I believe you will not find anywhere in the Pauline literature any aesthetic canons of approval. The terms that sometimes sound like this in our translations turn out to refer to moral criteria. So I should translate προσφιλῆ (Phil 4:8) not as 'lovely' (RSV) but, as in the epitaphs, 'loveable', and the following term εὔφημα not as 'gracious' (RSV) but 'honourable' (Good News Bible), both terms implying a moral judgement.

A recent study of the eulogistic terminology of Greek public inscriptions of the Roman empire in relation to the moral vocabulary of Plutarch provides a useful measure of Paul's vocabulary.[21] Of 75 terms examined, fewer than half are found anywhere in the NT, and then often as *hapax legomena* and mostly in Acts, Hebrews or the Pastorals (notably Titus). The Pauline *homologoumena* have relatively little in common with the eulogistic tradition. Noticeably lacking are the array of compounds in εὐ- and φιλ- which give expression to the prevailing nexus between aesthetic and moral approval (e.g. εὐκοσμία, εὐνομία, εὐταξία, φιλοδοξία, φιλοκαλία). Some of the alpha-privative terms that connote irreproachability do however go over (ἄμεμπτος, ἀνέγκλητος, ἀνεπίληπτος). This presumably deliberate and certainly heartfelt reaction against any kind of status based upon cultivation also helps to make sense of Paul's dilemmas over the ideal of wisdom (σοφία was one of the ideals of the eulogistic tradition to which Paul did wish to stake a claim, but on his own terms). It was a cultural revolution which still carries us all in its wake—if only in the convention of self-deprecation.[22]

The second conflict-point between Paul and the Corinthians lies in the field of cultural anthropology. It was over money. For reasons which

21 C. Panagopoulos, *Dialogues d'histoire ancienne* 5 (1977) 197–235, reviewed by E. A. Judge, *New Documents 1977*, no. 83.
22 E. A. Judge, *The Conversion of Rome: Ancient Sources of Modern Social Tensions* (North Ryde, N.S.W.: Macquarie Ancient History Association, 1980).

modern Western minds have often found difficult to grasp, they objected to him because he would *not* accept their support, but insisted on
paying his own way by physical labour. This again confronts a basic convention of status. In the non-productive cities of the Graeco-Roman
world, deriving their wealth basically from the labour of peasants on estates belonging to city magnates, social power was not exercised by taking profit from one's dependants (who often did little work anyway), but
by passing money down to them to keep up their subordinate dignity.
The niceties of this system were preserved by the conventions of what
was called friendship. This is a status conferred by the greater on the
lesser. It implied full conformity with the wishes of the initiator—as
Jesus stated when he formulated the terms upon which the disciples
would be counted as his friends ('if you do what I command you', John
15:14). It also carried the dangerous risk of renunciation, as Pilate was
once warned ('If you let this man go, you are not Caesar's friend', John
19:12). And if you refused an offer of friendship by not taking someone's
money you openly declared yourself his enemy. Enmity also entails a
painful and exhausting ritual of confrontation. P. Marshall has defined
from classical sources the social conventions governing the conduct of
friendship and enmity, and used them as a framework for explaining the
upheaval over Paul's refusal of support. Here is another point at which
Paul deliberately rejected the established system of status.[23]

The friendship-enmity system operates amongst those who are of
equal rank in class terms, providing them with a hierarchical principle
of collaboration or defining the terms of conflict if that is refused. Between people of different social ranks, status relations are best understood
in terms of the Roman patron-client system; at Rome one may be promoted from clientship to friendship if one's property ranking permits,
and the rules of *clientela* set the moral tone for the system of *amicitia*.
My use of the Roman institution of patronage to explain the sponsorship of New Testament communities has been called in question.[24] Did
Roman practice have effect in Greek states? From the legal point of view,
no doubt, only if they were also Roman colonies, as several New Testament cities were. But Roman citizens were found in slowly increasing
numbers almost everywhere else as well. The Pauline connection shows

[23] P. Marshall, *Enmity and Other Social Conventions in Paul's Relations with the Corinthians* (Ph.D. dissertation, Macquarie University 1980, to appear in the series Wissenschaftliche Untersuchungen zum Neuen Testament). [Ed.: Now available, *Enmity in Corinth: Social Conventions in Paul's Relations with the Corinthians* (WUNT II 23; Tübingen: Mohr, 1987).]

[24] A. Cameron, 'Neither Male nor Female', *Greece and Rome* 27 (1980) 62.

a frequency of Latin names ten times greater than the public inscriptions of the Eastern cities of the time (excluding the names of Greeks which explicitly identify them as possessing Roman citizenship). The only comparable frequency I have noticed is with the recently published set of manufacturers' signatures on Corinthian lamps.[25] I am inclined to explain this on the hypothesis that Paul was appealing to certain categories of Greeks who did in fact hold Roman citizenship, but acquired by the inferior processes of manumission or service in the auxiliary forces. The list of Pauline cognomina tallies quite well with that of the imperial soldiers' *cognomina*.[26] Such men must often have returned to settle in their home towns, but though now superior in civil rank they would have lacked the social status of the well-established Greeks who were still not commonly admitted to Roman citizenship.

The documentary evidence shows on the one hand that the Roman law of patronage was sufficiently distinctive to introduce into Greek the technical loan-word πάτρων instead of being covered by its approximate equivalent in Greek, προστάτης. On the other hand it became sufficiently familiar to acquire the Greek pattern of inflexions and derivatives and to be attested in Egyptian papyri and inscriptions at about 70 per cent of the frequency of προστάτης, with cases arising as early as the first century B.C.[27] The typical instance relates of course to the patronage of Roman citizens over their freedmen. προστάτης did not cover this, the original sense of *patronus,* since Greek law did not transmit citizenship by manumission. A Greek freedman passed under the protection of a god or magistrate,

---

25 E. A. Judge, *New Documents 1977,* no. 84.

26 Relating the figures recorded by L. R. Dean (*A Study of the Cognomina of Soldiers in the Roman Legions* [Ph.D. dissertation, Princeton University, 1916]) to those for the city of Rome derived from L. Vidman (*Corpus Inscriptionum Latinarum,* Vol. 6.6.2. *Index Cognominum* [Berlin/New York: de Gruyter, 1980]), we may rate the 17 Pauline *cognomina* in order of likelihood of their being of military origin, as follows: Crispus, Quartus, *Silvanus, Pudens,* Aquila, *Rufus, Secundus, Niger, Clement,* Urbanus, Crescens, Paul, Tertius, *Justus,* Fortunatus, Ampliatus, Achaicus. Those italicised are attested as soldiers' names in the East in the first century A.D. Achaicus is not listed in Dean and is presumably of servile origin, as is Ampliatus, which is rare as a soldier's name. If we take Dean's tallies as a percentage of Vidman's the range is otherwise from 56 per cent (Crispus) to 13 per cent (Fortunatus).

27 F. Preisigke and E. Kiessling, *Wörterbuch der griechischen Papyrusurkunden* (Heidelberg, Berlin: Preisigke, 1924–1944; Amsterdam: Hakkert, 1969); S. Daris, *Spoglio lessicale papirologico* (Milan: Istituto Papirologico dell' Università Cattolica del Sacro Cuore, 1968); idem, *Il lessico latino nel greco d'Egitto* (Barcelona: Papyrologica Castroctaviana, 1971); H. J. Mason, *Greek Terms for Roman Institutions* (Toronto: Hakkert, 1974).

whereas at Rome the *patronus* assumed legal and moral guardianship over the new freedman-citizen. This was one of the sources of the growing authoritarianism of Roman politics.[28] προστάτης was used to translate other Latin words *(praeses, princeps)* as well as having its pre-contact meanings, so that the need for the loan-word πάτρων is clear. But as late as A.D. 133–137 the translation of an unusual prefect's edict which lists cases to be referred to the higher court identifies complaints by patrons against their freedmen by using the participle ἐλευθερώσαντες instead of employing either noun.[29] By the third century, when everyone was Roman, there was a vogue for displacing πάτρων with προστάτης, and by the fourth century πάτρων is available as a general title of respect.

Yet the earlier letter to Sarapion, a πάτρων, gives no indication of Roman citizenship, though equally that cannot be excluded.[30] Could the later generalisation of the term already be in force? A clearer case is a second-century letter where the recipient is called πάτρων in the address, πατήρ in the prescript.[31] J. R. Rea has not discussed the coupling of πάτρων in *CPR* 5.19 with τροφεύς, which should also have a technical meaning. The τροφεύς, I take it, is the one who rears a foundling (θρεπτός), handing it to a nurse (τροφός) for suckling. It is interesting that Paul likens himself to the female τροφός rather than to the paternal τροφεύς (1 Thess 2:7). As the previous verse shows, he is consciously stepping down in status. We possess a number of papyrus nursing contracts, all from the period I B.C.–A.D. II.[32] Not surprisingly such an arrangement is attested only from Egypt. But it would have been general in the Greek East. The status of θρεπτός was not however familiar to Romans, to judge from Pliny's query to Trajan on the point.[33] Pliny

---

[28] J. W. Jones, *Law and Legal Theory of the Greeks* (Oxford: Clarendon, 1956) 284–85; D. M. MacDowell, *The Law in Classical Athens* (London: Thames & Hudson, 1978) 82–83. R. P. Saller (*Personal Patronage under the Early Empire* [Cambridge: CUP, 1982]) demonstrates that it cannot be assumed that the ideology of patronage was displaced by principles of seniority and merit as the basis of the political career during our period.

[29] F. Preisigke, F. Bilabel, E. Kiessling, and H.-A. Rupprecht, *Sammelbuch griechischer Urkunden aus Ägypten* 12.1 (1976) 10929 = *New Documents 1976,* p. 50, line 15.

[30] J. R. Rea, *Corpus Papyrorum Raineri* 5 (Vienna, 1976), no. 19 = *New Documents 1976,* no. 16, line18, dated I/II A.D.

[31] F. Bilabel, *Veröffentlichungen aus den badischen Papyrus-Sammlungen 2* (Heidelberg, 1923), no. 42, referred to by Rea.

[32] The latest is *Sammelbuch* 12.2 (1977), no. 11248 = *New Documents 1977,* no. 1.

[33] *Ep.* 10.65, with commentary by A. N. Sherwin-White (Oxford: Clarendon, 1966).

coyly uses the Greek word, and all the precedents cited relate to Roman administration of Greek states. Trajan declares in reply that people reared in this way are entitled to assert the liberty they were born with. But τροφεύς first appears in the documents as a metaphor in court life under the Ptolemies. An inscription of II B.C. honours Apollodorus as the relative, the τροφεύς and the foster-father of the king's son.[34] No foundling status or slavery is involved here. Similarly we have an Apollophanes who is τροφεύς to a Ptolemaic priest with named father.[35] In Roman times, the coins and inscriptions of Asia Minor show the word now coupled with εὐεργέτης for the benefactor of a city (had it displaced πάτρων in this respect?). L. Robert argues that it specifically recognises alimentary benefits.[36] But if so, not just in time of famine. Synnada honours an Aurelius Theodorus as hereditary τροφεύς and εὐεργέτης.[37] Where do we stand with CPR 5.19? Literally it implies that Sarapion has in the Greek manner taken up the writer as a foundling into slavery and then as a Roman citizen manumitted him into clientela. But nothing else about the letter requires or even suggests this. Since legalities are hardly in place in such a studiously vague letter, we may build rather on παρ᾽ ἕκαστα in line 9 and ask whether ἐμνήσθης is correctly translated 'make mention of us'. Was Sarapion perhaps sending regular money, in return for which the writer prays for his health?

My suggestion in any case is that we can assume a prevailing familiarity with Roman patronal practice and ideals, which were transposed also to international relations, so that they may be taken as a realistic guide to the ethical character of such other conventions of personal dependency as will have existed in the various Greek states. As early as 166 B.C. an inscription of Abdera describes the Roman noblemen who undertook the city's interests at Rome as πάτρωνας τῆς πατρίδος, and by the first century we have inscriptions honouring a Roman general as πάτρωνα καὶ εὐεργέτην, which neatly combines the Roman and the Greek styles of diplomacy.[38] By the beginning of I A.D. this usage is applied to private benefactors in Cyprus without any indication of Roman rank.[39]

---

[34] Sammelbuch 1 (1915), no. 1568, line 1.

[35] Sammelbuch 4 (1931), no. 7426, line 5.

[36] L. Robert, Monnaies grecques (Geneva/Paris: Droz, 1967) 66–67.

[37] W. H. Buckler and W. M. Calder, Monumenta Asiae Minoris Antiqua, Vol. 6 Monuments and Documents from Phrygia and Caria (Manchester: Manchester University, 1939), no. 375.

[38] L. Robert, Bulletin épigraphique (1972), no. 622a (P. Clodius Pulcher, cos. 92); (1970), no. 441 (Lucullus).

[39] Bulletin épigraphique (1962), no. 342, reporting T. B. Mitford, American Journal of Archaeology 65 (1961), no. 38, inscription erected by three Cypriot

The old-established Greek term προστάτης is used particularly of the sponsor of a private association. We may safely look to it also as a guide to the way social protection may have been provided for the Pauline churches. A tantalising textual deviation has always clouded the reference to Phoebe, διάκονος of the church at Cenchreae (Rom 16:1). Paul asks the addressees of the letter 'to receive her worthily of the saints' and to 'stand by her in whatever she requires of you'. This pulls both ways. 'Receiving' (αὐτὴν προσδέξησθε) might be taken to imply her social inferiority, but 'standing by her' (παραστῆτε αὐτῇ) implies that she will be looked up to. Wanting perhaps to make all things equal, two ninth-century MSS (F & G) read the following statement as saying that 'she has been the assistant (παραστάτις) of many and of me myself', and that might be held to correspond to the activities of a διάκονος, as indeed the Vulgate had taken it. Hence no doubt the RSV translation 'helper'. The better attested reading προστάτις ('protectress') suffered from appearing to assign Phoebe a much higher social status than might have been anticipated, and from the fact that no other individual woman could be found referred to by this term anywhere in ancient Greek. Its common use was for a patron-goddess.

The missing link has now appeared on a still not fully published papyrus held in Milan dating from 142 B.C.[40] A woman is said in a legal document to be the προστάτις of her fatherless son. It perhaps means that she has the formal responsibility of being his guardian (ἐπίτροπος), but that the broader term has been used because of the anomaly of a woman's being in this position. Whatever the explanation, the fact that the feminine form of προστάτης is now firmly attested for an individual confirms the judgement of C. K. Barrett and others that Paul is acknowledging his social dependence upon Phoebe.[41] We may safely add her to the array of honoured and therefore rich women who appear frequently in the documents.

women whom Mitford assumes to be freedwomen of a Roman citizen. On giving and receiving, see F. W. Danker, *Benefactor: Epigraphic Study of a Graeco-Roman and New Testament Semantic Field* (St Louis: Clayton, 1982) and S. C. Mott, 'The power of giving and receiving: Reciprocity in Hellenistic benevolence', in G. F. Hawthorne, ed., *Current Issues in Biblical and Patristic Interpretation: Studies in Honor of Merrill C. Tenney* (Grand Rapids: Eerdmans, 1975) 60–72.

[40] *P.Med. Bar.* 1, line 4, discussed by O. Montevecchi, *Aegyptus* 61 (1981) 103–15.

[41] C. K. Barrett, 'a protectress of many, and of me myself' (*A Commentary on the Epistle to the Romans* [London: Black, 1957] 283); C. E. B. Cranfield, 'Phoebe was possessed of some social position, wealth and independence' (*The Epistle to the Romans, II* [Edinburgh: T. & T. Clark, 1979] 783); E. Käsemann, 'the idea is that of the personal care which Paul and others have received at the hands of the deaconess' (*Commentary on Romans* [London: SCM, 1980] 411).

A recent case is Apollonis of Cyzicus whose statue was to preside for
ever over the marriage registry of the city.[42] Although the official citation
(line 55) attributes this distinction to her ancestors' and her husband's
merit (ἀρετή), while she is veiled in the more discreetly feminine quality
of σωφροσύνη (line 56), we can hardly doubt that in practice she had
been in her own right a figure of social influence in the city.[43] Nor were all
eminent ladies backward in coming forward. At Tlos in Lycia in I A.D. the
council and people bore witness to the skill of Antiochis in medical science, which she records in a statue put up by herself.[44] In the same city in
the next century the city clamoured for its priest of the Augusti to move
that Lalla be called 'mother of the city'.[45] In an inscription of II/III A.D.
from Tomis, a widow Epiphania is made by her second husband to say
that she was born among the Muses and shared in wisdom. 'And to
friends abandoned (namely, widowed?) as woman to women I provided
much with a view to piety'.[46] Her father and (first?) husband had been
shipowners, and she claims to have seen many a land and sailed every sea.
A long-published document of Assos attests the formalisation of such status as 'first of women', a phrase perhaps echoed in Acts 17:4 of the women
who protected Paul at Thessalonica.[47]

III. PAUL THE BUILDER

You will have noticed that we now seem to have got Paul firmly back
inside the securities of the patronal system, which I have proposed he

[42] E. Schwertheim, *Zeitschrift für Papyrologie und Epigraphik* 29 (1978)
213–16, line 69.

[43] J. Pircher, *Das Lob der Frau im vorchristlichen Grabepigramm der Griechen*
(Innsbruck: Wagner, 1979), no. 3, quotes H. North, *Sophrosyne: Self-knowledge
and Self-restraint in Greek Literature* (Ithaca: Cornell University, 1956) 253, n. 10,
'the primary virtue of women in Greek inscriptions', often mentioned as the
sole virtue. In Pircher, no. 3, it supplies 'immortal glory'.

[44] A. Wilhelm, *Jahrbuch des österreichischen archäologischen Instituts* 27
(1932) 83–84 = G. Pfohl, ed., *Inschriften der Griechen: Epigraphische Quellen zur
Geschichte der antiken Medizin* (Darmstadt: Wissenschaftliche Buchgesellschaft,
1977) 109–10 = *New Documents 1977*, no. 2, p. 17, where a number of other
women doctors are listed.

[45] C. Naour, *ZPE* 24 (1977), no. 1, reported in *New Documents 1977*, no. 60.

[46] A. Slabotsky, *Studii Clasice* 17 (1977) 117–38 = *New Documents 1977*,
no. 16.

[47] J. R. S. Sterrett, *Papers of the American School of Classical Studies in Athens* 1 (1882–83) no. 16 = R. Merkelbach, *Die Inschriften von Assos* (Bonn: Habelt,
1976) = *New Documents 1976*, no. 25 *bis*.

was to reject at Corinth. One may envisage the following historic development.[48] After the severe mistreatment he suffered in the Roman colonies of the Anatolian plateau on his first journey, when the social establishment was clearly worked against him, Paul adopted a different position, which we first notice at Philippi. He invokes his Roman citizenship and (as later in Romans) insists upon the integrity of Roman control. He also accepts the protection of socially well-placed households, and conspicuously of eminent women. But the Thessalonian letters, with their demand that people work to support themselves, at once show how he reacted against the parasitic aspects of the system. The Corinthian letters show him in a head-on confrontation with the mechanisms by which it imposed social power defined as moral superiority. His positive response to this collision was to build a remarkable new construction of social realities that both lay within the fabric of the old ranking system and yet transformed it by a revolution in social values.

The building terminology is used deliberately. Paul's notion of edification, which we have now reduced to a pale ideal of inward-looking personal development, is in his usage a graphic and innovatory formulation of how people were to manage their relations with each other. The very word οἰκοδομή is a solecism by Attic standards, but widely used in Paul's day as the ordinary term for the process of construction on a building site. Its extensive metaphorical development in Paul seems to be largely his own inspiration, going well beyond certain Old Testament anticipations.[49] In the earliest Pauline letters (1 Thess 5:11; Gal 2:18) the idea is also not extensively developed, but it is the great encounters in the church at Corinth which stimulate his reflection on constructive as opposed to destructive relations. The constructive spirit is that of love, by which each contributes to the others' good, as distinct from the 'puffed-up' spirit which pulls down the building (2 Cor 10:8; 13:10). In Romans the idea is largely neglected in the theological development of the parallel figure of the body, which must also be taken as an attempt to formulate the new principle of social relations (Rom 12:3–8). In Colossians (2:7) and especially Ephesians (4:12–16) the two figures are however elaborately drawn together. Ephesians 2:19–22 shows the most remarkable development of the idea. Here he moves from a starting-point in a metaphor drawn from the terminology of political alienation

---

[48] E. A. Judge, 'The social identity of the first Christians: a question of method in religious history', *Journal of Religious History* 11.2 (1980) 201–17, reviews twenty years of discussion of these matters.

[49] H. Pohlmann, 'Erbauung', *Reallexikon für Antike und Christentum* 5 (1962) 1043–70.

through progressive degrees of political and domestic assimilation to the figure of a new structure in which Christ is the cornerstone and all are built in to a harmonious growth.

This is Paul's answer to the deep-seated problem of human exploitation which Marxism in our age has construed as alienation from the product of our labour. Paul's solution is the reverse of Marx's. Man is not merely to be restored to self-fulfilment and the possession of what he himself produces. Paul's estimate of man's capacity is more radical in that it caters both for the socially destructive forces of self-assertion in us which reformism and even revolution cannot master, and for the need for a fresh endowment of spiritual resources from beyond ourselves if those better endowed by nature or education are not to assert themselves over us. The notion of the gifts of the Spirit opens to everyone, however limited in genetic endowment or social opportunity, the promise of being able to contribute to the upbuilding of a new structure of human relations. Such a mode of tackling the problems of oppression in human culture and society is an historical innovation of the first order. It may perhaps be called the first structural approach to human relations.

8

The Teacher as Moral Exemplar in Paul and in the Inscriptions of Ephesus

THE 'IMITATION OF Paul' is one of the struts in *Faith's Framework* that Donald Robinson has placed some stress upon. His structure of New Testament theology builds on 'Paul the exemplar'.[1] It is this modelling function imposed on the behaviour and experience of the apostle that helps to explain why certain early letters of Paul were kept, and became part of the new canon, even though they arose from very particular occasions. The structuring of New Testament theology is historical. It is not only a matter of elaborating ideas by argument from first principles, as with philosophy. The explanation is not essentially demonstrated by logic (as in the medical schools of the day). It arises experimentally, and is tested by life.

A contemporary historical analogy may thus help us to understand how this stance may have struck Paul's hearers in the Greek churches. If they were also attending the *ekklēsiai* of their cities, they would often have heard declaimed the ceremonial resolutions by which the tradition of civic virtue was imprinted upon the consciousness of the next generation. If they had idle moments in the market-place and colonnades they could scan the same texts inscribed on stone monuments, an array reaching back across centuries. Even the most detached inhabitant must have absorbed subliminally the overwhelming display of moral continuity the cities presented.

I. CIVIC VIRTUES IN EPHESUS

Public places were a parade-ground of statues. A policy of reciprocal interest was explicitly appealed to. The honour of a statue from the

---

[1] *Faith's Framework: The Structure of New Testament Theology* (Sutherland/ Exeter: Albatross/Paternoster, 1985), pp. 131–32.

grateful people was the incentive that would stimulate benefactors in the next generation. The immortality of renown underwrote public welfare. This policy is elaborately explained in the preamble of a decree in honour of C. Vibius Salutaris, passed by the Council and People of Ephesus in A.D. 104 or soon after.[2] He was an Ephesian who enjoyed Roman citizenship, and a career in the imperial administration. He was a repeated benefactor both of Artemis and of the city. Men who are 'devoted to honour' (*philotimoi*: Paul deflects the verb to quite different commitments, 1 Thess 4:11; 2 Cor 5:9; Rom 15:20) in public life, and have displayed the 'affection' (*storgē*: Paul once uses the adjective *philostorgoi*, Rom 12:10) of citizens who are 'genuinely' that (*gnēsioi*: a Pauline accent also, 2 Cor 8:8; Phil 2:20; 4:3; 1 Tim 1:2; Tit 1:4), must be honoured. Paul would have agreed: 'honour to whom honour is due' (Rom 13:7). But the Ephesians rely upon a principle foreign to him, that of reciprocity.

The honours are explicitly said to be 'reciprocal' (*amoibaiai*, line 9), in response to the 'affection' displayed by the 'genuine' citizens. The adjective is unique amongst the 3,000 inscriptions of Ephesus, but the sentiment is basic to them. Our inscription uses also the related verb and noun (lines 389, 392), which are commoner. The New Testament uses only the noun, of the reciprocation (of care) that children or grandchildren owe their widowed mother (1 Tim 5:4). But this is defined as 'an act of piety' (*eusebein*), acceptable in the sight of God. It is not conceived in terms of reciprocal self-interest. The same goes for the 'honour' of Romans 13:7. It is part of the order by which God maintains society.

The honours that reciprocate favours received are said by the Ephesians to be justified on two grounds. First, it is fitting that those who have already done well by the city should 'derive enjoyment from' (*apolauein*) that. The term is unique in the Ephesian inscriptions. But the benefactor's entitlement to enjoy the admiration of his fellow-citizens is the fundamental purpose of the civic inscriptions in the first place. The principle is criticised in the New Testament at 1 Timothy 6:17: wealth is not in fact a safe basis for the high and mighty, who should put their hope in God. He gives them everything richly for their 'enjoyment' (the same term, and only used here in the New Testament), and their wealth should be in good works, as they share it out and lay up treasure in heaven (v. 18). One might have thought the practical outcome was

---

[2] H. Wankel et al., *Die Inschriften von Ephesos*, vol. 1 (= *Inschriften griechischer Städte aus Kleinasien*, vol. 11) (Bonn: R. Habelt, 1979), no. 27 (first published in 1870), lines 8–14. This series provides the only extensive epigraphic documentation that we are ever likely to have for a major centre of Paul's ministry.

the same—a redistribution of wealth. But the approval in this case is to come from God; the political benefit to the donor is implicitly taken away; and the hard fact of excess wealth is accentuated. It is notable, on the other side, that the inscriptions, generated as they are by the studied use of wealth, absolutely avoid the characterisation of it in plain terms. Instead a courtly convention always describes the favours as acts of 'goodwill' *(eunoia)*, establishing the moral quality of the donor. Vibius is said to be 'distinguished in family and in worthiness', 'practising a good disposition', so as to 'adorn his superior advantages with serious-ness of character' (lines 15–19). Yet the whole inscription exists to reg-ister the details of his endowment of the city. The money has purchased merit.

The second justification for honouring benefactors is to stimulate others to 'compete' *(hamillasthai)* for such rewards (line 12). The term is once more unique here amongst the inscriptions of Ephesus, and not used in the New Testament at all. But it accurately pin-points one of the principal motives of civic generosity, to outshine one's peers in benefac-tions. Those who are zealous in honouring the goddess must be held in high regard by the city (line 13) to provide the incentive for others.

The ethical ideals of this civil contract were not only sanctified through the temple of the city's goddess (which functioned as a central bank), but taught in college (the gymnasium). The triple pillars of fi-nance, piety and training upon which the city was built are succinctly expressed in the funeral tribute to Heraclides Didymus of the first cen-tury A.D.[3] He is a 'benefactor' *(euergetēs)* of the people. This term nor-mally suffices to say it all. But in this case the donor is said to have shown his individual 'merit' *(aretē)* comprehensively. Three clauses then follow which spell this out. He showed 'piety' *(eusebeia)* to Artemis, and 'good-will' *(eunoia)* to the people. These are familiar enough elements in the formula. But between them stands an unusual tribute. Heraclides has been a benefactor of the people by reason also of the 'power' *(dynamis)* and 'trust' *(pistis)* shown in his 'learning' *(mathēma)*. This can hardly be construed as another form of financial gift. We do not know anything of Heraclides apart from this monument, but he must surely have been a professor in one of the schools of Ephesus. Since as a 'benefactor' he must have been financially generous, but would hardly have taken on the life of a teacher if he had had inherited means, one may suppose he had done very well at it. What then were the 'power' and 'trust' he showed? He was surely a sophist, specialising in the rhetorical training of tertiary

---

[3] *Inschriften von Ephesos*, vol. 3, 1980, no. 683A (first published in 1953).

students in the gymnasium. If so, he is being commemorated for the effectiveness of the skills in public leadership that he passed on to the next generation of young men from the well-to-do families of the capital of Asia. There are other tributes to teachers of this kind.

Around 140 B.C. Attalus II of Pergamum wrote to the Council and People of Ephesus praising one of their citizens.[4] The inscription does not preserve his name in full (it begins Aristo—), nor the reason for the king's writing to Ephesus (perhaps to secure some privilege for him). But the surviving lines formulate rather elegantly the principle of moral exemplification upon which Greek education relied. Aristo— had been judged 'worthy' *(axios)* by the king to look after the upbringing of his nephew, the future Attalus III (who was to bequeath the kingdom to Rome). He provided an 'appropriate' 'education' *(paideia)* for him. The king then explains that this arose not only from his 'skill' *(empeiria)* and 'tradition' *(paradosis)* with 'words' *(logoi)*, in which he was the superior of many, but also because in 'character' *(ēthos)* he was clearly very praiseworthy, and particularly suited to keeping company with the young man. Those of the younger generation who are 'naturally' *(ek physeōs)* 'gentlemen' *(kalokagathikoi)* are 'keen to emulate' *(zēlousi)* the 'life-styles' *(agōgai)* of their 'masters' *(epistatai)*. This is why not only the king, but the prince as well, has paid Aristo— 'compliments' *(episēmasiai)*.

Also from the second century B.C. comes a tribute by the Council and People of Ephesus to the gymnasiarch, Diodorus.[5] The thirty-six surviving lines are largely taken up by the citation of a speech made to the council by a deputation of students. (They had already, in their own union, resolved to set up a statue to Diodorus in the gymnasium, and have sent deputations both to the Council and to the People to co-opt their support as well.) It is a trend-setting showpiece of rhetorical training, as can be judged by the appearance of several terms that become hallmarks of the next couple of centuries—'reputation' *(axiōma)*, 'dignity' *(semnotēs)*.

Diodorus is concerned for the 'good bearing' *(eukosmia)* and 'manliness' *(euandria)* of the youth. He trains them in 'love of effort' *(philoponia)*, both bodily and psychic. He acts 'out of love of the good' *(philagathōs)*, 'neglecting nothing that relates to honour and glory, for the sake of the memorable and praiseworthy establishment of his existing preference *(haeresis)* for the best' (lines 22–24). It was his 'love of glory' *(philodoxia)* and 'righteousness' *(dikaiosynē)* that moved the people to endorse the statue. The young men want it 'with a view to ex-

---

[4] *Inschriften von Ephesos,* vol. 2, 1979, no. 202 (first published in 1964).
[5] *Inschriften von Ephesos,* vol. 1, 1979, no. 6 (first published in 1960).

horting' *(protrepomenoi)* everyone to become 'emulators' *(zēlōtai)* of the best practices.

These four inscriptions are each quite distinctive amongst the inscriptions of Ephesus. In no case are the particular circumstances exactly paralleled elsewhere, and each is strikingly rich in terms that were by no means routine. Yet we are dealing with a coherent ethical tradition. It is the mainstay of the long-established and flourishing social order of the Greek cities under the Roman hegemony. Fashions of expression may change, and individuals strive for distinction within its conventions, but it is fundamentally conservative. Any innovation is purely ceremonial. Certainly there is sharp criticism brought (in other inscriptions) against those who use their position extortionately, but there can be no question that the objective is to maintain the established order, and its privileges.

Paul also endorsed this stability. Social rank is one of the methods by which the world is governed under God. Yet at the same time a radical reordering of social relations is under way. It is being institutionalised within the churches, but Paul is already conscious that it will be noticed by outsiders. The privileges of education and wealth are being systematically discounted. A conflict of interest is arising over this within the churches.

II. FOLLOWING AND IMITATING

As with public education, Paul is developing a tradition that depends upon personal replication of its values. He both wishes to institute his practice as a tradition (2 Thess 2:15; 3:6; 1 Cor 11:2), and at the same time rejects the established ones (Gal 1:14; Col 2:8). In the Gospels the call is to 'follow' Jesus, but in Paul it is to 'imitate' him, through 'imitating' Paul. In neither case can it be shown that this reflects the pattern of the dominant culture. Neither type of expression is used for the process of social replication in the inscriptions of Ephesus, for example.

Yet it is not the words 'follow' and 'imitate' that are strange, nor the idea of following a master or imitating an ethical model in the sense of moral patterning. The two phrases come together in this sense in writers contemporary with Paul, where they are both clearly figures of speech for the same ideal. Arguing that Socrates may be called the disciple of Homer, Dio Chrysostom says:[6]

> . . . if a follower *(zēlōtēs)*, he would also be a pupil *(mathētēs)*. For whoever really follows anyone surely knows what that person was like, and by

---

[6] *Discourse* 55.4, trans. H. L. Crosby, Loeb Classical Library, vol. 4 (London: Heinemann, 1946), pp. 383, 385.

imitating *(mimoumenos)* his acts and words he tries as best he can to make himself like him.

Jewish writers were even willing to speak of the imitation of God, though that has been called 'the central paradox of Judaism'. For 'one can only imitate that of which one has an idea . . . but as soon as one forms an idea of God, it is no longer he whom one conceives'.[7] Philo explains that when Moses approached the thick cloud where God was, he entered 'into the unseen, invisible, incorporeal and archetypal essence of existing things'.[8]

> Thus he beheld what is hidden from the sight of mortal nature, and, in himself and his life displayed for all to see, he has set before us, like some well-wrought picture, a piece of work beautiful and godlike, a model *(paradeigma)* for those who are willing to copy *(mimeisthai)* it. Happy are they who imprint *(enapomaxasthai)* . . . that image *(typos)* in their souls.

Josephus writes similarly of the task of Moses:[9]

> . . . first to study the nature of God, and then, having contemplated his works with the eye of reason, to imitate *(mimeisthai)* so far as possible that best of all models *(paradeigma)* and endeavour to follow it *(katakolouthein)* . . . God, as the universal Father and Lord who beholds all things, grants to such as follow *(tois hepomenois)* him a life of bliss.

Already in the second century B.C., Aristeas has the Jewish spokesman answer the question of Ptolemy Philadelphus, 'How he might preserve his kingdom unimpaired to the end', with 'By imitating *(mimoumenos)* the constant gentleness of God'; and again, 'How he might be beyond outbursts of wrath', with 'You must realise that God governs the whole world with kindliness and without any passion; His example, Your Majesty, you must follow *(katakolouthein)*'.[10]

---

[7] M. Buber, 'Imitatio Dei', *Israel and the World: Essays in a Time of Crisis* (New York: Schocken Books, 1948), pp. 66–67. The reference, which I owe to H. D. Betz, is to p. 71 of this translation by G. Hort of the essay of 1926. Buber offers a way forward that is very suggestive for the understanding of the New Testament idea (pp. 76, 77): 'The secret of God which stood over Job's tent (Job 29:4) . . . can only be fathomed by suffering . . . only when the secret no longer stands over the tent, but breaks it, do we learn to know God's intercourse with us. And we learn to imitate God.'

[8] *Life of Moses* 1.28.158–59, trans. F. H. Colson, Loeb Classical Library, vol. 6 (London: Heinemann, 1935), p. 359.

[9] *Jewish Antiquities* 1.19, 20, trans. H. St. J. Thackeray, Loeb Classical Library, vol. 4 (London: Heinemann, 1930), p. 11.

[10] *Aristeas to Philocrates* 188, 254, trans. M. Hadas (New York: Harper & Brothers, 1951), pp. 175, 201.

Within the New Testament, however, the non-congruence of the calls to 'follow' *(akalouthein)* Jesus, but 'imitate' *(mimeisthai)* Paul, warns us not to assume that we are hearing a cliché of the times. The words are not interchangeable. In either case the meaning is peculiarly literal. Paul could not have asked his churches to follow him in the plain sense, as Jesus did with the disciples. The churches were expected to imitate Paul when he was not there, but following Jesus meant actually going after him.

Paul's call for imitation is unique. And it is only given to churches he had personally founded. He is not offering an ethical model for all in this particular term. There are, of course, numerous other ways in which he does mean to generalise from his teaching and practice, and it is in recognition of these that his various letters have been canonised.[11] How then does the call to 'follow' Jesus or 'imitate' Paul differ from the setting of an ethical pattern?

Jesus is sometimes addressed as *rabbi* (the Greek text using this loan-word), and the far commoner vocative *didaskale* ('teacher') no doubt represents this. In Luke he is several times addressed as *epistata* ('master'), the term used by Attalus (in the Ephesian inscription above) for the tutor of his nephew. The disciples *(mathētai)* thus seem to see themselves as students in a rabbinic school. But the repeated call to 'follow' Jesus sets them apart from rabbinic discipleship. Whatever the importance of the teaching and training, the test they must pass is whether to commit themselves to something radically different—a life dedicated to the coming Kingdom, stripped of the security and status that study normally bestowed. Nor was this simply a more drastic form of philosophy, as with the Cynics, for the call was to share personally the ambiguous prospects of their Master. Even the ultimate bonds were to be abandoned. To the one who said, 'Lord, let me first go and bury my father' (Matt 8:21), Jesus said, 'Follow me, and leave the dead to bury their dead.' This is not a discipleship of ethical modelling. Against Schulz and Betz, Hengel claims that 'there is no bridge from the rabbinate to Jesus'.[12]

The apocalyptic prophets, though offering at first sight an alternative categorisation for Jesus, are also fundamentally different. They aimed to lead out the masses, but Jesus avoided that in order to select a few who would go with him into the Kingdom. Nor, Hengel urges, can

---

[11] E.g. 1 Cor 4:6; Phil 4:9; for a full survey of the element of personal example in this see chapter 7 of B. Fiore, *Personal Example.*

[12] For this and the points in the following paragraph see pp. 86–87 of the English version of M. Hengel, *Nachfolgen und Nachahmen.*

the early church have read back such an idea into the Gospels, since it made no sense after the event to put the emphasis on a literal following of Jesus in his Messianic calling, when what was now required was a general guide to the life of faith.

Schulz argues that this has in fact emerged with Luke 14:27: 'Whoever does not bear his own cross and come after me, cannot be my disciple'. But the immediate context of this saying and of its parallels (Matt 10:38; Mark 8:34) shows that it is still decisively anchored in the immediate expectation of the Kingdom. With 1 Pet 2:21 a certain shift of perspective is noticeable. Christ's suffering is an 'example *(hypogrammos)*, that you should follow in *(epakolouthēsēte)* his footsteps', the immediate outcome being patient endurance. But the suffering is still only for 'a little while' (5:10) before 'the glory that is to be revealed' (5:1). The same applies to Rev 14:1, 'it is these who follow the Lamb wherever he goes', where, however, the accent has shifted to a life of personal purity.[13]

In the Apostolic Fathers, however, following has become an almost entirely ethical and disciplinary practice, detached even from the figure of Christ. Those that wait, says 1 Clement (35:4, 5), will receive a share of the promised gifts (alluding to 1 Cor 2:9):[14]

> But how shall this be, beloved? If our understanding be fixed faithfully on God; if we seek the things which are well-pleasing and acceptable to him . . . and follow *(akolouthēsōmen)* the way of truth . . .

The sacrifices and services must be at fixed times and hours (1 Clem 40:2–4). 'So then those who offer their oblations at the appointed seasons are blessed, for they follow the laws of the Master and do no sin.'

Clement may well not have in mind at all the call of Jesus to follow him, but merely be reflecting a conventional usage of the term. But this could hardly be said of Ignatius, when he writes to the Philadelphians (2:1, 2):

> And follow as sheep where the shepherd is. For there are many specious wolves who lead captive with evil pleasures the runners in God's race, but they will find no place if you are in unity.

This interpretation of the parable differs from that given by Jesus to the uncomprehending disciples (John 10:7–16) in several ways. As the

---

[13] For a tabulation of six different senses of 'following' in the Gospels, see pp. 115–17 of A. Schulz, *Nachfolge und Charisma*.

[14] Citations from 1 Clement and Ignatius below are generally taken from *The Apostolic Fathers*, trans. K. Lake, Loeb Classical Library, vol. 1 (London: Heinemann, 1912).

antithesis to the shepherd, the hireling has changed places with the wolves, a shift already contemplated in Paul's speech to the Ephesian elders (Acts 20:29, 30). The Pauline figure of the race (Acts 20:24 perhaps supplied the term *dromos)* has been brought in as the main picture of the life situation. But, most strikingly, the personal bond between shepherd and sheep (retained in Acts) has been lost to view in Ignatius, for whom 'following' the shepherd is understood as maintaining the solidarity of the flock in the good life. In his letter to the Smyrnaeans (8:1), Ignatius manages to dislocate the 'following' altogether from the shepherd: 'see that you all follow the bishop, as Jesus Christ follows the Father'. His focus has passed to ecclesiastical order.

A similar shift occurs in Ignatius with his treatment of the Pauline idea of imitation. There is no suggestion, of course, that one should imitate Paul. This confirms the observation that Paul had developed this particular point explicitly for the benefit of his own converts. But he had also linked their imitation of him with his of Christ (1 Cor 11:1; cf. 1 Thess 1:6), and there is a more general call to imitate God, as beloved children (Eph 5:1). Hebrews calls for imitation 'of those who through faith and patience inherit the promises' (6:12), and of the faith of 'those who spoke to you the word of God', that is, 'your leaders' (13:7). The beloved Gaius is urged, 'do not imitate evil but imitate good' (3 John 11). This increasingly broad notion of imitation helps us to understand how the idea appealed to Ignatius, who uses it more commonly than does Paul.

Clement of Rome (17:1) had called upon his audience to become imitators of the prophets, having in mind what the epistle to the Hebrews (11:37) had said about their wearing the skins of goats and sheep. This was a mark of humility, says Clement (16:17), of which the Lord himself had given an example *(hypogrammos).* Ignatius expresses the wish that all would imitate Burrhus, who was to carry back his letter to the Smyrnaeans (12:1). 'He is a pattern *(exemplarion)* of the ministry of God.' But it is rather with the direct imitation of God that Ignatius is concerned. The Ephesians (1:1) perfected that by sending their bishop, Onesimus, to see him. Ignatius wants them all to be like that (1:3). He had already received Crocus (2:1) as an example *(exemplarion)* of their love. To the Trallians (1:2) he says that their bishop, Polybius, had conveyed their godly 'benevolence' *(eunoia—a gift of money?),* which proved that they were imitators of God. Ignatius comments to the Magnesians (10:1) on the disaster it would be if God should imitate us—to avoid that we should become his disciples *(mathētai),* and learn to live according to Christianity *(Christianismos),* that tell-tale abstraction which first appears in his letters.

With the imitation of Christ, however, we can see that Ignatius has not wholly transposed the motif to the ethical plane. The Ephesians (10:2) are not to strive to 'counter-imitate' their critics, but to return gentleness for cruelty. Thus, we should become their brothers and strive to be imitators of Christ, to see who might suffer more wrong, be more destitute or more despised, says Ignatius (10:3). He is both grasping Paul's point and at the same time schematising it. He was, of course, like Paul, seized by the identification with Christ that he anticipated in his martyrdom. Pleading with the Romans (6:3) not to intervene in his favour, he begs, 'Let me be an imitator of the passion of my God'. But there is a more institutionalised imitation that also looms large in his mind. He writes to the Philadelphians (7:2) the message he has from the Spirit:

> Do nothing without the bishop, keep your flesh as the temple of God, love unity, flee divisions, be imitators of Jesus Christ, as he was also of the Father.

III. THE IMITATION OF PAUL

What, then, is distinctive with the imitation of Paul? The earliest instances of this terminology (1 Thess 1:6; 2:14) show two features that were never exactly repeated, whether in Paul or elsewhere. First, the imitation has already occurred—it does not arise as an exhortation to an on-going style of life. Secondly, there is a network of imitation, rather than one sequence in which all follow. The Thessalonians became imitators of 'us', not of Paul alone, but also of his fellow-authors of the letter, Silvanus and Timothy, 'and of the Lord' (1:6). They also became imitators of 'the churches of God in Judaea' (2:14).

In either passage the term 'imitators' *(mimētai)* arises with reference to the preaching of the gospel, and to its effects. It can be seen to be the word of God (not only the words of the preacher) because it 'is at work' *(energētai)* in the believers (2:13) and accompanied by a 'power' *(dynamis)* which can be assessed by 'what kind of men we proved to be' (1:5). Specifically, it appears to be the subsequent 'affliction' *(thlipsis)* (1:6) that is common to all believers and verifies their 'imitation' of the others, 'for you suffered the same things from your own countrymen' (2:14). In either passage the final allusion is to God's wrath (1:10; 2:16): it seems that the 'affliction' of believers (and consequential 'imitation' of each other) is a reaction against the judgment of God that the gospel preaching ushers in for the whole world (as explained by Paul in 2 Thess 1:4–10). As with the call to the disciples to 'follow' Jesus, then, the 'imitation' of Paul does not begin as the institutionalisation of a tradition of training, but is a sign of the imminent establishment of the kingdom of God.

This is not to say that Paul is not already conscious of the need for teaching 'traditions' (2 Thess 2:15; 3:6). The very fact that he has seized upon their being 'imitators' constitutes them also an 'example' *(typos)* for other believers, in respect of their 'trust' *(pistis*—in the sense of loyalty?) (1 Thess 1:7, 8). This is explicitly said to be a supplementary benefit to the sounding out of the word of the Lord, which is the principal effect of their being 'imitators'. Subsequently, however, the obligation to 'imitate' arises from the 'tradition' (2 Thess 3:6, 7), and relates to Paul's principle of living at his own expense, which he had adopted 'to give you in our conduct an example *(typos)* to imitate' (v. 9).

The same issue provokes Paul into a protest against the comfortable life of the Corinthians (1 Cor 4:12). Adopting the stance of their 'father' (vv. 14, 15), Paul urges them to be 'imitators' of him (v. 16). Timothy has been sent to remind them of his 'ways in Christ, as I teach them everywhere in every church' (v. 17). For those who still disagree, he threatens a test, which reflects his continuing sense of the imminence of God's direct rule, 'for the kingdom of God does not consist in talk but in power' (v. 20). There is a pattern of life indeed, but it is not seen in terms of education or ethical rules. A kindred practice gives rise to the injunction, 'Be imitators of me, as I am of Christ' (1 Cor 11:1). It is the matter of curbing one's own liberty of conscience for the sake of another's scruple (10:23–30). Paul justifies this also in terms of the priority of other people's salvation (vv. 31–33).

The abandonment of rights (in this case the privileges derived from circumcision) 'for the sake of Christ' (Phil 3:7) leads Paul into one of his great visions of identification with Christ in suffering (v. 10). The goal is indeed to be made perfect *(teleiousthai),* but in the resurrection (vv. 11, 12), so that the mark of being 'perfect' *(teleioi)* (v. 15) lies in the very abandonment of the security of this life. To this end Paul invites the 'brethren' to become 'joint-imitators' *(symmimētai)* of him, and watch those who so live *(peripatountes)* as they have an 'example' *(typos)* in 'us' (v. 17—drawing Timothy into the pattern?). Others are living as 'enemies of the cross of Christ' (v. 18) because they have not yet identified themselves with the 'community' *(politeuma)* in the heavens (v. 20). The emphatic rejection of a civil solution here shows that Paul's concept of imitation has not in the end moved far from its eschatological purpose.

Much the same applies to the Pastoral Epistles, with their conceptually related terminology. Paul had been made a 'pattern' *(hypotypōsis)* for those who were to believe (1 Tim 1:16), and the same term expresses the 'pattern of sound words' that had been entrusted to him (2 Tim 1:12, 13). His personal suffering and great expectations again provide the context (v. 11). But there is now also an articulated pattern of life. Timothy is to be an 'example' *(typos)* to the believers in 'speech, conduct, love, faith and purity' (1 Tim 4:12), and Titus even more comprehensively (Titus 2:7). (For Peter, setting the example, 1 Pet 5:3, was the alternative for elders to domineering over their flock.) There is a good 'doctrine' *(didaskalia)* dealing with many matters, that Timothy has 'followed' *(parēkolouthēkas)* (1 Tim 4:6); specifically, it is Paul's doctrine he has 'followed' (2 Tim 3:10), along with his 'life-style' *(agōgē)*, his 'aim in life' *(prothesis)*, as well as various virtues—but still not forgetting his persecution and sufferings (v. 11). Timothy has 'followed' these too, because they provide a key to understanding it all (v. 12). To the Lord's servant (2 Tim 2:24, 25) and to the grace of God itself (Titus 2:11) is assigned an educative function with an ethical outcome in terms that would have appealed directly to the Ephesian public (Titus 2:12). While awaiting their 'blessed hope' (v. 13) the people of God is to be an 'emulator' *(zēlōtēs)* of good deeds (v. 14). Peter makes the same point, but having his eye on self-defence against a sceptical public (1 Pet 3:13). Paul had made much of this word (also a favourite at Ephesus) but in quite different connections. He is very conscious of its ambiguities: it's fine if in a good cause (Gal 4:18), but one can go too far (Gal 1:14)—love does not 'emulate' (1 Cor 13:4).

What sort of example, then, might the Ephesians have seen in Paul? The writer of Acts professes to have been present at Paul's farewell speech to the elders of Ephesus (Acts 20:18–35). It is possible to argue that 'the parts of speaker and eye-witness recorder fell so close together from the outset that there is little scope for the attempt to separate their contributions'.[15] Paul reminds them of his lifestyle in Ephesus (v. 18). It was governed by humiliation at the hands of his opponents (v. 19). More is expected (v. 23). He does not rate his life highly, except to complete his race *(dromos)* to preach the gospel (v. 24). He has felt a responsibility for their very lives (v. 26). There will be troubles to come (v. 29). He has taken no advantage of their hospitality (v. 34). This leads to his final charge (v. 35):

> In all things I have shown you that by so toiling one must help the weak, remembering the words of the Lord Jesus, how he said, 'It is more blessed to give than to receive'.

---

[15] C. J. Hemer, 'The Speeches in Acts: I: The Ephesian Elders at Miletus', *Tyndale Bulletin* 40, 1989, pp. 77–85.

The letter traditionally assigned to the Ephesians (though it could originally have been addressed to Hierapolis and Laodicea—Col 4:13, 16)[16] expresses the essence of the Pauline doctrine (Eph 5:1, 2):

> Therefore be imitators of God, as beloved children. And walk in love, as Christ loved us and gave himself up for us, a fragrant offering and sacrifice to God.

These words conclude a lengthy description of the way the Gentiles 'walk', in the futility of their minds, and of the new life in Christ (Eph 4:17–32). It does not constitute so much a systematic ethical model as a pinpointing of the sources of the two lifestyles, with illustrative examples. The pattern is not set by Paul, but by God himself, as Father. It was Christ's self-sacrifice that manifested the true meaning of the love which now shapes our relations with each other.

Why, then, had Paul called for 'imitation' of himself? Although the term, as Betz has argued, may seem to echo the language of the mystery cults, his experience was no merely spiritual re-enactment or contemplation of Christ's. It cost him also the most extreme physical and social rebuffs. He could not, however, claim to 'follow' Christ, for he had appeared to him only 'as to one untimely born' (1 Cor 15:8). The idea of imitation offered a means of expressing the replication of Christ's experience, especially in social relations, that could be passed on in turn to those who believed in him. It created a tradition that could endorse much of the common stock of good behaviour in the public community. But its motivation was fundamentally different. In particular the call to sacrifice one's own reasonable interest to a higher objective was a bewildering up-ending of the ethical life as the Greeks had refined it.[17]

Publications since 1962 which have been generally drawn upon in preparation of this study:

E. Best, *Paul and His Converts* (Edinburgh: T&T Clark, 1988), pp. 59–72 ('Paul as Model').

H. D. Betz, *Nachfolge und Nachahmung Jesu Christi im Neuen Testament* (Tübingen: Mohr, 1967), passim.

W. P. de Boer, *The Imitation of Paul: An Exegetical Study* (Kampen: J. H. Kok N.V., 1962), passim.

---

[16] A. T. Lincoln, *Ephesians* (Dallas: Word Books, 1990), pp. 1–4.

[17] E. A. Judge, 'Cultural Conformity and Innovation in Paul: Some Clues from Contemporary Documents', *Tyndale Bulletin* 35, 1984, pp. 3–24.

B. Fiore, *The Function of Personal Example in the Socratic and Pastoral Epistles* (Rome: Biblical Institute Press, 1986).

P. Gutierrez, *La paternité spirituelle selon Saint Paul* (Paris: J. Gabalda, 1968), pp. 178–88 ('L'appel à l'imitation').

M. Hengel, *Nachfolge und Charisma: Eine exegetisch-religionsgeschichtliche Studie zu Mt 8:21f. und Jesu Ruf in die Nachfolge* (Berlin: Verlag Alfred Töpelmann, 1968), trans. J. C. G. Greig, *The Charismatic Leader and His Followers* (Edinburgh: T&T Clark, 1981), pp. 1–2, 84–88.

G. Lyons, *Pauline Autobiography: Towards a New Understanding* (Atlanta: Scholars Press, 1985), pp. 190–201 ('Paul's Exemplary Ethos').

A. Schulz, *Nachfolgen und Nachahmen: Studien über das Verhältnis der neutestamentlichen Jüngerschaft zur urchristlichen Vorbildethik* (München: Kösel-Verlag 1962), passim.

J. H. Schütz, *Paul and the Anatomy of Apostolic Authority* (Cambridge: CUP, 1975), pp. 226–32 ('The Imitation of Paul and of Christ').

D. Stanley, 'Imitation in Paul's Letters: Its Significance for His Relationship to Jesus and to His Own Christian Foundations', in P. Richardson and J. C. Hurd, eds., *From Jesus to Paul: Studies in Honour of Francis Wright Beare* (Waterloo: Wilfrid Laurier University Press, 1984), pp. 127–41.

A Comprehensive Bibliography of the Publications of Edwin A. Judge

COMPILED BY DAVID M. SCHOLER

IT IS MY intent to provide here a complete record of E. A. Judge's publications in chronological order. Under each year, items are arranged in the order of books, articles, book reviews. In the case of items that appeared in more than one place, cross references are provided to entry numbers. In a few cases, items for newspapers and other non-academic sources have been omitted, as well as a few items unrelated to the study of ancient history. In spite of the attempt to be accurate and inclusive, I know, as a bibliographer, that some things always seem to be missed and/or are listed with some errors. All shortcomings are my responsibility.

1956

1. "The Penetration of Graeco-Roman Society by Christianity," *Tyndale House Bulletin* 1 (1956): 5–6.

1958

2. "Amicitia and Clientela," *Bulletin of the Classical Association of NSW* 4 (1958): 8–14.
3. "Some Factors Affecting Success in Roman Politics," *Iris: Newssheet of the Classical Association of Victoria* 44 (1958): 3–4.
4. "'The Times of This Ignorance': Christian Education as a Reappraisal of History," *Journal of Christian Education* 1 (1958): 81–87, 127–36; 2 (1959), 28–31.

1959

5. " 'Contemptu famae contemni virtutes': On the Morality of Self-Advertisement among the Romans," *Mens Eadem* (Sydney, 1959), 24–29.

6. Review of E. M. Blaiklock, *The Acts of the Apostles: An Historical Commentary*, in *Journal of Christian Education* 2 (1959): 109–11.

1960

7. *The Social Pattern of the Christian Groups in the First Century: Some Prolegomena to the Study of New Testament Ideas of Social Obligation*. London: Tyndale, 1960. Equals *18*, cf. *144*.

8. "Christianity within the Framework of Ancient Society," *The Christian Graduate* 13 (1960): 53–57.

9. "The Early Christians as a Scholastic Community," *Journal of Religious History* 1 (1960/1961): 4–15; 125–37. Equals *69*.

10. Review of J. C. O'Neill, *The Theology of Acts in Its Historical Setting*, in *Journal of Religious History* 1 (1960): 152–54.

1961

11. "The Literature of Roman Political Self-Advertisement," paper summarized in *Proceedings of the Seventh Congress of AULLA* (Christchurch, 1961), 24.

12. "The Roman Theory of Historical Degeneration," *Hermes* 58 (1961): 5–8.

13. Review of M. Turnbull, *The Changing Land*, in *Teaching History* 3 (October 1961): 16–17.

14. Review of T. F. Glasson, *Greek Influence in Jewish Eschatology*, in *Reformed Theological Review* 20 (1961): 88.

1962

15. Articles in *The New Bible Dictionary* (ed. J. D. Douglas et al.; London: Inter-Varsity Fellowship,1962): "Achaia," 9; "Alexander the Great," 23–24; "Asia," 98; "Augustus," 111; "Bithynia," 158; "Caesar," 174; "Caesar's Household," 175; "Claudius," 238; "Colony," 242; "Government 2. In the New Testament," 489–90; "Greece," 493–94; "Judgment-Seat," 680; "Julius," 680; "Jupiter," 680; "Lystra," 761; "Macedonia," 764; "Mitylene," 832; "Mysia," 856; "Nero," 877–78; "Orator," 912; "Phrygia," 994–95; "Pontus," 1010; "Rhodes," 1096; "Roman Empire," 1099–1101; "Rome," 1105–7; "Rulers of the City," 1108; "Serjeants," 1161; "Slave II.

In the New Testament," 1198–99; "Theatre," 1270; "Thessalonica," 1272; "Thrace," 1274; "Tiberius," 1275–76; "Town Clerk," 1287.

1963

16. "Contemporary Political Models for the Inter-relations of the New Testament Churches," *Reformed Theological Review* 22 (1963): 65–76.

17. " 'Signs of the Times': The Role of the Portentous in Classical and Apostolic Narrative," *SCM Journal* 1 (1963): 20–24.

1964

18. *Christliche Gruppen in nichtchristlicher Gesellschaft: Die Sozialstruktur christlicher Gruppen im ersten Jahrhundert.* Übersetzt von Hilde Nordsieck. (Neue Studienreihe 4.) Wuppertal: R. Brockhaus, 1964. Equals 7.

19. "Problems of 'General Religious Teaching,'" *Journal of Christian Education* 7 (1964): 106–15.

20. "Roman Literary Memorials," paper summarized in *Proceedings of the Ninth Congress of AULLA* (Melbourne, 1964), 28–30.

21. Review of W. Warde Fowler, *Social Life in Rome in the Age of Cicero,* in *Teaching History* 12 (December 1964): 15–16.

1965

22. "The Place of Eyewitness Accounts in Classical History," *Teaching History* 13 (May 1965): 23–24.

1966

23. "Ancient History in forms V and VI," *Teaching History* 16 (May 1966): 5–6.

24. "The Conflict of Educational Aims in the New Testament," *Journal of Christian Education* 9 (1966): 32–45.

25. "The Origin of the Church at Rome: A New Solution?" *Reformed Theological Review* 25 (1966): 81–94 [with G. S. R. Thomas].

26. Review of F. V. Filson, *A New Testament History,* in *Reformed Theological Review* 24 (1966): 65–67.

1967

27. "Christian Education in the Early Church," *Syllabus for the Certificate in Christian Education* (Sydney, 1967), 1–8.

28. "Res publica restituta," paper summarized in *AULLA: Proceedings and Papers of the Eleventh Congress* (Sydney, 1967), 26–27.

1968

29. "Augustus' Conception of His Place in Roman History," *Ancient History Study Sessions of the HTA* (Sydney; July–August 1968): 30–48.

30. "Paul's Boasting in Relation to Contemporary Professional Practice," *Australian Biblical Review* 16 (1968): 37–50.

1969

31. "The Cities of the Bible/The Cities of the New Testament," Appendix One in *The Zondervan Pictorial Bible Atlas* (ed. E. M. Blaiklock; Grand Rapids: Zondervan, 1969): "Alexandria," 360–62; "Antioch of Pisidia," 362; "Antioch of Syria," 362–64; "Athens," 364–65; "Caesarea," 366–67; "Corinth," 368–69; "Damascus," 369–70; "Derbe," 370–71; "Ephesus," 371–72; "Iconium," 373; "Joppa," 380; "Laodicea," 380; "Lystra," 380–81; "Perga," 382; "Pergamum," 382; "Philadelphia," 382; "Philippi," 382–83; "Salamis," 384; "Sardis," 384; "Smyrna," 385; "Thessalonica," 385; "Thyatira," 385–86; "Troas," 386.

32. "The Hellenistic Empires," Chapter 12 in *The Zondervan Pictorial Bible Atlas* (ed. E. M. Blaiklock; Grand Rapids: Zondervan, 1969), 227–47.

33. "Judah's War of Independence," Chapter 13 in *The Zondervan Pictorial Bible Atlas* (ed. E. M. Blaiklock; Grand Rapids: Zondervan, 1969), 249–71.

1970

34. "First Impressions of St Paul," *Prudentia* 2 (1970): 52–58.

35. "The Gospel and Social Change," *InterVarsity* [Sydney] (1970): 4–7.

1971

36. "The Decrees of Caesar at Thessalonica," *Reformed Theological Review* 30 (1971): 1–7.

37. "Documents of Augustan Rome," *Ancient Society* 1:3 (1971): 20–38. Reprinted in *90, 113.*

38. "A Historian Answers the Question," in *Why I Am Still a Christian* (ed. E. M. Blaiklock; Grand Rapids: Zondervan, 1971), 97–108.

39. "The Set Authors for Ancient History: Some Current Translations," *Ancient Society* 1:1 (1971): 19–31.

40. "Tribute to David Geoffrey Evans," *Ancient Society* 1:1 (1971): 2–3.

41. Review of B. F. Harris, ed., *Auckland Classical Essays*, in *Ancient Society* 1:3 (1971): 39–42.

1972

42. "Demythologizing the Church: What Is the Meaning of 'the Body of Christ'?" *Interchange* 11 (1972): 155–67.

43. "Reflections from Germany upon Ancient History Today," *Ancient Society* 2:4 (1972): 27–42. Equals *51*.

44. "St Paul and Classical Society," *Jahrbuch für Antike und Christentum* 15 (1972): 19–36.

45. Review of F. F. Bruce, *New Testament History*, in *Journal of Religious History* 7 (1972): 163–65.

46. Review of Bo Reicke, *The New Testament Era*, in *TSF Bulletin* 64 (1972): 31–32.

1973

47. "'Antike und Christentum': Some Recent Work from Cologne," *Prudentia* 5 (1973): 1–13.

48. "Antike und Christentum: Towards a Definition of the Field," *Proceedings and Papers of the Fifteenth Congress of the Australasian Universities Language and Literature Association* (Sydney, 1973), 7.14. Superseded by *67*.

49. "St. Paul and Socrates," *Interchange* 14 (1973): 106–16.

50. "'Veni Vidi Vici', and the Inscription of Cornelius Gallus," *Vestigia* 17 (1973): 571–73 = *Akten des VI. Internationalen Kongresses für griechische und lateinische Epigraphik, München 1972*. Reprinted in *90, 113*.

1974

51. "Reflections from Germany upon Ancient History Today," *Mitteilungen der Alexander von Humboldt-Stiftung* 28 (1974), 13–20. Equals *43*.

52. "'Res Publica Restituta': A Modern Illusion?" in *Polis and Imperium: Studies in Honour of Edward Togo Salmon* (ed. J. A. S. Evans; Toronto: Hakkert, 1974), 279–311. Reprinted in *90, 113*.

53. "St Paul as a Radical Critic of Society," *Interchange* 16 (1974): 191–203.

1975

54. Articles in *The Zondervan Pictorial Encyclopedia of the Bible* (ed. M. C. Tenney et al.; 5 vols. Grand Rapids: Zondervan, 1975); all articles from Volume 1: "Alexander," 97–99; "Alexander Balas," 99; "Alexander the Son of Simon of Cyrene," 99; "Alexander the Member of the High-Priestly Family," 99; "Alexander the Jewish Spokesman at Ephesus," 99; "Alexander 'Delivered to Satan,'" 99; "Alexander the Coppersmith," 100; "Antioch, Chalice of," 182–83; "Antioch of Pisidia," 183–84; "Antioch in Syria," 185–89; "Antiochians," 189.

55. "The Acts of the Apostles," *Ancient Society* 5:2 (1975): 66–72.

56. "How to Check on a Translation," *Ancient Society* 5:2 (1975): 103–9.

57. Review of Alan Cameron, *Porphyrius the Charioteer,* in *Ancient Society* 5:2 (1975): 118–19.

58. Review of Arnold Toynbee, *Constantine Porphyrogenitus and His World,* in *Ancient Society* 5:2 (1975): 120–21.

1976

59. "Cicero, Selected Letters," in *Papers of the Macquarie University Continuing Education Conference for Ancient History Teachers* (Sydney, 1976), 135–40.

1977

60. "Caesar's Son and Heir," in *Papers of the Macquarie University Continuing Education Conference for Ancient History Teachers* (Sydney, 1977), 76–101. Reprinted in *90, 113.*

61. "The Earliest Use of Monachos for 'Monk' (P. Coll. Youtie 77) and the Origins of Monasticism," *Jahrbuch für Antike und Christentum* 20 (1977): 72–89.

62. "Papyrus Documentation of Church and Community in Egypt to the Mid-Fourth Century," *Jahrbuch für Antike und Christentum* 20 (1977): 47–71 [with S. R. Pickering].

63. "Self and Status in Greek and New Testament Thought," *Values Education* [University of Waikato, Hamilton] (1977), 111–26.

64. "Some Suggestions on Moral Education," *Values Education* [University of Waikato, Hamilton] (1977), 127–37.

1978

65. "Biblical Papyri Prior to Constantine: Some Cultural Implications of Their Physical Form," *Prudentia* 10 (1978): 1–13 [with S. R. Pickering].

66. "Julius Caesar's Solution to Rome's Problems," in *Papers of the Macquarie University Continuing Education Conference for Ancient History Teachers* (Sydney, 1978), 1–29.

1979

67. "'Antike und Christentum': Towards a Definition of the Field: A Bibliographical Survey," *ANRW* Principat 23/1 (1979): 3–58.

68. "Augustus in the Res Gestae," in *Papers of the Macquarie University Continuing Education Conference for Ancient History Teachers* (Sydney, 1979): 1–43. Reprinted in *90, 113*.

69. "Die frühen Christen als scholastische Gemeinschaft," in *Zur Soziologie des Urchristentums: Ausgewählte Beiträge zum frühchristlichen Gemeinschaftsleben in seiner gesellschaftlichen Umwelt* (ed. Wayne A. Meeks; trans. G. Memmert; Munich: Kaiser, 1979), 131–64. Equals *9*.

70. Review of R. M. Grant, *Early Christianity and Society*, in *Reformed Theological Review* 38 (1979): 55–56.

1980

71. *The Conversion of Rome: Ancient Sources of Modern Social Tensions.* (Publications of the Macquarie Ancient History Association 1.) North Ryde, NSW: Macquarie Ancient History Association, 1980.

72. "Augustus on Roman History," in *Papers of the Macquarie University Continuing Education Conference for Ancient History Teachers* (Sydney, 1980), 1–24. Reprinted in *90, 113* as "The Eulogistic Inscriptions of the Augustan Forum."

73. "The Social Identity of the First Christians: A Question of Method in Religious History," *Journal of Religious History* 11:2 (1980): 201–17.

74. Review of E. A. Livingstone, ed., *The Concise Oxford Dictionary of the Christian Church*, in *Journal of Christian Education* 67 (1980): 59–60.

1981

75. "The Date of Ezana, the 'Constantine' of Ethiopia," §94 bis in *New Documents Illustrating Early Christianity* 1 (1981): 143–44.

76. "The Earliest Attested Monk," §81 in *New Documents Illustrating Early Christianity* 1 (1981): 124–26.

77. "Fourth-Century Monasticism in the Papyri," in *Proceedings of the XVIth International Congress of Papyrology, New York, 24–31 July 1980* (ed. R. S. Bagnall et al.; Chico: Scholars Press, 1981), 613–20.

78. "Legislation on Abortion in the Ancient World," *Genesis Review* 1:1 (1981): 7–15.

79. "Preface" to *New Documents Illustrating Early Christianity* 1 (1981): iv–v.

80. "The Regional *kanon* for Requisitioned Transport," §9 in *New Documents Illustrating Early Christianity* 1 (1981): 36–45.

81. "Setting the Record Straight: Alternative Documents of a Protest in the Roman Army of Egypt," in *Papers of the Macquarie University Continuing Education Conference for Ancient History Teachers* (Sydney, 1981), 121–31.

82. "A State Schoolteacher Makes a Salary Bid," §26 in *New Documents Illustrating Early Christianity* 1 (1981): 72–78.

1982

83. *Rank and Status in the World of the Caesars and St. Paul.* University of Canterbury Publications 29. Christchurch: University of Canterbury, 1982.

84. "Divine Constantine," §107 in *New Documents Illustrating Early Christianity* 2 (1982): 191–92.

85. "Government in New Testament Times," in *The Book of Bible Knowledge* (London, 1982), 153–59.

86. "Greek Names of Latin Origin," §84 in *New Documents Illustrating Early Christianity* 2 (1982): 106–8.

87. "In What Sense Did the Roman Republic Collapse?" in *Papers of the Macquarie University Continuing Education Conference for Ancient History Teachers* (Sydney, 1982), 70–79.

88. "Moral Terms in the Eulogistic Tradition," §83 in *New Documents Illustrating Early Christianity* 2 (1982): 105–6.

89. "Preface" to *New Documents Illustrating Early Christianity* 2 (1982): 1.

1983

90. *Augustus and Roman History: Documents and Papers for Student Use* (Macquarie University, Sydney, 1983). Includes reprints of *37, 50, 52, 60, 68, 72*; cf. second ed., *113*.

91. "Christian Innovation and Its Contemporary Observers," in *History and Historians in Late Antiquity* (ed. B. Croke and A. M. Emmett; Sydney/New York: Pergamon, 1983), 13–29.

92. "The Interaction of Biblical and Classical Education in the Fourth Century," *Journal of Christian Education* 77 (1983): 31–37.

93. "The Reaction against Classical Education in the New Testament," *Journal of Christian Education* 77 (1983), 7–14. Equals *105, 149*.

94. (a) "Social Status in Church Life"; (b) "Did the Apostles Bow to Caesar?" (c) "A Sceptical Look at Worship in the New Testament," in *The New Testament World: Seminar Papers for Course 08.12 of the Continuing Education Program* (Macquarie University, Sydney, 1983).

1984

95. "Cultural Conformity and Innovation in Paul: Some Clues from Contemporary Documents," *Tyndale Bulletin* 35 (1984): 3–24.

96. "Gesellschaft und Christentum III: Neues Testament," in *Theologische Realenzyklopädie*, vol. 12 (Berlin and New York: Walter de Gruyter, 1984), 764–69.

97. "Gesellschaft und Christentum IV: Alte Kirche," in *Theologische Realenzyklopädie*, vol. 12 (Berlin and New York: Walter de Gruyter, 1984), 769–73.

98. "The Infallibility of Scripture," *Issues in the Authority of Scripture* (Zadok Centre, Series 2, Papers, T 21; Canberra, 1984), 12–14.

99. "New Documents of Triumviral Foreign Policy," in *Papers of the Macquarie University Continuing Education Conference for Ancient History Teachers* (Sydney, 1984), 39–57.

100. "Selection Criteria for the *Corpus Papyrorum Christianorum*," in *Atti del XVII Congresso Internazionale di Papirologia, Napoli, 19–26 Maggio, 1983* (ed. M. Gigante; Naples: Centro Internazionale per lo studio dei papiri ercolanesi, 1984), 117–22.

1985

101. "The Churches and the Teaching of Paul on Women," in *Women in the World of the New Testament: Seminar Papers for Course 08.05 of the Continuing Education Program* (Macquarie University, Sydney, 1985), 8–16.

102. "The House Next to the Augustan Forum," paper summarized in *AULLA XXIII Conference Proceedings and Papers* (Melbourne, 1985), 10–11.

103. "'The Most Important Part of Roman History'—Cornelius Gallus on Augustus?" in *Papers of the Macquarie University Continuing Education Conference for Ancient History Teachers* (Sydney, 1985), 60–71.

104. "On Judging the Merits of Augustus," *Colloquy* 49 (Center for Hermeneutical Studies in Hellenistic and Modern Culture, Berkeley, Calif., 1985). Reprinted in *113*.

105. "The Reaction against Classical Education in the New Testament," *Evangelical Review of Theology* 9 (1985): 166–74. Equals *93, 149*.

106. "Response to Bruce J. Malina on the Gospel of John in Sociolinguistic Perspective," *Colloquy* 48 (Center for Hermeneutical Studies in Hellenistic and Modern Culture, Berkeley, Calif., 1985), 24–29.

1986

107. "Introduction" to Gordon Moyes, *Discovering Paul* (Sydney: Albatross, 1986), 8–9.

108. "Jesus Outside the Gospels," in *History and the Gospels: Seminar Papers for Course 08.06 of the Continuing Education Program* (Macquarie University, Sydney, 1985), 12–26.

109. "The Quest for Mercy in Late Antiquity," in *God Who Is Rich in Mercy: Essays Presented to D. B. Knox* (ed. P. T. O'Brien and D. G. Peterson; Homebush West, NSW: Lancer Books, 1986), 107–21.

110. "Roman Administration and the Trial of Jesus," in *History and the Gospels: Seminar Papers for Course 08.06 of the Continuing Education Program* (Macquarie University, Sydney, 1985) [pages unknown].

111. "A Tribute to B. F. Harris," *Ancient Society* 16.1 (1986): 2–7.

112. "'We Have No King but Caesar'—When Was Caesar First Seen as a King?" in *Papers of the Macquarie University Continuing Education Conference for Ancient History Teachers* (Sydney, 1986), 108–19. Reprinted in *113*.

1987

113. *Augustus and Roman History: Documents and Papers for Student Use*, 2nd ed. (Macquarie University, Sydney, 1987). Second ed. of *90*; includes reprints of *37, 50, 52, 60, 68, 72, 104, 112*.

114. "Agrippina as Ruler of Rome?" in *Papers of the Macquarie University Continuing Education Conference for Ancient History Teachers* (Sydney, 1987), 123–30. Equals *118*.

115. "A Latin Inscription in the Ancient History Teaching Collection," *Ancient Society* 17:1 (1987): 4.

116. "The Magical Use of Scripture in the Papyri," in *Perspectives on Language and Text: Essays and Poems in Honor of Francis I. Andersen's Sixtieth Birthday, July 28, 1985* (ed. E. W. Conrad and E. G. Newing; Winona Lake, Ind.: Eisenbrauns, 1987), 339–49.

117. "Πραΰτης," §80 in *New Documents Illustrating Early Christianity* 4 (1987): 169–70.

1988

118. "Agrippina as Ruler of Rome?" *Teaching History* 22:1 (1988): 13–16. Equals *114.*

119. "Tiberius Gracchus and Numantia," in *Papers of the Macquarie University Continuing Education Conference for Ancient History Teachers* (Sydney, 1988), 33–41.

120. "Why They Were Left Out: The Formation of the Canon," in *Papers of the Society for Early Christianity Seminar 'Books They Left Out'* (Sydney, 1988), 1–20; summarized in *Newsletter* 3 (1988), 3–4.

1989

121. "The Beginning of Religious History," *Journal of Religious History* 15 (1989): 394–412.

122. "The Gentile Response to Judaism in the First Century," in *Papers of the Society for Early Christianity Seminar 'Jews and Christians: The First-Century Dilemma'* (Sydney, 1989), 19–27; summarized in *Newsletter* 6 (1989): 5–6.

123. "Tiberius Caesar: The Refusal of Power," in *Papers of the Macquarie University Continuing Education Conference for Ancient History Teachers* (Sydney, 1989), 73–78.

1990

124. "Athens and Jerusalem," in *Past, Present and Future: Ancient World Studies in Australia* (ed. R. K. Sinclair; Sydney: Australian Society for Classical Studies, 1990), 90–98.

125. "Julius Caesar: His Place in Roman History," in *Papers of the Macquarie University Continuing Education Conference for Ancient History Teachers* (Sydney, 1990), 35–46.

126. "The Mark of the Beast," in *Papers of the Society for Early Christianity Seminar 'The Book of Revelation in Its Roman Setting'* (Sydney, 1990), 29–30; summarized in *Newsletter* 10 (1990), 9–11. Cf. *130.*

127. "Papyri," in *Encyclopedia of Early Christianity* (ed. E. Ferguson et al.; New York & London: Garland, 1990), 686–91.

1991

128. "Benefactors at Ephesus: Ethical Ideals in St Paul and the Inscriptions of Ephesus," in *Papers of the La Trobe University Seminar 'Ephesus and the World of St Paul'* (Melbourne, 1991), 21–31, 53–58. Equals *137*.

129. "Claudius on Roman History," in *Papers of the Macquarie University Continuing Education Conference for Ancient History Teachers* (Sydney, 1991), 87–95.

130. "The Mark of the Beast, Revelation 13:16," *Tyndale Bulletin* 42 (1991): 158–60. Cf. *126*.

131. "Why Did the Romans Not Confuse Christians with Jews?" in *Papers of the Society for the Study of Early Christianity Seminar 'Conflict, Compromise, Consensus'* (Sydney, 1991), [pages unknown]; summarized in *Newsletter* 13 (1991): 2–3.

1992

132. "The Criticism of the New Testament in Late Antiquity," in *Papers of the Society for the Study of Early Christianity Seminar 'What Happened to the New Testament in Late Antiquity?'* (Sydney, 1992), 1–6; summarized in *Newsletter* 15 (1992): 5–6.

133. "Reading the New Testament in Late Antiquity," in *Papers of the Society for the Study of Early Christianity Seminar 'What Happened to the New Testament in Late Antiquity?'* (Sydney, 1992), 32–38; summarized in *Newsletter* 16 (1992): 3–5.

134. "The Teacher as Moral Exemplar in Paul and in the Inscriptions of Ephesus," Chapter 12 in *In the Fullness of Time: Biblical Studies in Honour of Archbishop Donald Robinson* (ed. D. Peterson and J. Pryor; Homebush West, NSW: Lancer/Anzea, 1992), 185–201.

135. "A Woman's Behaviour," §2 in *New Documents Illustrating Early Christianity* 6 (1992): 18–23.

1993

136. "Ancient Beginnings of the Modern World," *Ancient History* 23 (1993): 125–48. Cf. *155*.

137. "Benefactors at Ephesus: Ethical Ideals in St Paul and the Inscriptions of Ephesus," in *Papers of the Macquarie University Semi-*

nar 'Ephesus and the World of St Paul' (Sydney, 1993), 19–29, 45–49. Equals *128*.

138. "Judaism and the Rise of Christianity: A Roman Perspective," *Australian Journal of Jewish Studies* 7 (1993): 82–98. Cf. *143*.

139. "Pilate, Pontius," in *The Oxford Companion to the Bible* (ed. B. M. Metzger and M. D. Coogan; New York/Oxford: Oxford University Press, 1993), 594–95.

140. Review of C. Crabtree et al., eds., *Lessons from History: Essential Understandings and Historical Perspectives Students Should Acquire*, "Should History Teach the National Truth?" *Education Monitor* (Summer 1993/ 1994): 30–32.

1994

141. "City Life in the Roman Empire as Seen in the Acts of the Apostles," in *Papers of the Macquarie University Continuing Education Conference for Ancient History Teachers* (Sydney, 1994), 31–32.

142. "Foreword" to P. W. Barnett, *The Truth about Jesus: The Challenge of the Evidence* (Sydney: Aquila, 1994), iii–iv.

143. "Judaism and the Rise of Christianity: A Roman Perspective," *Tyndale Bulletin* 45 (1994): 355–68. Cf. *138*.

1995

144. "Interpreting New Testament Ideas," Chapter 3 in *Understanding Paul's Ethics: Twentieth-Century Approaches* (ed. B. S. Rosner; Grand Rapids: Eerdmans/Carlisle: Paternoster, 1995), 75–84. Reprint of pp. 7–17 in *7*.

145. "The Meaning of 'Ministry,'" *St Andrews Quarterly* (1995): [n.p.].

146. "The Motives of Tiberius Gracchus," in *Papers of the Macquarie University Continuing Education Conference for Ancient History Teachers* (Sydney, 1995), 17–19.

1996

147. "The Biblical Shape of Modern Culture," *Kategoria* 3 (1996): 9–30. Equals *156*.

148. "Multiculturalism: Where Does the Gospel Belong?" *Southern Cross Quarterly* (Sydney; Summer 1996–1997): 4–9.

149. "The Reaction against Classical Education in the New Testament," in *Theological Perspectives on Christian Formation* (ed. J. Astley, L. J. Francis, and C. Crowder; Grand Rapids: Eerdmans, 1996), 80–87. Equals *93, 105*.

150. Review of Jørgen Podemann Sørensen, ed., *Rethinking Religion: Studies in the Hellenistic Process*, in *Journal of Religious History* 20 (1996): 246–47.

1997

151. "Papyri," *Encyclopedia of Early Christianity* (ed. E. Ferguson et al.; 2d ed.; New York & London: Garland, 1997), 867–72.

152. "The Rhetoric of Inscriptions," Chapter 29 in *Handbook of Classical Rhetoric in the Hellenistic Period 330 B.C.–A.D. 400* (ed. S. E. Porter; Leiden/New York: Brill, 1997), 807–28.

153. "The Second Thoughts of Syme on Augustus," *Ancient History* 27 (1997): 43–75.

154. Review of P. W. Barnett, *The Second Epistle to the Corinthians*, in *Southern Cross Quarterly* (Sydney; Summer 1997): 28–29.

1998

155. "Ancient Beginnings of the Modern World," in *Ancient History in a Modern University*, Volume 2: *Early Christianity, Late Antiquity and Beyond* (ed. T. W. Hillard et al.; Ancient History Documentary Research Centre, Macquarie University, NSW Australia/Grand Rapids/Cambridge, UK: Eerdmans, 1998), 468–82. Cf. *136*.

156. "The Biblical Shape of Modern Culture," *Evangelical Review of Theology* 22 (1998): 292–306. Equals *147*.

157. "Conversion in the Ancient World," in Society for the Study of Early Christianity *Newsletter* 32 (1998): 3–4.

158. "With Whom Did the Cults Compete?" in *Papers of the Society for the Study of Early Christianity Seminar 'Christianity and Competing Cults'* (Sydney: Macquarie University, 1998), 3–5.

1999

159. "Biblical Sources of Historical Method," *Kategoria* 15 (1999): 33–39.

160. "Foreword" to F. Münzer, *Roman Aristocratic Parties and Families* (trans. T. Ridley; Baltimore and London: Johns Hopkins University Press, 1999), xv–xvii.

161. "Introduction" to C. G. Heyne's address on Roman Deportation: A 1791 Comparison with Botany Bay, trans. P. M. McCallum, in *Ancient History* 29 (1999): 118–28.

162. Review of Ramsay MacMullen, *Christianity and Paganism in the Fourth to Eighth Centuries*, in *Journal of Religious History* 23 (1999): 240–41.

2000

163. "The Impact of Paul's Gospel on Ancient Society," Chapter 20 in *The Gospel to the Nations: Perspectives on Paul's Mission in Honour of Peter T. O'Brien* (ed. P. G. Bolt and M. Thompson; Downers Grove: InterVarsity/Leicester: Apollos, 2000), 297–308.

164. "The Period of Augustus and the Julio-Claudians," in *Papers of the Macquarie University Ancient History Teachers Conference* (Sydney, 2000), 123–28.

165. Review of P. W. Barnett, *Jesus and the Rise of Early Christianity* . . . , in *Southern Cross Quarterly* (Sydney; Autumn 2000): 7.

2001

166. "Ancient Contradictions in the Australian Soul," lecture for the Institute for the Study of Christianity in an Age of Science and Technology (Brisbane, 2001), summarized in their *Bulletin* 33 (Canberra, Winter 2001): 7–9; reprinted in the Christian Librarians' Network *Newsletter* 4.1 (Winter/Spring, 2001): 18–22.

167. "Athena, the Unknown God of the Churches," lecture for the Institute for the Study of Christianity in an Age of Science and Technology (Brisbane, 2001), summarized in their *Bulletin* 33 (Canberra, Winter 2001): 6–7; reprinted in the Society for the Study of Early Christianity *Newsletter* 40 (Sydney, 2001): 3–4.

168. "Paul Barnett's Historic Contribution," *Southern Cross Quarterly* (Sydney; October 2001), 27.

169. Review of C. A. Evans and S. F. Porter, eds., *Dictionary of New Testament Background,* "Changing the Scenery," *Evangelicals Now* (August 2001): 22.

2002

170. "The Ecumenical Synod of Dionysiac Artists," §23 in *New Documents Illustrating Early Christianity* 9 (2002): 67–68.

171. "Her Soul Went up on High," §8 in *New Documents Illustrating Early Christianity* 9 (2002): 19.

172. "Jews, Proselytes and God-fearers Club Together," §25 in *New Documents Illustrating Early Christianity* 9 (2002): 73–80.

173. "Paul Barnett and New Testament History," *New Documents Illustrating Early Christianity* 9 (2002): ix–xii.

174. "Should We Drop BC/AD for B.C.E./C.E.?" Society for the Study of Early Christianity *Newsletter* 43 (2002): 4.

175. "Thanksgiving to the Benefactor of the World, Tiberius Caesar," §10 in *New Documents Illustrating Early Christianity* 9 (2002): 22.

176. Review of Nicholas Horsfall, *The Culture of the Roman Plebs*, in *Ancient History* 32 (2002): 195–200.

2003

177. "Did the Churches Compete with Cult Groups?" in *Early Christianity and Classical Culture: Comparative Studies in Honor of Abraham J. Malherbe* (ed. J. T. Fitzgerald, T. H. Olbricht, and L. M. White; NovTSup 110; Leiden/Boston: Brill, 2003), 501–24.

178. "Ergänzung. Australien und Neuseeland," *Der Neue Pauly* 15/3 (2003): 1247–50.

179. "The Private Sources of Force in Roman Politics," *Ancient History* 33 (2003): 135–52.

180. "Setting the Record Straight: Alternative Documents of a Protest in the Roman Army of Egypt," *Ancient History* 33 (2003): 153–59.

181. Review of B. W. Ball and W. G. Johnsson, eds., *The Essential Jesus: The Man, His Message, His Mission*, in Society for the Study of Early Christianity *Newsletter* 45 (2003): 4–7.

2004

182. "The Absence of Religion, Even in Ammianus?" in *Making History for God: Essays . . . in Honour of Stuart Piggin* (ed. G. R. Treloar and R. D. Linder; Sydney: Robert Menzies College, 2004), 295–308.

183. "The Appeal to Convention in Paul," in *The New Testament in Its First Century Setting: Essays on Context and Background in Honour of B. W. Winter on His 65th Birthday* (ed. P. J. Williams, A. D. Clarke, P. M. Head, and D. Instone-Brewer; Grand Rapids/Cambridge, UK: Eerdmans, 2004), 178–89.

184. "Latin Names around a Counter-Cultural Paul," in *The Bible and the Business of Life: Essays in Honour of Robert J. Banks's Sixty-Fifth Birthday* (ed. S. C. Holt and G. Preece; Australian Theological Forum Series 12; Adelaide: Australian Theological Forum Press, 2004), 68–84.

185. "McDonald, Alexander Hugh," *Dictionary of British Classicists*, vol. 2 (ed. R. B. Todd; Bristol: Thoemmes Continuum, 2004), 604–6.

2005

186. "The Mind of Tiberius Gracchus," in *Papers of the Macquarie University Ancient History Teachers Conference* (Sydney, 2005), 73–90.
187. "On This Rock I Will Build My *Ekklesia.* Counter-Cultic Springs of Multiculturalism?" *Buried History* 41 (2005): 3–28.
188. "The Roman Base of Paul's Mission," *Tyndale Bulletin* 56 (2005): 103–17.

2006

189. "Was Christianity a Religion?" Society for the Study of Early Christianity *Newsletter* 56 (2006): 4–7.
190. "Was Paul Really a Pioneer?" in *Papers of the Society for the Study of Early Christianity Seminar 'Pioneers and Pilgrims'* (Sydney: Macquarie University, 2006), 6–7; expanded in *Newsletter* 55 (2006): 3–6.
191. "Who Programs Our Values?" CASE 10 (2006), 23–26, 5.

Forthcoming

192. "Kultgemeinde," in *Reallexikon für Antike und Christentum* (ed. G. Schöllingen; vol. 22; Stuttgart: Anton Hiersemann).
193. "Cicero and Augustus," "The 'Settlements' of Augustus," "The Real Basis of Augustan Power," "Augustus and the Roman Nobility," "What Kind of Ruler Did the Greeks Think Augustus Was?" "The Augustan Republic; Tiberius and Claudius on Roman History," in *The First Christians in the Roman World: Augustan and New Testament Studies* (ed. J. R. Harrison; Tübingen: Mohr Siebeck).

Reviews of Judge's seminal 1960 book, *The Social Pattern of the Christian Groups in the First Century* and its German translation.

Badian, E. *Durham University Journal* 53 (1961): 140–42.
Frend, W. H. C. *Journal of Roman Studies* 50 (1960): 283.
Kerber, W. *Scholastik* 40 (1965): 477–78.
Klein, G. *Zeitschrift für Kirchengeschichte* 195 (1962): 210.
Marrou, H. I. *Revue des Études Anciennes* 63 (1961): 225–28.
Marshall, I. H. *Evangelical Quarterly* 33 (1961): 57–58.
McCaughey, J. D. *Aumla* 16 (1961): 194–96.
Nicholls, J. J. *Journal of Religious History* 1 (1960): 115–17.
Philippi, P. *Pastoraltheologie* 54 (1965): [n.p.].

Pokorný, P. *Communio Viatorum* 7 (1964): 317–18.
Schippers, R. *Gereformeerd Theologisch Tijdschrift* 65 (1965): 164.
Simon, M. *Latomus* 19 (1960): 603–5.
Smith, R. E. *Journal of Ecclesiastical History* 12 (1961): 87–88.
Warren, C. A. *St Marks Review* 20 (1960): 29–31.
Wiefel, W. *Helikon* 5 (1965): 684–87.
Yule, G. *Historical Studies* 10 (1961): 124.

Index of Modern Authors

Index of Subjects

adoption, 23, 26
Aelius Aristides, 13, 67
Aeropagus, 49
Alexandria, Judaism in, 60, 140n
alienation, 19, 126
amicitia, 167
Anatolia, 82, 173
anthropology, 11
    Platonic, 153
Antioch, 8, 31, 41
    Hellenic community at, 88
    leaders in, 41
Antipater of Tarsus, 112
antiptosis, 63
Antonines, 13
apathy, 104
Apollonis of Cyzicus, 172
Apollos, 43, 61
apotheosis, 16
Aramaic, 9
archaeology, 138
Aretas (King of the Nabataean
    Arabs), 14
Aristotle, 62, 140
    on women, 110
associations, 118
    Jewish, 28–31
asteismos, 57, 58
astrology, 94n77
Athenian democracy, 11–12
Athens, 19
    classical, 76
atonement, 105
Atticism, 76, 91
Augustine, 58–60, 61, 63, 65, 68–71,
    164

Augustus, 13, 21–22, 23, 24, 76, 82, 146
    opposition to, 22
authority
    sociology of, 128
autonomy, 13, 15

baptism, 25, 26, 33
Barnabas, 41, 44
    as divine, 17
beauty, 104
benefactor, 177
Bithynia, 30
body, 104

Caesar, 18
    oath of personal loyalty to, 83
    slaves of, 148
Caesarea, 7–8, 9, 14, 16
Caesarism, 21–24, 118
canon, 175
Celsus, 140
character, 178
charisma, Paul's theology of, 127
"Chicago School," xiv
chleuasmos, 57
chora, 158
Christendom, 130
Christianity, 119
    early expansion of, 36–37, 41
    origins of, 4
    See also Christians (early)
Christians (early)
    associations/communities of, 7,
        31–34, 120
    and communism, 157–58
    in Egypt, 140n

entertainment, 41
  Roman, 85
Ephesus, 17, 18, 26, 50
  civic virtues in, 175–79
  Paul fighting with beasts at, 83, 85
  republic at, 15
  silversmiths at, 27, 28
epicrisis, 146
Epictetus, 19
Epicurean(s), 104, 123
Epicurus, 111
epideictic oratory, 63
epidiorthosis, 67
epikertomesis, 57
eschatology, 3, 34, 35, 122
  in ancient Palestine, 6
  See also under disciples
ethics, 92–93, 134
  Greek, 103

Fachprosa, 90
family
  in classical world, 111
  in Greek society, 27
Favorinus, 66
Felix (procurator of Judaea), 23, 145,
  164
Feuerbach, 157
figura iusiurandi, 68
Flavians, 13
foreigners, 19
freedom, 107, 161, 162
friendship, 23, 26, 132, 155, 167
  classical theory of, 105–6
friendship-enmity system, 167

Gadarenes, 9
Gaius Gracchus, 26, 63–64
Galilee, 7, 9, 39
Gallio, 50, 54
Gentiles, 9, 16
  mission to, 101
Gerasenes, 9
gladiators, 85
gnosticism, 94n77
God, 160
  executes justice, 115
  imitation of, 180
  rule of, over the world, 162
god(s), favor of the, 16
goodwill, 177

gospel(s), 125
  and the law, 89
government, 5, 8, 10, 18, 53–54, 115
  in Christian assemblies in Jeru-
    salem, 32
  constitutional, 22
  Jewish, in Jerusalem, 14
governors, 38
Greece (ancient), 27, 115
  and Judaism, 87–89
  law in, 84n36, 84n37
  literature in, 77, 90–91
  political theory in, 11
  states, 83, 86
Greek (language), 64–65, 87, 90, 142
  Koine, 64–65
Gregory of Nyssa, 61, 65

Hellenism, 4, 5, 6, 8, 33, 74, 76, 126
  citizen class, 9–10
hermeneutics, 2–5, 35
Herod Agrippa I, 14, 16
Herod the Tetrarch, 23, 41, 48
historiography, 3, 118
history, 80, 90, 118, 134, 135
History of New Testament Times
  School, 80–81
History of Religions School, 79, 93
Holy Spirit. *See* Spirit
Homer, 20, 177
honor, 178
horkou schema, 68
house churches, 123. *See also* Christians (early); church; house-
  hold(s)
household(s), 20, 25, 44, 118, 119, 133
  autonomy of, 20
  community, 133–34
  relationship with republic, 20–26,
    27
  terminology in NT, 26
human condition/nature, 11, 102
human exploitation, 174
humanitarianism, 19

idiotes, 58
imperial cult(s), 16–17, 24. *See also*
  Isis, cult of; mystery cults;
  religion

schemata, 63, 65
scribes, 5
Sebaste, 7
self
  abandonment of, by Paul, 103–5
  development, 103–4
  See also individual
self-protection, 104
self-restraint, 152
Semitisms, 87n54
Seneca, 61, 113, 125
Sergius Paulus, 37
servants, 26
service, 115, 152
servitude, 108
sex, 111
Sidon, 8, 9, 14
Silas, 49
skill, 178
slavery, 108–9, 120, 148, 161, 170
  in ancient world, 19, 21, 23, 44,
    86, 164
  emancipation from, 142, 144
  in New Testament, 55, 86, 107–9,
    114–15, 161–62
  metaphors, 27
  view of early Christians, 19
social determinism, 140
social rank, 56
society, 1, 129
sociology of religion, 129
Socrates, 179
sophism, 62, 92, 165, 177
sortition, 11, 32
soul, 104
Spirit, 16, 64
  gifts of the, 107, 174
status, 139, 155, 159, 165, 170
  abandonment of, by Paul, 105–9
  in classical world, 105–6
  converted to rank, 141, 145, 159
  foundling, 170
  See also rank

Stephanas, 26
Stephen, 41, 48
  execution of, 47–48
stewardship, 108
Stoic(s), 19, 101, 130, 104, 123
  divine providence in, 154
suasoriae, 63
synagogue(s), 25, 41, 101

Tacitus, 119
Tertullus, 16
tetrarch, 5
Thessalonica, 18, 49
  decrees of Caesar at, 83
Thyatira, 25
Tiberias, sea of, 9
Tiberius, 15
tradition, 178
Trajan, 17, 30, 34, 51, 169–70
tropoi, 63
trust, 177
typos, 185–86
Tyre, 8, 9, 14

utopianism, 11

virtue, 104
Vulgate, 171

wealth, 56, 125, 145, 167, 176–77
wisdom, 104, 166
women
  Aristotle's views of, 110–11
  in the early church, 114
  Greek views of, 110–13, 115
  Paul's views of, 86–87, 112
  Plato's views of, 110–11
  Roman aristocratic, 37
worship, 160

Zeno, 111
Zeus Propolis, 17

Index of Ancient Sources

Philo

Life of Moses
1.28.158–159   180

EARLY CHRISTIAN WRITINGS

Augustine of Hippo

de Doctrina Christiana
4.6.9   58
4.7.10   58
4.7.11   58
4.7.12   68–71
4.7.14   58
4.7.15   58
4.10.24   58
6.9   65, 76n12
7.11   65
8.22   65, 76n12
9.23   65, 76n12
12.27   59
17.64   59
20.40–41   65, 76n12
20.42   59
20.44   59
24.53   59–60

Clement of Alexandria

Epistles of Paul and Seneca
9   61
13   61

Paedagogus
2.70–76   152n37

Gregory of Nyssa

adversus Eunomium
I, 253B   61

Jerome

Commentariorum in Epistulam ad Ephesios libri III
3.5   62

Commentariorum in Epistulam ad Galatas libri III
2.4   61–62
3.6   62

John Chrysostom

De sacerdotio
4.5f   61

Tertullian

De corona militis
2   152n37
7   152n37

GRECO-ROMAN LITERATURE

Cassius Dio

Roman History
60.17.5   142n16

Cicero

Epistulae ad Atticum
2.1.8   11

Orator
21.69   59
23.77   58
29.101   58
63.214   63n7

Dio Chrysostom

Corinthiaca (Or. 37)
66, 97n84

De Homero et Socrate (Or. 55)
179–80

Dialexis (Or. 42)
58

Gaius

Digest of Justinian
3.4.1   28

Heliodorus

Aethiopica
2.25.1–6   161

Longus

Daphnis and Chloe
3.33   151

Juvenal

Satirae
3.62   8

Oxyrhynchus Papyri
P.Oxy. 3057   148–49
P.Oxy. 3271   141
P.Oxy. 3273   144, 145
P.Oxy. 3279   146
P.Oxy. 3283   145–46
P.Oxy. 3312   147
P.Oxy. 3313   151

Palatine Anthology
11.384   153n40

Plato

Republic
11

Pliny the Younger

Epistulae
10.34   30
10.65   169–70
10.93   30
10.96   33
10.97   17
47   13
48   13
92   13
93   13

Plutarch

Cicero
49.5   61

Tiberius et Caius Gracchus
2.6   64n8

Scriptores Historiae Augustae, Probus
6.1   67

Suetonius

Divus Claudius
25.3   141n13

Tacitus

Annales
15.44   31, 51

Historiae
5.9   15